America, War and Power

T0346557

This book addresses the role of armed force, and attitudes toward it, in shaping and defining the United States. The first six chapters, arranged in chronological order, reflect on this central question, focusing on the American Revolution and Early Republic; American antebellum adventurism, especially regarding Latin America; the American Civil War and its impact on US attitudes toward foreign entanglements, down to World War II; the convergence of military and domestic issues during Dwight D. Eisenhower's career as general and US president; the American experience of the Cold War; and the Vietnam War as a "television war," with consideration of its impact on the Iraq War. The last three chapters offer views on the topic in light of global systems theory, US domestic opinion and governance, and soft power theory. This collection will be of much interest to students of US military history, US politics and military history and strategy in general.

Lawrence Sondhaus is Professor of History at the University of Indianapolis, where he serves as chair of the History and Political Science Department and director of the Institute for the Study of War and Diplomacy. He is the author of nine books, including *Strategic Culture and Ways of War* (2006). **A. James Fuller** is Associate Professor of History at the University of Indianapolis. He is the author of *Chaplain to the Confederacy: Basil Manly and Baptist Life in the Old South* (2000) and co-author (with John Hollitz) of *Contending Voices: Biographical Explorations of the American Past* (2003).

War, history and politics series
Series editor: Jeremy Black

Trade, Empire and British Foreign Policy, 1689–1815
Politics of a commercial state
Jeremy Black

Citizens, Soldiers and National Armies
Military service in France and Germany, 1789–1830
Thomas Hippler

America, War and Power
Defining the state, 1775–2005
Edited by Lawrence Sondhaus and A. James Fuller

America, War and Power

Defining the state, 1775–2005

**Edited by Lawrence Sondhaus
and A. James Fuller**

Routledge
Taylor & Francis Group

LONDON AND NEW YORK

First published 2007
by Routledge
2 Park Square, Milton Park, Abingdon, Oxon, OX14 4RN

Simultaneously published in the USA and Canada
by Routledge
270 Madison Ave, New York NY 10016

Routledge is an imprint of the Taylor & Francis Group, an informa business

Transferred to Digital Printing 2009

Typeset in Baskerville by Wearset Ltd, Boldon, Tyne and Wear

British Library Cataloguing in Publication Data
A catalogue record for this book is available from the British Library

Library of Congress Cataloging in Publication Data
America, war and power : defining the state, 1775–2005 / [edited
by] Lawrence Sondhaus and A. James Fuller.
  p. cm.
 1. Power (Social sciences)–United States–History.
 2. War and society–United States–History. 3. United States–History,
 Military. I. Sondhaus, Lawrence, 1958– II. Fuller, A. James
HN90.P6A44 2007
973–dc22   2006034195

ISBN10: 0–415–77214–1 (hbk)
ISBN10: 0–415–54533–1 (pbk)
ISBN10: 0–203–08907–3 (ebk)

ISBN13: 978–0–415–77214–3 (hbk)
ISBN13: 978–0–415–54533–4 (pbk)
ISBN 13: 978–0–203–08907–1 (ebk)

Contents

List of contributors   vii

Foreword   x
FRED ANDERSON AND ANDREW CAYTON

Acknowledgments   xiii

**Introduction: perspectives on American power and
empire**   1
A. JAMES FULLER

1   **Defining a new empire: the new power takes shape,
    1775–1815**   11
    JEREMY BLACK

2   **The United States as rogue state: gunboat persuasion,
    citizen marauders, and the limits of antebellum
    American imperialism**   29
    ROBERT E. MAY

3   **Billy Yank and Johnny Reb take on the world: Civil
    War veterans' views of war, liberty, and empire**   64
    CAROL REARDON

4   **Defining Eisenhower's America: war, power, and
    race relations, 1941–1961**   88
    EDWARD O. FRANTZ

5   **Cold War perceptions and the American experience
    of war**   106
    R. WILLIAM AYRES

6 **From Vietnam to Iraq: the first television war and its legacies** 125

CHESTER PACH

7 **Global war and the foundations of US systemic leadership** 146

WILLIAM R. THOMPSON

8 **Domestic challenges to American hegemony** 169

STEVEN W. HOOK

9 **Soft power, hard power, and the Pax Americana** 201

LAWRENCE SONDHAUS

Index 218

Contributors

Fred Anderson is Professor of History at the University of Colorado, Boulder. His publications include *The Dominion of War: Empire and Liberty in North America, 1500–2000*, with Andrew Cayton (2005), *The War That Made America: a Short History of the Seven Years' War* (2005), *Crucible of War: the Seven Years' War and the Fate of Empire in British North America, 1754–1766* (2000), the *Oxford Companion to American Military History*, with John Whiteclay Chambers (1999), and *A People's Army: Massachusetts Soldiers and Society in the Seven Years' War* (1984; reprint edn 2001).

R. William Ayres is Associate Professor of International Relations at Elizabethtown College, where he serves as director of the Center for Global Citizenship. He has published articles in the *Journal of Politics, Nationalism and Ethnic Politics, International Journal of Peace Studies, Journal of Peace Research, International Politics*, and *International Interactions*.

Jeremy Black is Professor of History at the University of Exeter, and author or editor of more than eighty books. His most recent works include *George III: America's Last King* (2006), *War in European History, 1494–1660* (2006), *The Age of Total War, 1860–1945* (2006), *The Continental Commitment: Britain, Hanover, and Interventionism, 1714–1793* (2005), *Introduction to Global Military History, 1775–present* (2005), *Warfare in Europe, 1650–1792* (2005), and *War and the New Disorder in the 21st Century* (2005).

Andrew Cayton, Distinguished Professor of History at Miami University, Ohio, has served as visiting professor at the University of Leiden, where he held the John Adams chair in American Studies. His most recent publications include *The Dominion of War: Empire and Liberty in North America, 1500–2000*, with Fred Anderson (2005), *The Center of a Great Empire: the Ohio Country in the Early American Republic*, with Stuart D. Hobbs (2005), *Ohio: the History of a People* (2002), and *The American Midwest: Essays on Regional History*, with Susan E. Gray (2001).

Edward O. Frantz is Assistant Professor of History at the University of Indianapolis. He specializes in the history of the Republican party, with special attention to its policies toward the southern United States and race relations. His publications include "A March of Triumph? Benjamin Harrison's Southern Tour and the Limits of Racial and Regional Reconciliation," *Indiana Magazine of History* (2004).

A. James Fuller is Associate Professor of History at the University of Indianapolis. His publications include *Contending Voices: Biographical Explorations of the American Past*, with John Erwin Hollitz (2002), and *Chaplain to the Confederacy: Basil Manly and Baptist Life in the Old South* (2000).

Steven W. Hook is Associate Professor of Political Science at Kent State University, and past president of the Foreign Policy Analysis sections of the American Political Science Association and the International Studies Association. He has authored or edited five books: *US Foreign Policy: the Paradox of World Power* (2005), *American Foreign Policy since World War II*, with John Spanier (16th edn 2002), *Comparative Foreign Policy: Adaptation Strategies of the Great and Emerging Powers* (2002), *Foreign Aid Toward the Millennium* (1996), and *National Interest and Foreign Aid* (1995).

Robert E. May is Professor of History at Purdue University. He is author or editor of four books: *Manifest Destiny's Underworld: Filibustering in Antebellum America* (2002; reprint edn 2004), *The Union, the Confederacy, and the Atlantic Rim* (1995), *John A. Quitman: Old South Crusader* (1985; reprint edn 1989), and *The Southern Dream of a Caribbean Empire, 1854–1861* (1973; reprint edn 2002).

Chester J. Pach is Associate Professor of History at Ohio University. He has authored or edited four books: *The Presidency of Ronald Reagan* (2006), *The Johnson Years* (2006), *The Presidency of Dwight D. Eisenhower*, with Elmo Richardson (2nd edn 1991), and *Arming the Free World: the Origins of the United States Military Assistance Program, 1945–50* (1991).

Carol Reardon is Associate Professor of History at Penn State University, and past president of the Society for Military History (2005–7). She has served as visiting professor at the US Military Academy and the US Army War College. Her publications include *Launch the Intruders: a Naval Attack Squadron in the Vietnam War, 1972* (2005), *Pickett's Charge in History and Memory* (1997), and *Soldiers and Scholars: the US Army and the Uses of Military History, 1865–1920* (1990).

Lawrence Sondhaus is Professor of History at the University of Indianapolis, where he serves as director of the Institute for the Study of War and Diplomacy. He is the author of nine books, most recently *Strategic Culture and Ways of War* (2006), *Navies in Modern World History* (2004), *Navies of Europe* (2002), and *Naval Warfare, 1815–1914* (2001).

William R. Thompson is Professor of Political Science at Indiana University, and past president of the International Studies Association (2005–6). He has authored or edited seventeen books, most recently *The Evolution of War*, with Jack S. Levy (2006), *Globalization and Global History*, with Barry Gills (2005), *Puzzles of the Democratic Peace: Theory, Geopolitics, and the Transformation of World Politics*, with Karen Rasler (2005), and *Growth, Trade, and Systemic Leadership*, with Rafael Reuveny (2004).

Foreword

Fred Anderson and Andrew Cayton

Comparatively few generalizations about human beings hold up well under scrutiny; one that seems to do better than most is that people are inveterate story-makers. As far back in time as we can reach, and as widely across the world's cultures as we can range, we find women and men constructing narratives that create a sense of drama and convey their notions of meaning and significance to wider audiences. At least since Thucydides, historians have participated in this larger enterprise by telling stories within a framework of rules that constrain the imagination in certain ways – for example, by refusing to make things up, and by not omitting people or events merely because they happen to be inconvenient – in return for a singularly important promise: that the things they say about the world, how it came to be as it is, and what past events signify, will possess the power of truth, or at least as much of the truth as they can grasp. Academic historians, as the modern practitioners of that ancient craft, impose the highest possible standards of evidence and logical analysis as they scrutinize received narratives, interrogating them for consistency with the evidence that they unearth in their own researches, asking if there may be other, more accurate and coherent, ways to understand the world and its shaping. Ultimately the specific, highly focused questions that modern historians ask of the past, then, depend upon the pre-existing stories they seek to test for coherence and truth.

Our starting point in writing *The Dominion of War: Empire and Liberty in North America, 1500–2000* was to posit the existence of one such received narrative of United States history, a national story in which three great wars for liberty punctuate an otherwise fundamentally peaceful pattern of settlement and economic growth. In this narrative, the Revolutionary War establishes the Republic on the basis of theoretically universal values of liberty and equality, but leaves unsettled the issue of slavery, which fundamentally contradicts them; after nearly a century, the Civil War finally makes those political values universal by abolishing slavery, albeit at the price of a tremendous collective blood sacrifice, a tragic act of national atonement; and World War II generalizes those values as Americans defend liberty against the dual tyrannies of fascism and militarism that threaten to enslave the world as a whole. Many of the specific questions that professional historians have asked about the history of the United States over the last century, we believed, have arisen from their efforts to examine and to question this *ur*-plot of America's past.

Many of the closely focused monographs that resulted from these inquiries seemed to us to imply that another kind of "grand narrative" could be constructed for North American history. Examined in a way that did not privilege the three great wars of liberation as exceptions that proved the rule of a fundamentally peaceful national development, the history of North America (within which the United States could be situated) began to look like one in which many *kinds* of wars had played central roles in shaping the continent and its peoples. We came to believe that wars for empire, which in the received narrative tended to be assigned to the margins and treated as aberrant events, might well imply another set of meanings if they were resituated at the center of the American story. Ultimately the book we wrote, by attending closely to the character, impact, and implications of events like the Seven Years' War, the War of 1812, the Mexican War, the Spanish–American War, and the twentieth century's many wars of intervention, offered a narrative in which the three great wars of liberation could be seen as unintended, revolutionary consequences of previous attempts to achieve imperial mastery. Empire and liberty, we argued, were complementary aspects of American development in a history characterized fully as much by the pursuit of power as by the pursuit of happiness; war itself had exerted a virtually continuous, catalyzing influence on the development of North America and its peoples.

We did not set out to write a polemic in *The Dominion of War*, but rather hoped to re-tell a familiar story in a way that would provoke other historians (and perhaps even general readers) to re-examine their assumptions about the character of American history and to think anew about the kinds of questions they asked about it. What we hoped for, in short, is the sort of thing that typically takes years to happen, if it happens at all. This is particularly the case with an academic book, where the reviews that matter most take more than a year to appear after the date of publication, in specialist venues like *The Journal of American History* and *The American Historical Review*. Thus we were extraordinarily pleased, and more than a little surprised, to learn that the Institute for the Study of War and Diplomacy at the University of Indianapolis proposed to bring together several noted historians and scholars of international relations for a symposium on the book in the fall of 2005. The organizers, Professors A. James Fuller and Lawrence Sondhaus, invited the participants, whose revised work appears in this volume, to address issues of concern to themselves and their fields in the context of the book's arguments and larger narrative.

The role that Jim and Larry assigned to us was the simple and pleasurable one of responding to their papers in general sessions that lasted the whole of Saturday, September 24, 2005. We were as happy to do so as any pair of flattered professors would be, but ultimately our reactions went well beyond the comments we offered and heard that day. The chapters that follow – on warfare in the early republic, the private imperialism of the Jacksonian filibusters, Civil War veterans' views of late nineteenth- and early twentieth-century imperialism, Dwight D. Eisenhower's caution in the use of power, the role of psychology and perception in the shaping of foreign policy, the role of television in wartime, the temptations of exceptionalism in American history, the domestic constraints on American power, and the issue of power within American strategic culture – have given us far more to think about than we would have imagined possible. Nothing could be more gratifying than to see such a feast of ideas and approaches emerge from an invitation to respond to *The Dominion of War*. Yet, as will be clear to any reader of this volume, there is much more to it than that. In the pages that follow, you will find superb scholars grappling with important issues in the history of North America, and in the relations of Americans with other peoples, coming up with work that goes far beyond anything that we had imagined might emerge from the symposium. Far more than merely being responses to our work, these chapters are reminders of the creative power of scholarship to illuminate the past – and the present – with the flashes of insight and the kinds of meticulously developed arguments that can only be found in the work of gifted and creative scholars. We are honored to have played even the modest part we did in the making of this book.

Acknowledgments

The papers included in this volume had their origins in the symposium "War and Power: Defining the American State," hosted on September 23–24, 2005, by the Institute for the Study of War and Diplomacy of the University of Indianapolis, and funded by an InQuery Grant from the Lilly Endowment. Jeremy Black, Robert E. May, Carol Reardon, Chester Pach, William R. Thompson, and Steven W. Hook submitted papers that appear, in revised form, in this volume. Panel discussants included Fred Anderson and Andrew Cayton, whose book *The Dominion of War: Empire and Liberty in North America, 1500–2000* (2005) served as the common reading for the symposium. Participants from the Institute for the Study of War and Diplomacy included the editors and four of our colleagues – Jyotika Saksena, Milind Thakar, R. William Ayres, and Edward O. Frantz – of whom the latter two contributed chapters to this volume. We are grateful to all of our colleagues and invited guests for their contributions to the symposium and subsequent efforts to see the project through to publication. We would also like to acknowledge the members of the staff of the University of Indianapolis and its supporting services who helped make our symposium a successful event, in particular Laura Irmer and Ted Polk. Finally, we would like to thank our spouses, Brenda and Rovena, for their patience and moral support during the eighteen months it took to plan the symposium and produce this volume.

A. James Fuller
Lawrence Sondhaus

Introduction

Perspectives on American power and empire

A. James Fuller

In *The Dominion of War: Empire and Liberty in North America 1500–2000*, Fred
Anderson and Andrew Cayton attempt to reshape our understanding of
American history by arguing that republican ideas of freedom and imperialism are two sides of the same coin. In their view, American imperialism
was not an aberration for a country that fought wars only for liberty.
Rather, they suggest that American empire was part of "the progressive
extension of a polity's, or a people's, dominion over the lands or lives of
others, as a means of imposing what the builders of empires understand as
order and peace on dangerous or unstable peripheral regions." As Anderson and Cayton are quick to point out, "to found a narrative of American
development on the concept of dominion is to forgo the exceptionalist
traditions of American culture – those durable notions that the United
States is essentially not like other nations but rather an example for them
to emulate, a "shining city on a hill." Instead, they dismiss American
exceptionalism "in favor of a perspective more like the one from which
historians routinely survey long periods of European, African, or Asian
history."[1]

Most of the chapters in this book carry on this endeavor of forgoing
American exceptionalism. Throughout the following pages, the reader
will find challenges to one of the most enduring concepts in American
culture: the idea that the United States is different from the rest of the
world. Challenging American exceptionalism is not a new enterprise nor
does this book hope to put it to rest once and for all. But these chapters
do offer fresh insights into the nature of US foreign policy, war, and the
meaning of American history and society.

Alexis de Tocqueville first introduced the terminology of American
exceptionalism in *Democracy in America*, his classic observation based on his
travels throughout the United States in 1831–1832. For Tocqueville,
America was different from Europe for two main reasons, "the *spirit of religion* and the *spirit of liberty*." In his view, the values of Protestant Christian-
ity and individual liberty stemmed from New England and
"interpenetrated" the rest of society. He did not compare the US to any
specific country, but his notes indicated that he was obviously thinking of

his native France as he wrote about America. The point he made was that America was different. That did not always mean that America was better than Europe. Indeed, Tocqueville and other European travelers often looked down their noses at their American hosts and sneered at what they understood to be American inferiority.[2]

But over time, American exceptionalism came to mean something more, to imply that the United States was superior to the rest of the world. Many of America's early leaders clearly thought in ways that included both definitions of the Tocquevillian term. They believed their new nation was different from Europe, that they were leading the way to a new age in which the world would look to the United States as a model. This did not mean that America would involve itself in the international arena. Instead, the US hoped to maintain its neutrality. The most famous formulation of this policy appeared in George Washington's Farewell Address, but perhaps the best statement came from John Quincy Adams:

> America does not go abroad in search of monsters to destroy. She is the well-wisher to the freedom and independence of all. She is the champion only of her own. She will recommend the general cause by the countenance of her voice, and benignant sympathy of her example.[3]

By the twentieth century, American exceptionalism was a tradition, part of the national identity. To be sure, its expression in foreign policy changed over time. Whether or not the nation's involvement in wars and territorial expansion meant an abandonment of exceptionalism is a question often considered by diplomatic historians.[4] Reconciling empire with the tradition of American exceptionalism was not always easy to accomplish, but it was surely attempted by scholars and politicians alike. Nationalist interpretations of history and politics arose from the foundation of exceptionalism and explained American expansion and empire as a new kind of international involvement.

In this view, the United States did not build its empire for traditional reasons, but to defend and extend liberty. During the mid-twentieth century, liberal consensus scholars like Richard Hofstadter, Daniel Boorstin, and Louis Hartz produced often-sophisticated interpretations that both analyzed and supported the idea of exceptionalism. Hofstadter explained American history as a pragmatic consensus in which idealists were realists and liberals were conservatives and conservatives were liberals. His analysis emphasized the ways in which American political leaders operated pragmatically in order to further the ideology upheld by all of them and the majority of Americans. Politics required practical measures to maintain liberty, equality, and capitalism. Shaped largely by Franklin Delano Roosevelt and the New Deal as well as his personal political views that moved from radicalism to liberalism, Hofstadter's work helped to build the liberal-consensus interpretation that supported the nationalist defense of exceptionalism.[5]

Daniel Boorstin, another former radical, is best remembered for his trilogy, *The Americans*, a nationalist history of the United States, but he published more than twenty books and explored important issues in intellectual history. Boorstin asserted that the United States never experienced a democratic revolution because it was essentially democratic from its inception. He also argued that America had no grand political theories, but that the development of the country came during periods of action under stress, pointing to the New Deal as an example. This fits well with Hofstadter's argument about pragmatism, as did Boorstin's insistence that American thought was unique. His assertion that other countries could learn much from American politics and culture placed his interpretations clearly within the exceptionalist camp. Boorstin's work not only contributed to the nationalist interpretation created by the consensus historians, but also helped to popularize it, as his many books became bestsellers.[6]

Political scientist Louis Hartz published a classic statement of the liberal consensus interpretation in his 1955 book, *The Liberal Tradition in America*. Like Boorstin, Hartz believed that the American Revolution was not really revolutionary, but was a war for independence. He argued that the absence of feudalism meant that American politics was dominated by a pervasive liberalism. At base, the political battles between American parties were an illusion, as politicians used rhetoric to cover the sham. In reality, the major parties were part of the same consensus tradition. Terms like "liberal" and "conservative" meant little and were used by politicians to suit their purposes. In his view, there were no real differences in American politics. While he may have been correct in asserting that earlier scholars had overstated the case for conflict in American history, Hartz may well have gone too far in stressing the framework of consensus. Hofstadter, Boorstin, and Hartz joined many others in forging the consensus interpretation that staunchly defended both nationalism and American exceptionalism. The consensus view dominated the academy from 1945 to at least 1965, although many of the scholars in this school of thought continued to publish well into the 1980s and 1990s.[7]

Meanwhile, some on the left also used exceptionalism as a means to interpretation. These radicals asked, "Why is there no socialist movement in America?" and they often based their answers to this central question on the notion of exceptionalism. In the nineteenth century, Karl Marx and Friedrich Engels struggled with exceptionalism themselves and tried to explain the lack of socialism in America by arguing that Americans had "their own social democratic school." They worried about "special American conditions" and believed that America was so bourgeois that such prejudices pervaded the working class, preventing a revolution.[8] Italian Marxist theorist Antonio Gramsci argued that exceptionalism was based on a distinctive American ideology rooted in its values and revolutionary origins. This ideology emphasized hard work, an ethic that was accepted by the working classes as well as the bourgeoisie.

Recently, exceptionalism has fallen from favor in many scholarly circles, especially on the left. New Left scholars influenced by the 1960s rejected the nationalist view and the consensus interpretation of history. They emphasized conflict and their criticism raised serious doubts about the synthesis that the consensus school had forged, including American exceptionalism. Today, attacking exceptionalism is quite popular among academics. Radical historian Howard Zinn delivered a venomous diatribe against exceptionalism in a speech at MIT in 2005. Later published, the speech is typical of the leftist distaste for the nationalist tradition: Zinn defined American exceptionalism to fit his own purposes and railed against both religion and military power. He asserted that exceptionalism should be defined as the notion that "the United States alone has the right whether by divine sanction or moral obligation, to bring civilization, or democracy, or liberty to the rest of the world, by violence if necessary." This definition ignores the traditional term's admission that Americans do not always live up to their own standards. Nor does it recognize the ways in which exceptionalism has changed over the course of the country's history. His criticism of George W. Bush and other American presidents who have invoked God compares American religion to Hitler's Germany: "Anyone today who claims the support of God might be embarrassed to recall that the Nazi storm troopers had inscribed on their belts, 'Gott mit uns' ('God with us')." He then launches into a long jeremiad about American military aggression without regard to context. Surely, Zinn's radical critique is too extreme for most historians, even those who identify with the left. But his speech is indicative of a broader criticism of exceptionalism.[9]

Still, the tradition endures, and there is a growing movement to defend it. As writer John Fonte outlined in an article in the conservative *Policy Review* (now published by the Hoover Institution), the debate over American exceptionalism lies at the heart of today's culture wars. In his analysis, the battle lines are drawn between Tocquevillians and Gramscians. The Tocquevillians are a loose coalition of liberals and neo-conservatives who defend American exceptionalism against the radical attacks of Gramscian leftists. The radicals rely on Antonio Gramsci's notion of hegemony to interpret American culture. In this view, the privileged classes exercise power in multiple ways, including hegemony, which combines ideology and values in such a way that the oppressed and subordinate groups in society often consent to their own exploitation. To overcome this, Gramsci argued that it was necessary to "delegitimize the dominant belief systems of the predominant groups and to create a 'counter-hegemony' (i.e., a new system of values for the subordinate groups) before the marginalized could be empowered." Because hegemony is so entrenched throughout "all spheres of civil society – schools, churches, the media, voluntary associations – civil society itself," Gramsci argued, "is the great battleground in the struggle for hegemony." Gramsci believed that intellectuals positioned within the established institutions would lead the way to class consciousness and revolution. Thus, the defenders of American exceptionalism see themselves pitted against the forces of political correctness and perceive attacks on the exceptionalist tradition as nothing less than a socialist plot to bring down America. In response, they have taken up the cause with renewed vigor.[10]

Perhaps the most influential statement of American exceptionalism in recent years came in political scientist Samuel P. Huntington's 1996 book, *The Clash of Civilizations and the Remaking of the World Order*. An expansion of an article he wrote in 1993, Huntington's interpretation challenged the ideas of other post-Cold War theorists like Francis Fukuyama, whose 1992 book, *The End of History and the Last Man*, proposed the triumph of liberalism and the end of ideological conflict. Huntington argued that the new era would be marked by wars between cultures as the forces of China, India, and the Muslim world assaulted Western civilization (led by the United States). Ideology no longer dominated world politics, he warned, and America needed to prepare itself for the coming clash of cultures. While some critics accused him of creating the intellectual foundation for a more aggressive US foreign policy, Huntington himself focused on the internal aspects of his theory and called for less intervention internationally rather than more. Thus, he called for a vigorous strengthening of American culture. This theme continued in his 2004 book, *Who Are We? The Threat to American Identity*, as he argued that the large number of Hispanic immigrants to the United States threatened to divide the country and destroy its culture. Denounced as a Nativist, anti-Catholic tract by many on the left, the book is probably more properly seen as a continuation of his concern about the internal survival of exceptionalism. Huntington emphasized the sheer diversity of the power of the United States, including the appeal of its culture and institutions as well as its military and economic might. His work led a resurgence of liberal ideas in the wake of New Left criticism.[11]

Another important examination of American exceptionalism appeared in Seymour Martin Lipset's *American Exceptionalism: a Double-Edged Sword*. Lipset built on the work of Huntington in arguing that exceptionalism is based on an American ideology centered on five concepts: liberty, egalitarianism, individualism, populism, and laissez faire. Relying heavily on the work of other political scientists, his own previous scholarship and on international comparative surveys, Lipset argued that American exceptionalism was very real and very much alive and well in the late twentieth century. He dismissed the notion that exceptionalism means consensus history and politics, arguing that, while Americans agree on principles, they disagree strongly on how to apply those same principles. He also returned to one of the foundational doctrines of exceptionalism in arguing that difference did not always mean better, noting that American distinctiveness often includes negative characteristics.[12]

Historian Walter A. McDougall recently emerged as another defender of American exceptionalism. Widely regarded for his Pulitzer Prize-winning history of the space race and his work on foreign policy, McDougall published *Freedom Just Around the Corner: a New American History, 1585–1828*, the first of a proposed three-volume history of the United States. He opens the books with a powerful statement of exceptionalism: "The creation of the United States of America is the central event of the past four hundred years." His interpretation rests on the idea that the "American character" is unique, that Americans have enjoyed more opportunity than others, and that they have shaped a distinct history in their efforts as hustlers. McDougall, like Lipset, relies on values and beliefs, on broad terms that are often deliberately left vague. But his emphasis on the dynamism of American history rings true with many liberals and libertarians. And, like Lipset, he includes the negative as well as the positive, pointing out that "what is novel about Americans ... is not that they are better or worse than peoples of other places and times (100 percent of whose genes they share), but that they are *freer* than other peoples to pursue happiness and yet are no happier for it." Here, McDougall quotes Huntington, who argued that in order to be a disappointment America had to offer hope. Pointing out American disappointment and the downside of American society as part of exceptionalism is one way to correct the nationalist tendency toward a triumphal history that ignores the negative.[13]

This, then, is the broad context for the chapters included in this volume. Beyond the matter of American exceptionalism, the authors also address questions and problems specific to their subjects. The result is a collection that sometimes challenges accepted interpretations, often extends our understanding with insightful analysis, and raises new questions to consider.

In the opening chapter, historian Jeremy Black blasts away at the notion of American exceptionalism. He rejects exceptionalism and argues that we need to consider America as a participant, willing and unwilling, in a complex and multipolar international system. From the outset, participation in the international system helped to set the parameters and sometimes the contents of American history, in the domestic realm as well as in foreign policy. The author thus challenges the exceptionalist argument that US foreign policy during the early American republic resulted directly from a concern for the preservation of liberty at home and that the new nation acted abroad only when internal liberty was at stake.

Historian Robert E. May also rejects the exceptionalist tradition in his treatment of US diplomacy and military affairs in the pre-Civil War years in Chapter 2. He interprets these events in relation to post-9/11 discourses about terrorism and rogue states. Although formal US government policies (gunboat intimidation and aggressive diplomacy) serve as his backdrop, May focuses on privately organized US "filibustering" expeditions against other countries, mostly in Latin America. He emphasizes the irony (given US leadership in the twenty-first-century "war on terror") that in the mid-nineteenth century the United States was regarded as the rogue nation of the Western world – a state that promoted international terrorism in pursuit of its own national goals of territorial expansionism. Far from being exceptional, in May's analysis, the United States fits with broader patterns in world history, both in its experiments with filibustering and in its appetite for empire.

American support for empire is examined in Chapter 3, as historian Carol Reardon rejects the widely held belief that the Spanish–American War healed traditional sectional differences, especially among veterans of the Civil War, and paved the way for a common vision of American interests abroad thereafter. In 1898, Union veterans supported the Spanish–American War and the creation of the American empire that followed. In contrast, Southern veterans' organizations remained unconvinced that sectional ill-will had died or that the North appreciate Southern loyalty to the nation since 1865. These former Confederates continued to show little interest in debating the causes, conduct, or consequences of the Spanish–American War. The veterans of both sides united in support of American intervention during World War I, but only after the German declaration of unrestricted submarine warfare. This reconciliation proved temporary, however, and, after the war, the veterans again followed section-specific courses. While Northerners condemned the antiwar movement of the 1920s as disloyal and naive, the official position of the United Confederate Veterans called for resolution of global conflicts without resort to war. Their experiences in 1861–1865 and the bitter aftermath of the Civil War continued to color the views of veterans on questions of war and peace until age silenced their collective voice on the eve of World War II. Reardon's chapter takes its place in the literature on reconciliation by extending our understanding of the complex ways in which the Civil War shaped post-war sensibilities. In so doing, she adds to the sophisticated analysis of historians like David W. Blight, whose book, *Race and Reunion*, traced the tragic course of racism in the quest for reconciliation.[14]

Race is the central theme of historian Edward Frantz's work in Chapter 4. The author shows how decades of service in a segregated US army shaped Dwight D. Eisenhower's vision of America to a far greater extent than most historians have acknowledged. In contrast to most assessments of Eisenhower, which treat his presidency in isolation from his military career, this chapter demonstrates the clear domestic policy impact of attitudes he developed while in the armed forces, especially regarding Civil Rights. Frantz thus contextualizes Eisenhower's moderate policies as president and demonstrates what we can learn about individuals who decide not to use the power that they accumulated as a military leader.

Individual leaders, their perceptions, and their role in wielding US power is the focus of international relations scholar R. William Ayre's study in Chapter 5. He argues that the post-World War II period and the beginning of the Cold War brought US policy-makers into an active role in international affairs on a previously unprecedented scale. The Cold War also brought a new dimension to US foreign policy – a stable enemy – and with it new ways of thinking about and perceiving the world. Delving into political psychology, he argues that the foreign policy perceptions of US leaders, more fluid in previous eras, became fixed around a set of images of the enemy and derivative perceptions linked to the central conflict with Soviet Communism. These images affected the perceptual judgments of leaders about a whole range of issues and those judgments, in turn, drove US foreign policy in the 1950s and 1960s and shaped the nation's experience of war throughout the following decades.

The power of perception is also at the heart of Chapter 6, as historian Chester J. Pach looks at the role of the media. Pach argues that the loss in Vietnam influenced subsequent US military actions by concentrating on the controversies that arose over television coverage of the war. Vietnam was the first US war to receive extensive, daily coverage on network newscasts and the first during which a majority of Americans said that they relied on television as their principal source of news. Both Lyndon B. Johnson and Richard M. Nixon thought that TV news presented an oversimplified, distorted, or biased view of the war that was responsible for eroding popular support for the US war effort. Pach concludes with a comparison between the coverage of the Vietnam War and the current war in Iraq, including some discussion of the debate over whether the latest war is "another Vietnam."

Political scientist William R. Thompson returns to the matter of American exceptionalism in Chapter 7. Thompson argues that the US ascent story can be told relying on a systemic perspective and leadership long cycle theory. He rejects the customary exceptionalist approach to accounting for the rise of the United States to global primacy as descriptive, American-centric, and heavily reliant on the distinctiveness of the ascent. The author focuses on the effects of wars on development, especially the period of global war between 1914–1945. While conceding that there are unique aspects to the US ascent, he concludes that the general nature of its trajectory was less distinctive than is usually supposed.

In Chapter 8, political scientist Steven W. Hook focuses on domestic pressures on US foreign policy at two levels of analysis: political culture and the state. He touches on a pervading aspect of American exceptionalism in identifying a cultural pattern of detachment from world politics that stems from the nation's origins and early development. This detachment is reflected in recent indicators of international education, public opinion, and news media coverage of foreign affairs. Hook then turns to aspects of US domestic governance, particularly the diffusion of foreign-policy authority, that further hinder the conduct of foreign policy. Throughout the chapter, he takes issue with the assumptions of the exceptionalist tradition expounded by scholars like Huntington and Lipset, especially its reliance on a consensus of Americans in their world views. Arguing that American exceptionalism is an enduring and costly cultural delusion, his conclusion looks at an uncertain future for the maintenance of the present US hegemony. In the end, despite his reservations about exceptionalism, he accepts the neoliberal view that soft power is of greater importance today than the traditional hard power of military superiority.

The basis of US hegemony is explored by historian Lawrence Sondhaus in Chapter 9. He criticizes the post-Cold War positions of realists as well as neoliberals; the former for predicting that the demise of the Soviet Union would lead to a revival of a multipolar world order, the latter for misjudging what really matters about contemporary US power. In particular, Sondhaus focuses on the neoliberal premise that soft power now matters more than traditional hard power. He traces the changes in the discourse on soft power in reaction to three major international crises – the Kosovo crisis of 1999, the terrorist attacks of September 11, 2001, and the US invasion of Iraq in 2003 – before concluding that soft power theory has significant weaknesses, some of which stem from Joseph Nye's aversion to long-cycle theory, others from the general liberal preference to undervalue the significance of military power. In turning to the more distant past to examine the nature of power, he challenges American exceptionalism by finding similarities between contemporary US hegemony and the pervasive strength of the British Empire a century or more ago. He concludes that, just as the considerable soft power dimension of British hegemony could not save the Pax Britannica in the face of a relative decline of British hard power, the soft power aspects of contemporary US hegemony, no matter how well cultivated, are no substitute for military strength.

And so the book returns to its beginning, the tension between the idea of liberty and the realities of war, and the matter of American exceptionalism. Critical of the exceptionalist tradition, these authors nevertheless respect its power and the ways in which it has intersected with foreign policy. The interdisciplinary nature of these chapters results in a book that includes analysis of individuals alongside systemic theory, looks to the past and to the future, explores psychology and military strategy, examines perceptions and reality. Taken together, these chapters offer new insights into the ways in which war and power defined the American state, and in which the American state and culture defined both war and power. In doing so, these scholars have taken up the task of interpreting the American past as Fred Anderson and Andrew Cayton suggested, "in light of a pattern of development in which the values of republicanism and empire have consistently complemented one another, a history in which war and freedom have long intertwined."[15]

Notes

1 Fred Anderson and Andrew Cayton, *The Dominion of War: Empire and Liberty in North America, 1500–2000* (New York: Viking Books, 2005), xiv–xv.
2 Alexis de Tocqueville, *Democracy in America* (reprint, New York: Vintage Books, 1990), 43, 31.
3 John Quincy Adams, *An Address Delivered at the Request of the Citizens of Washington; on the Occasion of Reading the Declaration of Independence, on the Fourth of July, 1821* (Washington, DC: Davis and Force, 1821), quoted in Walter A. McDougall, *Promised Land, Crusader State: the American Encounter With the World Since 1776* (New York: Mariner Books of Houghton Mifflin, 1997), 36.
4 For an example of this, see McDougall, *Promised Land, Crusader State.*
5 Richard Hofstadter, *The American Political Tradition and the Men Who Made It* (New York: Alfred Knopf, 1948).
6 Daniel Boorstin, *The Genius of American Politics* (Chicago: University of Chicago Press, 1958). It should be noted that many American academics flirted with socialism and communism in the decades before World War II. Thus, the path away from radicalism taken by Hofstadter and Boorstin was not unusual. Boorstin apologized for his involvement with the Communist Party and gave names of communists to the government during the Red Scare of the 1950s. He became a conservative and was much reviled by the left. In many ways, these scholars foreshadowed the later neo-conservative movement that abandoned liberalism in reaction to the New Left.
7 Louis Hartz, *The Liberal Tradition in America* (New York: Harcourt Brace, 1955).
8 Karl Marx and Friedrich Engels, quoted in Seymour Martin Lipset, *American Exceptionalism: a Double-Edged Sword* (New York: W.W. Norton, 1996), 78–79. For a brief outline of Gramsci's views on this matter, see ibid., 87. For more on Marx and Engels grappling with exceptionalism, see ibid., 77–109.
9 Howard Zinn, "The Power and the Glory: Myths of American Exceptionalism," *Boston Review: a Political and Literary Forum* 30 (Summer 2005), 3–4: 20–22.
10 John Fonte, "Why There Is A Culture War: Gramsci and Tocqueville in America," *Policy Review* 104 (December 2000 and January 2001), 15–31. For examples of the Tocquevillian response to attacks on exceptionalism, see: *A Call to Civil Society: Why Democracy Needs Moral Truths* (Chicago: Council on Civil Society, 1998).
11 Samuel P. Huntington, *The Clash of Civilizations and the Remaking of the World Order* (New York: Simon & Schuster, 1996); Francis Fukuyama, *The End of History and the Last Man* (New York: Free Press, 1992); Samuel P. Huntington, *Who Are We? The Challenges to America's National Identity* (New York: Simon & Schuster, 2004).
12 Lipset, *American Exceptionalism.*
13 Walter A. McDougall, *Freedom Just Around the Corner: a New American History, 1585–1828* (New York: HarperCollins, 2004), xiii, 16. For McDougall's analysis of American foreign policy, which includes a revisionist organization of US diplomatic traditions, see Walter A. McDougall, *Promised Land, Crusader State.*
14 David W. Blight, *Race and Reunion: the Civil War in American Memory.* Boston: Harvard University Press, 2001.
15 Anderson and Cayton, *The Dominion of War,* 424.

1 Defining a new empire

The new power takes shape, 1775–1815

Jeremy Black

Editor's introduction

Taking an outsider's view, the author focuses on the context of inter-national competition in which the United States formed. Challenging the traditional exceptionalist view, he argues that the first decades of the new republic were marked by war. To the degree that they helped to define the perspectives of the Federalists and the Democratic-Republicans, debates over military power were central to the politics of the early republic.

America was a state born in war, and its early decades as an independent state involved the assertion of power through force, against both foreign and domestic challenges. Indeed, exigencies and debates focused on force, and how best to secure, sustain and use it, were crucial in the polit-ical and governmental history of these decades. This subject is generally neglected these days because of a preference, in accounts of the American Revolution and subsequent years, for social themes, especially topical ones of gender and race. Furthermore, among political historians, and, here again, there is no American exceptionalism, there has traditionally been a degree of reluctance in coming to terms with the formative context of international competition and military need. In seeking as a foreigner to discuss the subject, there is a danger that the opposite approach is taken, with an excessive focus on this context, at the expense, in particular, of the role of domestic political debate, in not only framing but also deter-mining the understanding of this context, and therefore in providing the essential narrative. Yet, there is first-rate American work on the topic,[1] and this chapter is intended as a contribution to be read alongside this literature.

If contexts are the order at the outset, then the interpretative context also requires understanding. Here the key problem is posed by American exceptionalism, an approach that both discourages American scholars from looking for parallels that might add comparative insights, and foreign scholars from doing the same. The key context for this period is that, between 1776 and 1815, America was not alone in having to define itself as a new state in an acutely threatening international order, for this was also true of a host of states and would-be-states across the Western world; while all existing states, in responding to challenges, did likewise, albeit within far more established political patterns. The usual comparison for the American Revolution is with the French Revolution that began in 1789, but that, in fact, was only one among a number of European revolutionary or radical movements, and, in several countries in the 1780s, short-lived radical governments were established. These included Geneva, the United Provinces (modern Netherlands) and the Austrian Netherlands (modern Belgium), in all of which the new order was suppressed by counter-revolutionary force. The destruction of Polish independence early the following decade can also be located in this context, as the reform movement that had drawn up a new constitution in 1791 was a particular issue for Catherine the Great of Russia. Furthermore, as another comparative element, the range of territories affected by secessionist movements in the European colonial world also included Ireland (against British rule in 1798) and Haiti (against the French).

It was also necessary for colonial authorities to respond to the de facto independence thrust upon them by the overthrow of metropoles by French forces during the French Revolutionary and Napoleonic Wars (1792–1815). This was a problem throughout the Spanish empire, as the Bourbon dynasty there was overthrown by Napoleon in 1808 and replaced by his own brother, Joseph, and also, to a lesser extent, in its Portuguese counterpart. The extent to which these colonial authorities had to devise diplomatic and military policies has been underrated, because new states were not created until after the Napoleonic Wars, but independence was not the necessary precondition for these policies.

As yet, there is not the basis for a systematic comparative study of this issue, while a chapter-length is insufficient for this purpose. Nevertheless, across the Western world, a sense of incipience accompanied by urgency was general, and the issues were similar. In particular, as with all revolutionary periods, irrespective of the goals of policy, there was the question of how best to control military forces. This involved both the specific issue of loyalty, with the political consequences that might arise, and the more general one of long-term political and social impact. The issue of loyalty was most acute if the new political system was felt to be under threat. That led, for example, to the killing of French Revolutionary generals for being unsuccessful, as Theobald Dillon was in 1792, and Adam Philippe de Custine in 1793, because a lack of success was held to betoken an absence of zeal, if not worse. Such an approach would have played havoc with American commanders in 1775–83 and 1812–15: Philip Schuyler, Benjamin Lincoln and Horatio Gates would have been prominent victims, and George Washington could have been executed for failing to save New York City in 1776 and Philadelphia in 1777, or for not crushing Sir Henry Clinton at Monmouth Court House in 1778.

Alongside ensuring effectiveness, a failure to control the military was clearly a serious problem for new governments and states. Napoleon's coup in 1799 revealed this in France, while successive caudillos were to make it apparent in Spanish America, and the civil sphere in Haiti suffered greatly from the same problem. The US was far from removed from this process. Brigadier General James Wilkinson, Governor of the Louisiana Territory, was heavily involved with the plans associated with Vice President Aaron Burr in 1804–6, which included the secession of New York and New England (1804),[2] and, with subsequently, the "Spanish Conspiracy," which appears to have included plans for a Western secession. Wilkinson hoped to seize Santa Fé from the Spaniards for his own ends. Indeed, Wilkinson's self-serving treason was not dependent on Burr, nor restricted to his schemes. Furthermore, they nearly put paid to the career of the best American general prior to the Civil War for, in 1810, Winfield Scott was court martialled and suspended for a year for criticizing Wilkinson's involvement.[3] At the same time, successive versions of the Mississippi Question reflected the volatility of loyalties in the hinterland.

Alongside the fear of military force subverting the republic, of a Benedict Arnold, Oliver Cromwell or Napoleon Bonaparte, or their equivalent, indeed, in religious terms, of an ungodly "Man of Blood" acting as an un-Christian tyrant, there was also a profound anxiety about the problems for American public life that would come from the military, irrespective of the intentions of its commanders. In part, this stemmed from the origins of the American state (the federal entity as well as the individual states), both as a product of British political culture and as a reaction against the supposed authoritarian practices of the metropole, not least in its use of military force, in its expectations of financial support for the military, and in its readiness to rely on military governance.

The political culture was that of opposition to a standing army. This was the product of a seventeenth-century English tradition, directed against Stuart and Cromwellian autocracy, that had been revivified in the "Commonwealth" and country-party critique of supposed "Old Corps" Whig governmental practices and intentions during the reigns of George I (1714–27) and George II (1727–60). From the imperial perspective, this might appear surprising, as British regulars had played a key role in the conquest of French Canada in 1758–60, thus ending the challenge to British North America's most vulnerable borders. However, the British military had won few plaudits from the colonists, being widely seen, particularly by self-conscious local politicians, as autocratic in intention and manner. Some British officers indeed loathed the American troops and thought them incompetent, a judgment that the French and Indian War did not bear out, but one that reflected not so much a hostile response to an American proto-nationalism, as the view that many regulars held of militia and, indeed, of civil society.[4] Under George III, American hostility to the British military had risen when it had been associated, first as cause and, subsequently, as support, for an unpopular process of taxation; and this was to be accentuated by the experience of war and occupation.[5]

This was not the best background for any attempt to create a standing force to fight for American independence. This problem was exacerbated by the extent to which assumptions and practices about military goals and activity were colony-based and militia-orientated.[6] The US therefore represented an accentuation of the commonplace reluctance to see regular forces as anything other than supporters of centralization and arbitrary government. In forming this attitude, the acceptance of the theory of natural rights or natural law in the Declaration of Independence questioned the legitimacy of all authority, especially central authority, and the discrediting of executive power was also important.

Yet, more than a militia would be required to fight the British regulars. This was urgent from the outset, both because the British had a substantial force in Boston, and as a result of the great vulnerability of America, its lack of a battle fleet. Whatever the strength of individual American warships, as seen in 1812 when three British frigates were captured, and whatever the potential of American privateers, the Americans lacked a fleet able to block the use of the Atlantic by the British, both as a means of communication, partly solving logistical issues, and as the basis for a strategic dimension. In the nineteenth century, this was to lead to a heavy emphasis in the US on coastal fortifications in doctrine, force structure, and expenditure, a policy clearly directed against Britain, the leading naval power, but this was not a viable solution during the War of Independence. The relevant forts were lacking at the strategic level, and, operationally, garrisons in positions such as Fort Washington and Ticonderoga were unable to prevent British advances, as the campaigns of 1776 and 1777, respectively, demonstrated. Instead, by fixing garrisons, forts were actually a source of vulnerability, which the fall of Fort Washington in 1776 demonstrated. Similarly, the forts that blocked the river approaches to Philadelphia were captured in 1777.

On June 14, 1775, Congress decided to raise the Continental Army and, the following day, appointed George Washington commander of "all the Continental forces, raised, or to be raised, for the defense of American liberty." Understandably, he was unwilling to see militiamen as a substitute for Continentals. However, the powerful American ideological–political preference for militia over a trained army continued throughout the war. Creating numerous problems for Washington, this made it difficult to complete the Continental regiments.

It is possible either to emphasize the extent to which a new army was forged, serving as the basis for a new consciousness, or, alternatively, to stress deficiencies. The degree to which the army represented a new political identity and social practice certainly helped to sustain its cohesion, and even the continuation of the Revolutionary cause when the war went badly, as in the winter of 1777–8, when the army camped at Valley Forge. The formation of the army indeed was a political act: the army, a force that would not dissolve at the end of the year, even if individual terms of service came to an end, symbolized the united nature of the struggle by the Thirteen Colonies, and was a vital move in the effort to win foreign recognition and support.

It was not itself necessary to have such an army in order for individual colonies/states to assist each other militarily. Prior to the American Revolution, military units had been deployed outside the boundaries of individual colonies, against both Native American attacks and French and Spanish targets. Furthermore, during the Revolution, militia units under the control of state governments were sent to assist other states, as indeed they were sent to the Continental Army. However, by having such an army, military decisions were in large part taken out of the ambit of state government. Furthermore, individual military careers indicated the growing role of American, rather than state, considerations, and helped to make the new state a functioning reality capable of eliciting loyalty. For example, Benjamin Lincoln, in 1775 a councilor in the Upper Chamber of the new Massachusetts state government, and in 1776 a Major General in the Massachusetts force, was appointed to command the Massachusetts recruits levied to reinforce the Continental Army and, in 1778, was chosen to command the Southern Department. Politically, this helped to tie New England to the South, although his defense of Charleston in 1780 was a conspicuous failure. In 1781–3, however, Lincoln served as the First Secretary at War.

In theory, creating the Continental Army made the planning of strategy easier, freeing generals in some measure from the direction of state governments and allowing them to consider clashing demands for action and assistance. In practice, the creation of the army, although essential to the dissemination of a new notion of nationhood, did not free military operations from the views of state government, nor from the political disputes of the Continental Congress.

The complex relationships between force, nationhood and liberty were also seen in struggles over raising and supplying forces. Washington was obliged to deal with a form of government in which Congress could do little more than request men, funds and supplies from the states. The response varied considerably. Virginia was a state that provided much support for the Revolution, but, when, in April 1777, Congress recommended drafts from the militia to fill the Continental Army, Thomas Jefferson opposed them, arguing that they would be very unpopular. That November, the General Assembly to Virginia resolved that county lieutenants should collect clothing for the Continental troops raised in the county and send them to the army, but little was sent. In 1779, when a boat with 5,000 stand-of-arms imported for use by the Continental Congress arrived in Virginia, the arms were seized by the state government, leading to a serious dispute. There were riots against the draft in Virginia in 1780.

Virginia was not the only state to pose problems. South Carolina and Rhode Island did not introduce conscription, while, in the winter of 1777–8, General Anthony Wayne blamed what he saw as a lack of support from Pennsylvania on anti-military feeling in its government. Lincoln found the South Carolina militia unwilling to accept the command of Continental officers, while, in 1780, Horatio Gates, his successor as commander in the south, found his orders to the North Carolina militia countermanded by the state's Board of War. Gates had to threaten the Board with dismissal, and pressure from the North Carolina legislature played a role in his removal from command. In New York state, in early 1781, several local committees stirred up opposition to the impressments of supplies by the army. The strong sense of state identity and interests restricted any attempt to lessen state power in favor of Congress. Generals such as Nathaniel Greene criticized politicians and civilians, reflecting a tension between the civilian political control that characterized the Revolution and the sense among generals that they could handle matters better.

The success of the Revolution did not end disputes over how best to organize the military; indeed, it encouraged them, as there was room for political debate without the exigencies of war lessening the range of options, while the degree of federal responsibility proved a particular issue of controversy. With both the military and foreign policy, the Americans avoided the fissiparous consequences of a federal system, by giving the key power to federal, not state, government. In 1778, Congress banned individual congressmen from talking to the Carlisle Commission, sent by the British government in an unsuccessful attempt to try to negotiate an end to the war. In part as a result of the Longchamps affair in 1784, in which a French diplomat was attacked, an ad hoc congressional court was given jurisdiction over international law, and the authority of the individual states was subordinated. However, the authority of the Supreme Court (established in 1789) in international cases, expressed in the Constitution in 1787, also drew on broader cases and considerations. Individual states lacked the right to negotiate "foreign" treaties or to make war, although their relations with Native Americans initially threatened to permit both. Thus, in the mid-1780s, Georgia raised state forces for duty against the Cherokee.

The nature and size of the national army was particularly controversial, Henry Knox, a keen Federalist, pressed hard for a stronger federal government and a national military establishment while heading the War Department in 1785–94. In 1783, he had aroused concern by founding the Society of Cincinnati as a body for officers from the War of Independence and their descendants. This was seen as a threat to the Confederation government. Knox faced opposition to a permanent force, as well as the financial weakness of the federal government.

On June 3, 1784, the day after decreeing that the last units of the Continental Army be disbanded, the Confederation Congress, nevertheless, voted to establish a 700-strong regiment of one-year volunteers in order to strengthen America's presence in the Ohio Valley. In 1784–6, three treaties ceded much of southern and eastern Ohio to American settlement. This settlement was seen by most Americans as a rightful response to the God-given opportunities for expansion, and this expansion was itself seen as a recompense of their struggle for independence. In July 1787, Congress passed the Northwest Ordinance. This not only reasserted American sovereignty over the region, but also made it clear that this sovereignty was to be the prelude to settlement. The Ordinance provided for the establishment of new states there, and thus for an advancing frontier of settlement combined with a dynamic political structure. The Ordinance declared that Native rights would only be infringed "in just and lawful wars authorized by Congress," and that Native lands would only be acquired with their consent. This was a policy that was to be widely honored in the breach, helping to lead to conflict.[7]

The absence, until the constitution was settled and established, of a well organized government or a system of direct taxation, was a fundamental limit to military capability. By the end of 1786, the regiment consisted of only 565 officers and men. The army was subsequently expanded as relations slipped into an initially unsuccessful war with Native Americans, but, after peace was negotiated, the army was cut to 3,359 men in 1796.

The army was then expanded by the Federalists in 1798, during the Quasi War with France, with Washington as Commander-in-Chief and Alexander Hamilton as senior ranking Major General.[8] The latter sought to develop the force as a powerful permanent body able to unite America against internal subversion and foreign threat, but his intentions were suspect to many. The difference over force structure was politically very divisive. Opposed to France in the late 1790s, the governing Federalists linked foreign and domestic policies closely to military preparedness, and built up both army and navy. "Millions for defense, but not one cent for tribute" became their slogan,[9] and the government also passed the Alien and Sedition Acts in order to strengthen it against internal opposition. This was a divisive step. Kentucky and Virginia denounced the Acts in the name of states rights and thus, in effect, pressed the role of state governments in deciding the constitutional character of federal actions.

Differences in part rested on very different conceptions of the international system. Whereas Hamilton advanced a pessimistic interpretation of competing states and the need for preparedness, critics felt that a benign system was possible. Whereas Hamilton was in favor of a strong military, President John Adams was more concerned to restrict preparedness to a powerful navy.

Jefferson and the Republicans, who gained power after the election of 1800, limited the peacetime military establishment to 3,284. They were not interested in a European-style military nor an army of imperial size, were opposed to the taxes they entailed, and were suspicious of the existing army, not least because most of the senior officers were Federalists.[10] Instead, Jefferson preferred to rely on national unity, an example of the comforting illusion that virtue would necessarily prevail. This led Jefferson, in his Inaugural Address in 1801, to claim that America was the strongest country in the world. Keeping a large military establishment at a distance, however, was related to practices that were not conducive to professionalism, and therefore effectiveness. In the early Republican period, the practice of commissioning men directly from civil life, rather than promoting from the ranks in peacetime, led to a stress on political affiliation, social connections, and appropriate conduct. All of these brought the military close to civil society but with deleterious consequences for military effectiveness, as was seen in the War of 1812. However, the general political atmosphere was not one that identified professionalism with effectiveness.

Similarly, the Federalist plan to build up the navy was stopped when the Jeffersonians took power. Jefferson favored coastal gunboats, rather than the more expensive frigates with their oceanic range.[11] The emphasis on gunboats conformed to the militia tradition of American republicanism. Militia could use gunboats to defend the fortifications being built. However, the overall emphasis on the defensive was not the best preparation for an effective operational army, nor, specifically, for an invasion of Canada. Far from such political distinctions being an aspect of American exceptionalism, they were reflected in serious divisions over foreign policy and defense in other states with public politics, such as Britain, the United Provinces (Netherlands) in the 1780s and France in the early 1790s.

The indeterminacy that stems from the major role of politics has recently been outlined by Douglas Egerton in an essay worth quoting at length. Writing of the possibility of the re-election of Adams in 1800, he argues:

> Expansion into the American Midwest was sure to have continued regardless of what party controlled Washington. But with Adams in power the Louisiana Territory might have arrived on very different terms, due to Federalist détente with Toussaint Louverture.... Haitian independence in, say, 1801 under a President Louverture, protected by an Anglo-American naval agreement, might have prevented the final implementation of the treaty of San Ildefonso, in which Spain transferred control of Louisiana to France ... a possible Federalist acquisition of the Louisiana Territory from Spain under free-soil conditions.[12]

The last was unlikely not least because slaveholders in the border regions, such as Natchez in the 1790s, and Louisiana later, were determined to hold on to their property. Even antislavery Federalist officials in the Southwest recognized this political reality, such that any challenge to slavery would prompt secession or, at least, disunion. Nevertheless, counterfactuals bear consideration as a reminder of the number of different trajectories that were possible.

The American army was built up in 1808, as relations deteriorated with Britain and as an internal police force to enforce the embargo. In November 1811, in his annual address to Congress, President James Madison proposed increasing the army and recruiting a large number of volunteers, but, in 1812, the army establishment was only 6,686 officers and men, while the navy had seven frigates, ten sloops and sixty-two gunboats, but no ships of the line. This was not the sort of force that could mount transoceanic amphibious operations, and indeed this crucial lack of capability helped to ensure that American power was restricted to "near America." Sending three frigates and a schooner to the Mediterranean in 1801 was scarcely sufficient for any major scheme. Similarly, the overland force under William Eaton that marched from Alexandria in Egypt to help capture Derna contained only ten American marines, alongside thirty-eight Greeks and about 300 Arabs. This scarcely compared with the overseas forces that Britain deployed: in 1807, 6,000 troops were sent to capture Alexandria, while 4,800 troops stormed Montevideo that year, a force reinforced to 8,000 before the unsuccessful British attack on Buenos Aires. In 1809, 10,000 British troops captured Martinique from the French, while, in 1814, 4,500 troops landed in Chesapeake Bay.

Aside from the small size of the American military, American military capacity suffered from the lack of any equivalent to the ancillary forces that greatly enhanced British capability. This was particularly seen around the Indian Ocean. The mostly native British East India Company army was 18,200 strong in 1763, 115,400 in 1782 and 154,000 in 1805. Indian troops also played a major role in operations outside India: in Ceylon (Sri Lanka), the East Indies, Egypt and Mauritius. The Mauritius expedition in 1810 included 3,000 Indian troops, there were 5,770 Indian as well as 5,344 British troops in the expedition that took Batavia (modern Djakarta), the leading Dutch position in the East Indies, in 1811, and 1,800 Indian troops, as well as 900 British, in the force that conquered the inland Sri Lankan kingdom of Kandy in 1815.

The Americans had no equivalent. There was a use of Native American allies, Andrew Jackson benefiting from the support of about 500 Cherokee and Creek when he stormed the Creek camp at Horseshoe Bend in March 1814. Jackson profited from the debilitating Creek divisions into Lower/White and Upper/Red towns, with the former siding for the most part with the Americans, as again in 1818 when Jackson invaded Florida in the First Seminole War. However, numbers were small, and this did not represent an appreciable offensive capability, other than against nearby areas.

Slave troops had been used with some success in the West Indies by both Britain and France in the 1790s, the British raising twelve regiments in 1798, and the success of the Haitian Revolution in what had been the leading French slave economy – Saint Domingue – underlined the military proficiency of slaves and their ecological suitability for campaigning in the West Indies. Yet, this very revolution underlined the American revulsion against arming slaves that had been seen in the reaction to the adoption of such a policy in 1775–6 by John, fourth Earl of Dunmore, the last Royal Governor of Virginia. Thus, the Americans were not to create a slave army to campaign in the West Indies, a key instance of strategic culture being molded by domestic ideology. Aside from ideological opposition, there was not the institutional basis for such a policy. Slavery in North American was private, not public; it was an aspect of investment, not of governmental utility. There was no half-way house equivalent to the system run by the East India Company. John Carnac, a major in its army, saw the Company's organizational system as crucial in 1761: "If we are to keep our new countries, it will be absolutely necessary to have in pay a large body of sepoys."

A comparable force was certainly necessary if the Americans were to be able to mount a large-scale policy of conquest. The numbers of British troops sent to (and lost in) the West Indies – including 33,000 sent in 1795, and 45,000 lost in 1793–1801 – indicated the challenge if the US was to mount any viable program of Caribbean conquest. The American filibusters were less numerous, though they had some success in extending American power in the Gulf Region in the 1800s and 1810s, and, in 1813, temporarily gained control of Texas, but a larger loyalist force marched north from Mexico later that year and regained control. It was far less possible for filibusters to challenge the British in Canada successfully.

Numbers were an issue for the US in the War of 1812,[13] which led to increased reliance on the regulars, seen most clearly in James Monroe's call for an army of 100,000, and led to reform of the military system. However, this did not extend to a sweeping reform, either in terms of the organization of large-scale power projection or with regard to the militia. This left America in a weak position in the event of any future great power war.

The War of 1812 reflected the popularity of expansionism in some American political circles. For the Americans, however, this was a very divisive war, and one in which many refused to help. The Federalists, who were heavily represented in New England, were opposed to war with Britain, which they correctly saw as likely to harm trade. The Federalists also saw territorial expansion as likely to benefit the rival Republicans. In addition, New England interests had only limited concern in the British relations with Native Americans that troubled frontier regions. Commentators, indeed, had long detected regional sectionalism and rifts within the US.

In 1812, the Federalists were out-voted by the Republicans, but the divisions on declaring war – seventy-nine to forty-eight in the House of Representatives, and nineteen to three in the Senate – reflected the depth of disquiet. It was difficult to create both a nation-state and a nationality that worked. As the constitution expressly conferred the power to declare war on Congress, and Congress alone could vote money to pay for the war and the military, the potentially unifying position of the presidency was heavily qualified. Nevertheless, in 1812, division did not lead to civil conflict, and it is still appropriate to refer to American goals, albeit accepting that the depth of division not only limited the availability of resources, but also affected strategic options. The prime American goal was the conquest of Canada, an issue that symbolized the extent to which the American Revolution seemed unfinished abroad and, therefore, in some eyes unrealized at home. It is unclear whether the Madison government wished to retain Canada, or to use it merely as a pawn in negotiations over impressments, and the latter has been stressed in accounts that emphasize the defensive character of American policy; but both goals required the seizure of Canada.

Its defense was a difficult task: Canada seemed both vulnerable to American attack and of limited importance to Britain. It was vulnerable because the frontier was extensive, there were clear lines of American attack, not least the Champlain corridor, the British regulars available for defense were few, and the Canadian militia was untried. Canada, furthermore, was relatively unimportant to Britain compared to the war with Napoleon. The latter demanded the commitment of most of the British army. France, however, had already been defeated by the British at sea, decisively so at Trafalgar in 1805, and subsequent French attempts to rebuild their navy had not been particularly successful, not least in terms of fighting effectiveness. This naval relationship is a reminder of the extent to which American history was dependent on relations between other powers. This meant that it was possible for Britain to put maritime pressure on America, not least by mounting a blockade. In contrast, because warships of any size could not pass the St. Lawrence rapids from the Atlantic to the Great Lakes, the British were unable to send their ocean-going fleet there.

Although Canada provided the Americans with a clear strategic goal to permit the pursuit of imperial schemes, the Americans were unable to devise an effective means to obtain this goal. The size of Canada helped to make strategic planning difficult, as did the nature of contemporary communications, command and control, as well as relationships between individual commanders. For these reasons, there was little prospect of coordinated campaigning, which would have been the best way to take advantage of the distribution of American resources. The alternative, their massing in a single concentration of power, was not possible for political reasons, as well as not being feasible in logistical terms. A deficiency in planning, moreover, accompanied the organizational and political limitations affecting the war effort. The absence of an effective strategy made it difficult to make use of tactical and operational successes: those comprised parts in a whole that was absent. More particularly, multi-pronged attacks were not coordinated, and did not exert simultaneous or sequential pressure on the British. Such a strategy would have been difficult to execute given the extent of operations, but functional problems alone were not responsible for the American failure of coordination.

There were also serious political divisions over strategy. There was much support for a focus on the Champlain corridor in order to divide Montréal from Québec. Henry Dearborn, Secretary of War (1801–9), who, in 1812 was appointed senior Major-General in charge of the northern border, agreed that the main thrust should be there, but also pressed for ancillary assaults from Detroit and the Niagara frontier. Westerners were opposed to an emphasis on the Champlain corridor and, instead, wanted to prevent British help to the Native Americans, in particular by advancing on Fort Malden from Detroit.

Nevertheless, there was no shortage of optimism. It was widely assumed that the British could be beaten. Henry Clay, the Speaker of the House (and a Kentuckian), declared in 1812 that the Kentucky militia alone could conquer Montréal and Upper Canada. Jefferson hoped to drive the British from North America: Québec was to be taken in 1812 and Halifax in 1813.

Political issues can be set in a wider context. Whereas, from 1760 until 1775, there had been no effective rivalry among the European powers in North America, the situation had changed thereafter because the Americans failed to expel the British from Canada. This was a major constraint on American power, but crises in Anglo-American relations, including the War of 1812, were too brief and limited to lead to the sweeping political and governmental changes that the protracted character of the French Revolutionary and Napoleonic Wars led to in Europe. Despite a measure of American integration through economic growth and better communications (although far less than was to follow the War of 1812), the state/regional forces of loyalties and identities had been shown to be a challenge to American political coherence and military effectiveness, and nothing was done to alter the situation. The Federalists offered an agenda for governmental change designed to deal with the protracted crisis that arose from American vulnerability and international tension, but the crisis never became sufficiently severe to lead to a major reconfiguration of government.

In the War of 1812, the Federalists did not offer a successful political challenge at the national level, although the fissiparous tendencies integral to authority at the level of individual states were fully revealed. During what they termed "Mr. Madison's War," New Englanders, especially in Connecticut, Massachusetts and Rhode Island, were opposed to the conflict, unhelpful to the war effort and keen to retain links with Britain.[14] In those three states, and especially in Rhode Island, there was opposition to the use of the militia in the war. This made it harder to raise the manpower and logistical support for striking at the St. Lawrence artery of British power in North America; although, as in other crises in Anglo-American relations, a lack of the relevant naval capacity was also a key issue, as it made it necessary to strike overland.

In November 1812, the American attack from New England towards Montréal, the most vulnerable point in the British defense system for Canada as a whole, collapsed due to inadequate logistics and poor command. A year later, a similar attempt was abandoned when Wilkinson realized that there was going to be no overwhelming concentration of strength near Montréal. Thus, American strategic options were directly related to the domestic political situation. There was an emphasis on invading Canada further west than was militarily most wise, along with logistical and other problems relating to using New England as a base for operations. The British sought to exacerbate American divisions with their blockade, because, initially, "licensed" neutral commerce was permitted with New England. Indeed, economic links between the two sides remained important, and Canadian deficiencies in food and other supplies were rectified by American smuggling by sea and land.

Federalist opposition to the war led to a convention at Hartford in late 1814 that proposed changes to the constitution, but this was colored in the public eye by extremist talk of secession by New England.[15] This compromised the Federalists, helping James Monroe to win the 1816 and 1820 presidential elections. These victories ensured not only a continuity in Jeffersonian Democratic–Republican government, but also control by the group that had waged the recent war. Although the Democratic–Republicans adopted a number of Federalist views and programs once in power – the Bank, a standing army, and, after 1812, an oceanic navy and a general staff (created in 1813) – their inclinations, attitudes and ambitions were very different to those of Hamilton.

The 1812 war had left a conviction that America required a stronger military and, although it was followed by post-war demobilization, with the army cut from its official authorized size of 62,674 men (troop strength was actually lower), there was a determination not to return to the pre-war situation. The core of the wartime staff system was retained, with a new reform leadership instigating new procedures for efficiency and accountability, and a *de facto* acceptance of the regular army as the true first line of land defense. On March 3, 1815, Congress voted for a new peacetime establishment of 12,383 troops (as opposed to the 3,284 in 1807), and in 1816 voted $1 million per annum for eight years to construct a navy, including nine seventy-four-gun ships of the line.

By 1815, war had helped to define the American state, both externally and internally. The key episodes in the latter were Shays' Rebellion in

Massachusetts in 1786–7 and the Whiskey Rebellion in Pennsylvania in 1794. In the former, heavily debt-ridden farmers rebelled in order to stop the confiscation of their property to pay debts and taxes they could not meet. The rebellion was put down in early 1787, when about 1,500 rebellious Regulators, armed with pitchforks and other weapons of limited effectiveness, dispersed, after a 4,400-strong volunteer militia force under Benjamin Lincoln opened fire, including cannon fire. A bold advance by Lincoln, ten days later, surprised and disrupted an attempt to regroup, effectively ending the rebellion.

The role of Massachusetts volunteers, rather than federal troops, in suppressing the rebellion reflected the absence of a significant standing army. In 1786, the federal government tried to respond to the Massachusetts disturbances. Its decision, on 20 October, to recruit 2,040 troops was explained with reference to the crisis with the Native Americans in the Northwest,[16] but it also owed much to concern about the situation in Massachusetts. The number raised, however, fell far short of this figure, and, although regulars were dispatched, the rebellion was suppressed by the militia, and the Act was repealed on April 4, 1787. The rebellion had not served as an excuse to develop a powerful military.

The Whiskey Rebellion was a response to an excise tax on spirits introduced in 1791. In scenes similar to those that had confronted British policy prior to the War of Independence, tax collectors and their allies were again tarred and feathered. There was scant sympathy for the government's desire to use taxes to help address the national debt and to support the federal government. Conflict broke out with an attack on an excise inspector's house that was resisted with the aid of soldiers. As tension mounted, about 6,000 men attended a meeting at Braddock's Field near Pittsburgh, but they did not use the opportunity to take any political or military initiatives, and, instead, dispersed. The federal government called out the militia, but when they reached Pittsburgh, they encountered scant resistance.[17]

Challenges to the Union were more important and sustained than these tax revolts. Sectionalism, which was in part a function of commercial relations in the Atlantic trading system, was particularly severe. Nevertheless, compared to the serious and persistent civil violence throughout Latin America that followed independence, both separatist and struggles for political control within individual states, the situation in the US was relatively peaceful. Indeed, any reading of the history of Colombia or Mexico, Honduras or Peru, serves as a salutary comparison to the political history of the US. Although smaller, these states also had serious sectional divisions, as well as differences over ideology, and, furthermore, serious problems over how to control generals and other military leaders.[18] Presidents were not apt to give up power.

Crises in the US were resolved without much violence. Thus, Vermont separatism, which dated back to the beginning of the Revolution, did not, despite an upsurge in the late 1780s, lead to significant problems, and, in 1791, Vermont joined the union as the fourteenth state: it was not conquered. This level of comparative success can be seen as arising from the political culture and dispersed governmental power of the new country, although contingent factors were also important. The failure of the Shays' and Whiskey rebellions ensured that there was no pressure for a strong federal force capable of enforcing government power; nor a "balkanization" akin to that which affected Mexico, where local militias and strongmen enjoyed great power in the 1820s. Political differences were institutionalized in a federal system of shared sovereignty which made it easier to express interests and manage disputes short of conflict.

Externally, the key definition of the US was the winning of independence, but in circumstances that did not lead to the creation of a significant military able to give effect to bold expansionist plans. Instead, considerable difficulties were encountered in taking war to the Native Americans and, even more, the British in Canada, while, against the British elsewhere, only defensive successes could be achieved: Lake Champlain and Fort McHenry, in 1814, New Orleans in 1815.

The war, instead, that defined American liberty and empire was the longstanding one in which America's role was marginal or non-existent: that between Britain and France, a perspective again that qualifies American exceptionalism, or, at least, triumphalism. It was this conflict that ensured that the French were unable to maintain their positions in North America, losing Canada in 1760 and feeling it necessary to sell vulnerable Louisiana in 1803, just as it was the resumption of war between Britain and France in 1803 that doomed the French attempt to reconquer Saint Domingue/Haiti.

War between Britain and France also ensured that the former could devote only part of its attention to war with the US in 1778–83 and, even more, 1812–14; and, more generally, lessened the chances for British pressure on the US on other occasions. Indeed, the British had only been able to make a major effort to regain North America (including Canada) in 1776 because they were not then at war with France. This was amply recognized at the time and helped to make French entry a crucial goal for the Americans.

Indeed, French entry ensured that the conflict became a world war. In military, strategic and political terms, it provided force, range and options that the Americans on their own could not deploy. Politically, this included a representation in international power politics that rebels could not obtain on their own. Crucially, French entry also cleared the hurdle to Spanish entry, for Spain had been worried about supporting rebels. Spanish entry in 1779 made a major difference to the arithmetic of naval strength.

This does not tend to concern scholars of the American Revolution whose focus, unsurprisingly, is the Thirteen Colonies, but in order to understand both sides of the conflict, it is necessary to appreciate the implications of the widening of the war. American naval strength was not strategically important. It could not threaten the British Isles; indeed, the contrast with the situation in 1945 when the invasion of the Japanese home islands appeared a prospect within a year is striking. In contrast, in 1779, France and Spain made an attempt to invade southern England. It was unsuccessful, but reiterated the lesson of 1759 that Britain had to balance transoceanic expansion with the threat to the home base. This indeed prefigured the situation for America until relations with Britain improved. In the event of conflict with Britain, the latter could threaten America with naval action, ranging from blockade to invasion. Indeed, the role of naval power ensured that America was not protected from the power politics of the Western world by distance or the moat of the Atlantic: it was easier for Britain, France or Spain to intervene in the New World than in Eastern Europe, as Mexico discovered in the 1860s. The equations of distance were altered by railways – steam power affected land and sea force projection, but had a greater relative impact on land, followed by the petrol engine – but it was not until air warfare became a strategic tool that the situation was fundamentally transformed.

The need, in assessing American exceptionalism, to consider the impact on the international system of factors of relative power is not intended to remove the issue from the world of political thought and cultural identity, but, rather, to emphasize that the key aspect of this world was the strategic culture of the great powers, and that America had to act within this system. In part, the very rhetoric of standing outside it was an expression of aspirations and anger, and not the description of reality. We need to remember the distinction.

The role of international power politics in American history was such that, once the War of American Independence was over, there was no possibility of any *revanche*, not only because of British political attitudes, but also because Britain had to consider the possibility of revived confrontation with the French. Indeed, the two came close to war in 1787 in the Dutch Crisis, and, again, in 1790, when France promised support to Spain when the latter came close to war with Britain in the Nootka Sound Crisis. As a sign of improved Anglo-American relations in the shadow of Anglo-Bourbon confrontation, the latter crisis opened up the possibility of Anglo-American cooperation against Spain. George Beckwith, a British agent in New York, although not an accredited envoy, explored possibilities in discussion with Hamilton, then Secretary of the Treasury, although different views about the fate of any conquests from Spain prevented these talks from being taken further. At war with France from 1793, the British government was ready to improve relations with the US, negotiating Jay's Treaty, which settled, or at least eased, commercial and territorial disputes. Similarly, although too little and too late, the British government sought to avoid war with the US in 1812.

The Anglo-French context repeatedly encompassed Spain. As an ally of Britain in the latter stages of the Napoleonic Wars, Spain benefited from a measure of British support, and this restrained the US. Conversely, the situation changed after the end of the wars, and the British provided no protection for Florida as American annexationist pressures grew.

The wars that defined America were not yet those in which the country played a central role, a situation that, at least to an extent, continued until 1914–17. The assumption of American exceptionalism (for it is usually argument by assertion, rather than an explicit theoretical and empirical analysis), thus clashes with a need to consider America as a participant, willing and unwilling, in a complex and multipolar international system. Eliga Gould has seen the US as part of an Atlantic system but one that was in a distinct zone to Europe "with fewer obstacles to the exploitation of slaves, the removal of Indians, and expansion beyond its borders."[19] From the perspective of a native Tasmanian or a slave in Mauritius, the distinction might have appeared far less apparent. Alongside this qualification of American exceptionalism, participation in the international system helped to set the parameters and sometimes the content of American domestic history as well.

Notes

The author is most grateful to Peter Onuf for his comments on an earlier version of this chapter.

 1 It can be approached through Eliga H. Gould and Peter S. Onuf (eds), *Empire and Nation: the American Revolution in the Atlantic World* (Baltimore: Johns Hopkins University Press, 2005).
 2 Thomas Perkins Abernethy, *The Burr Conspiracy* (New York: Oxford University Press, 1954).
 3 James Ripley Jacobs, *Tarnished Warrior: Major-General James Wilkinson* (New York: Macmillan, 1938).
 4 Fred Anderson, *A People's Army: Massachusetts Soldiers and Society in the Seven Years' War* (Chapel Hill: University of North Carolina Press, 1984).
 5 Fred Anderson and Andrew R.L. Cayton, *Dominion of War: Empire and Liberty in North America, 1500–2000* (New York: Viking, 2005), 210.
 6 Lawrence Delbert Cress, "Radically Whiggery on the Role of the Military: Ideological Roots of the American Revolutionary Militia," *Journal of the History of Ideas* 40 (1979): 43–60; ibid., *Citizens in Arms: the Army and Militia in American Society to the War of 1812* (Chapel Hill: University of North Carolina Press, 1982).
 7 Article III of "The Northwest Ordinance," July 13, 1787, text in *Major Problems in the Era of the American Revolution, 1760–1791*, 2nd edn (Boston: Houghton Mifflin, 2000), 350–353.
 8 Richard H. Kohn, *Eagle and Sword: the Federalists and the Creation of the Military Establishment in America, 1783–1802* (New York: Free Press, 1975).
 9 Attributed to Charles Cotesworth Pinckney, 1796, when serving as US Ambassador to France.
10 Theodore J. Crackel, *Mr. Jefferson's Army: Political and Social Reform of the Military Establishment, 1801–1809* (New York: New York University Press, 1989).

11 Spencer C. Tucker, *The Jeffersonian Gunboat Navy* (Columbia: University of South Carolina Press, 1993).
12 Douglas R. Egerton, "The Empire of Liberty Reconsidered," in *The Revolution of 1800: Democracy, Race, and the New Republic,* James P.P. Horn, Jan Lewis and Peter S. Onuf (eds) (Charlottesville: University of Virginia Press, 2002), 309.
13 For an introduction to the extensive literature, see J. Mackay Hitsman, *The Incredible War of 1812: a Military History* (Toronto: University of Toronto Press, 1965) and George Francis Gillman Stanley, *The War of 1812: Land Operations* (Toronto: Macmillan, 1983).
14 Reginald C. Stuart, "Special Interests and National Authority in Foreign Policy: American–British Provincial Links during the Embargo and the War of 1812," *Diplomatic History* 8 (1984): 311–328.
15 James M. Banner, *To the Hartford Convention: The Federalists and the Origins of Party Politics in Massachusetts, 1789–1815* (New York: Knopf, 1970).
16 Wiley Sword, *President Washington's Indian War: the Struggle for the Old Northwest, 1790–1795* (Norman: University of Oklahoma Press, 1985).
17 Thomas P. Slaughter, *The Whiskey Rebellion: Frontier Epilogue to the American Revolution* (New York: Oxford University Press, 1986).
18 John Lynch, *Caudillos in Spanish America, 1800–1850* (New York: Oxford University Press, 1992); Miguel Angel Centeno, "War in Modern Latin America," in *War in the Modern World Since 1815*, Jeremy Black (ed.) (London: Routledge, 2003), 149–164.
19 Eliga H. Gould, "The Making of an Atlantic State System. Britain and the United States, 1795–1825," in *Britain and the America Go to War: The Impact of War and Warfare, 1755–1815*, Julie Flavell and Stephen Conway (eds) (Gainesville: University Press of Florida, 2004), 260.

2 The United States as rogue state

Gunboat persuasion, citizen marauders, and the limits of antebellum American imperialism

Robert E. May

Editor's introduction

> Analyzing the infamous filibustering expeditions of the mid-nineteenth century, the author lays bare the irony of contemporary rhetoric about rogue states and terrorism. The actions of private citizens and the American government's inability or lack of desire to control them caused other countries to consider the US a rogue nation that supported terrorism. Nevertheless, he concludes that foreign commentators and officials erred in suspecting that the expeditions had the covert support of the US government. He speculates that, just as foreigners misunderstood US policy in the 1850s, so today US national security analysts and the mass media may underestimate the commitment of governments such as Pakistan and Saudi Arabia in the war against terrorism.

The punishment was hardly proportionate to the crime. On July 13, 1854, US naval commander George N. Hollins, an officer long frustrated by his failure to be promoted out of rank, committed a startling act of aggression on a defenseless Central American target. That day, his two-gun war sloop, the USS *Cyane*, opened fire on Greytown, a small port on what is today Nicaragua's Caribbean coast, that had been known as San Juan del Norte before the British temporarily commandeered it several years previously and named it for a colonial official. Hours later, with much of Greytown already leveled, Hollins sent marines to burn buildings that had survived the bombardment. Throughout the affair, which did an estimated $3 million in damage, Hollins encountered no resistance from the inhabitants, who fled the attack.[1]

What provoked Hollins' wrath? Officially, his attack represented the US government's reprisal for a supposed insult to America's national honor at Greytown in May. Solon Borland, the outgoing US minister to Nicaragua and former US senator from Arkansas, had been on board an American-owned steamer making its way from the Central American interior down the San Juan River toward the coast, when the vessel rammed a freight-carrying bongo.[2] Following the impact, the steamer's captain, one T.T. Smith, had shot to death the native owner of the bongo, after the latter castigated him in Spanish for the mishap. Once the steamer arrived down-river, a marshal and deputies from Greytown tried to arrest Smith, but Borland, who had a history of brawling, held them at bay with a rifle. Afterwards, Borland went to the home of Joseph W. Fabens, the US commercial agent at Greytown. When the mayor and other officials of Greytown turned up to apprehend Borland, the minister claimed diplomatic immunity from arrest. During the dispute, someone threw a bottle at the minister, grazing his face, before the gathering broke up. The very next day, Borland sailed to the United States, where he lodged a complaint with President Franklin Pierce's administration against the authorities at Greytown, claiming that he had been held illegally under house arrest at Fabens' residence. Pierce's naval secretary, James C. Dobbin, then dispatched Hollins with instructions to teach Greytown's residents that the US government considered such "outrages" unacceptable. Although Dobbin expressed a preference that Hollins do this without resorting to violence, Hollins made minimal effort to avert the use of force. Rather, upon arrival, he had posted notice in Greytown that he expected the townspeople to apologize for the insult to Borland and pay $24,000 for cumulative damages to US property. When the inhabitants neither responded to Hollins' placards nor his subsequent proclamation that he would bombard the town the next day if his demands were not immediately satisfied, Hollins carried out his threat.

In retrospect, the *Cyane*'s guns represent something larger than retaliation for a relatively trivial affront to America's diplomatic dignity. Rather, the assault expressed the growing assertiveness of American capitalists and commercial expansionism in foreign countries in the mid-nineteenth century – in this case the investment of US businessmen in schemes of transportation across the Central American isthmus during the heyday of the California Gold Rush. During the years prior to the attack, the American business that owned Smith's river craft, the Accessory Transit Company, had experienced an adversarial relationship with officials in Greytown, then a self-governing, duty-free port within the boundaries of the indeterminate "Mosquito" protectorate claimed by the British over much of Central America's eastern coast. According to charter rights acquired by the Accessory Transit Company from the government of Nicaragua (which never recognized Britain's protectorate) in 1851, the Company held the right to transport passengers and goods across Nicaragua via the San Juan River and other routes. But in 1851, a British naval vessel had fired on the company steamboat *Prometheus* to enforce harbor dues imposed by Greytown authorities on incoming vessels. Since the US government, like Nicaragua, had never formally recognized Britain's protectorate, it denied Greytown's right to tax US commerce and protested what it considered an act of aggression. Although this crisis was defused when Britain disavowed the attack and agreed to refrain from enforcing such dues in the future, town–company relations remained tense, and were exacerbated when the company transferred its operational base from Greytown itself to Punta Arenas, a sand spit across the bay. There, the company erected a hotel, docks, and warehouses. Since passengers in transit across Central America would no longer need to stay or spend money in Greytown, its merchants faced a considerable loss of potential income; 23,957 travelers crossed Nicaragua via the Greytown area in 1853 alone. Greytown's council – ironically dominated by Americans – responded in February 1853 by demanding that the company immediately tear down some of its facilities at Punta Arenas and totally abandon the site within a month. Intervention by Captain Hollins had temporarily postponed a show-down. Still, from the company's perspective, the crisis demonstrated that the denizens of Greytown needed to be intimidated, with the company gaining mastery over the port. To this end, company president Joseph L. White had gone to Washington and lobbied the Pierce administration for assistance. The Borland matter played into his hands, and he made the most of it. In a letter to Fabens dated June 16, 1854, White explained that Hollins' instructions left much discretion to Fabens, and that White did not want Hollins to show mercy to the town. It would be better for Greytown's "scoundrels" to be punished severely, enabling the company to "build it up as a business place" and install its own officials there. Hollins dutifully had consulted with Fabens prior to the bombardment, and Fabens had helped to frame Hollins's demands on the town.[3]

At a time when many Americans are possibly becoming inured to the "collateral damage" of US military operations abroad, it is instructive to ruminate upon the Greytown affair, an assault so heavy-handed that even Hollins's confidant, naval officer Samuel Francis Du Pont, questioned the necessity of Hollins being so "fierce" against Greytown's "nest." While this single instance of the pre-Civil War abuse of US power abroad had no particular significance in its own right, the bombardment signified an emergent pattern in US foreign affairs.[4]

Although in hindsight, as the eminent historian David Potter pointed out so lucidly many years ago, it is natural to regard the years before the Civil War as a troubled period when domestic disputes over slavery surely dominated American national discourse, one can just as easily regard the 1850s as a time when many Americans had other things on their minds, and when the expansionist ideology of Manifest Destiny "still had much luster." In the mere six decades from the ratification of the US Constitution to the enormous land cession from Mexico in the 1848 treaty ending the US–Mexican War, the nation had grown from about 890,000 square miles to some 2,997,000 square miles. Furthermore, American armed forces, a high percentage of them volunteer amateurs, had just defeated a Mexican army that many astute European military observers considered superior to the American establishment. What new territory might the nation acquire in the decades ahead? What new markets might the nation open overseas for its surpluses? Despite escalating sectional tensions, it was only clear to the most far-sighted Americans in the early 1850s that civil war lay just beyond the chronological corner. Rather, many Americans instead considered it likely that their united nation, recently enriched by the discovery of gold in newly acquired California, would probably grow considerably in territorial mass and commercial influence abroad in the years to come.[5]

Consider in this light Commodore Matthew C. Perry's famous expedition to "open" Japan, a country closed to foreign intercourse (with the exception of a limited Dutch trade based on an island off Nagasaki) since the 1600s. Perry's venture reached its culmination on March 31, 1854, a season before Hollins obliterated Greytown. On that date, with American warships lurking offshore, Japanese officials signed with Perry the Treaty of Kanagawa, allowing the opening of two Japanese ports for provisioning American ships. Perry's limited agreement, which also included provisions protecting US seamen stranded in Japan, in turn paved the way for a major trade agreement with Japan several years later. Significantly, although Perry successfully cultivated the goodwill of Japanese officials and the treaty ceremony occurred in an atmosphere devoid of blatant acrimony, the document resulted from intimidation. The Millard Fillmore administration had sent Perry to Japan as commander of a significantly reinforced East India Squadron, with instructions (apparently drafted by Perry himself) to impress the Japanese with America's "power and greatness." In 1853, after reaching Asian waters via the Cape of Good Hope, Perry had landed troops in violation of the wishes of local officials at the port of Naha on the nominally Japanese Great Lew Chew Island (today Okinawa), and then shrewdly deployed his warships, sailors and marines at Edo (Tokyo) Bay. This display of strength persuaded Japanese officials to enter into the preliminary negotiations that established the foundation for the 1854 treaty. And, as with the Greytown bombardment, Perry's expedition had an imperial edge to it. During his mission, Perry put in at the British-claimed Bonin Islands (northeast of Grand Lew Chew Island), and subsequently advised their acquisition by the US so that Port Lloyd there might become a significant coaling station for mail steamers. Perry's official narrative of his mission, which was published by Congress, advised Americans to regard the term "colony" favorably and consider establishing a settlement on Formosa. In fact, in a post-expedition address to the American Geographical Society of New York, Perry prophesied that Americans, "in some form or other," would "extend their dominion" to include the Pacific islands and even get the "Saxon race" upon Asia's eastern shore.[6]

Consider also the "Ostend Manifesto" – the product of a conclave of the US ministers to Great Britain, France, and Spain actually drafted at Aix-la-Chapelle in Prussia[7] in October 1854, a season after the incident at Greytown. The Manifesto argued arrogantly that the United States, by the logic of self-preservation, could legitimately seize the Spanish colony of Cuba if Spain declined to sell it. Moreover, in 1855, when cruising in the

Fiji Islands in the South Pacific, Commander Edward B. Boutwell of the US Navy disregarded Navy Department orders that, in the course of investigating American complaints against Fijians and demanding reparations for damages to US property, he should not simply assume the veracity of reports about native depredations. Rather, Boutwell burned several places without legitimate evidence against the inhabitants. Appropriately, an Australian newspaper quipped that an officer of America's "model republic" had been carrying on in a "Greytown style among the Fijians." The historian David F. Long, surveying US naval missions in the South Pacific for the entire period 1826–1858, found such numbing evidence of American aggressions against natives that he could only lament that one officer who carried out mercy missions in New Zealand in 1845 represented a glaring exception to the rule.[8]

Such acts of governmental military zeal and verbal aggression against foreign states and populations are revealing enough. But, simultaneously, numbers of Americans were deeply enmeshed in plotting and carrying out "filibusters" – a form of private, unauthorized aggression abroad. Filibustering, a term that entered the English language soon after the Mexican War, generally referred in the late antebellum years to persons who planned or participated in private military expeditions against foreign countries or foreign colonies at peace with their own nations. Filibustering not only transgressed international law but was also prohibited by the US Neutrality Act of 1818, which mandated fines and jail terms for such criminal behavior. Thousands of Americans nonetheless broke the law and became involved in such plots, most of which involved strikes on Mexico, Central America, and the Spanish colony of Cuba. Press rumors, additionally, had Americans plotting such assaults across oceans against Ireland, Hawaii, and other places. In fact, there were so many such expeditions it is safe to assume that on virtually any day between the Mexican and Civil wars at least one of them was going on or was in its formative stages.[9]

Using Hollins' bombardment of Greytown in July 1854 as a chronological anchor, it is easy to probe antebellum filibustering's frequency and transparency, despite the efforts of some filibuster leaders to keep their planning secret so as to avoid arrest and prosecution. July 1854 marked about the midway point in the 1853–1855 plot of former Mississippi governor and Mexican War hero, John A. Quitman, to mount a filibuster to free Cuba from Spanish rule and eventually annex it to the United States. In the summer of 1853, General Quitman, as he was commonly addressed despite having been out of the army for years, had consented to requests from Cuban exiles in New York City to command an expedition. By July 1854, he had developed an extensive network of co-conspirators and made considerable progress in fund-raising and recruitment.

Documents dated throughout the month leave a paper trail on Quitman's plot. On July 1, for instance, a graduate of the Kentucky Military Institute sent Quitman an unsolicited letter saying that he had learned through the grapevine that Quitman had become the leader "of the Cuban patriots of the south," and that he would raise a "gallant band of sharp shooters" from his part of Kentucky to serve the "patriot cause." Five days later, a correspondent of one of Quitman's agents sent news from St. Joseph, Louisiana, that if Quitman would promise that his departure for Cuba was imminent, two local gentlemen would purchase $30,000 worth of bonds that Quitman was hawking to finance the expedition. On July 10, the notorious territorial expansionist and New York City journalist John L. O'Sullivan advised Quitman from his diplomatic post as US chargé d'affaires in Lisbon, Portugal, regarding the status of reported Spanish military reinforcements for Havana. O'Sullivan wished that Quitman would "prosper" in all his "works." Less than a week later, a cadet at the Virginia Military Institute solicited Quitman, saying he could be of considerable service since he knew Spanish and had been partially raised in Cuba. He hoped Quitman would grant him at least a lieutenancy in the invasion. On July 18, an influential Texan newspaperman dated a letter to Quitman saying that he had met their mutual friend, former US Treasury secretary Robert J. Walker, in Galveston. Walker not only favored Quitman's plans but also expressed a regret that he could not risk his fortune and life in the cause because he was too deeply engaged, at that particular moment, in a Texas railroad promotion. And so it went. On the last day of the month, Louisiana planter Samuel J. Walker reported to Quitman about his current activities in New York and Washington on behalf of the anticipated invasion.[10]

Quitman was hardly the only filibuster leader active that month. By July 1854, Henry L. Kinney, the Corpus Christi, Texas, entrepreneur had initiated a project that would result, the next year, in his filibuster to the Mosquito Coast and his occupation of Greytown. In May, Nicaragua's minister to the United States lodged a complaint with the US Department of State about Kinney's front organization, the Central American Land and Mining Company, which was seeking backing by falsely claiming title to a massive land grant on the Mosquito Coast. It would not be long, moreover, before William Walker, the most famous filibuster in US history, would invade Nicaragua. On December 28, an acquaintance of his would sign a contract with one of the factions in Nicaragua's ongoing civil war that provided for Walker's bringing 300 men to intervene in the strife. Walker, who was just back from an invasion of Mexico in 1853, would indeed sail to filibuster in Nicaragua, though with only fifty-six men. He left San Francisco in May 1855 on a brig bound for Nicaragua's Pacific coast, and played an important part in the warfare there over the following months. Although Walker initially served in a subordinate position to Nicaraguan natives, first in military units, later within a coalition government, he eventually seized power by stages, culminating in his being inaugurated Nicaragua's president in the summer of 1856, following his victory in a manipulated election. An allied Central American military force, with some British naval assistance, defeated Walker by the spring of 1857, and he was evacuated to the United States, as were most of his surviving followers, in the months following his capitulation on May 1, 1857. Still, Walker had controlled much of Nicaragua, and he would filibuster there again.[11]

In the Hawaiian kingdom, meanwhile, government officials anxiously followed news reports about Walker's invasion of Mexico, wondering whether California's filibusters would strike at their islands next. In January 1854, David L. Gregg, the new US commissioner to Hawaii, informed the US State Department that Walker's "recent operations in Lower California" had "somewhat excited" Hawaiian prince Alexander Liholiho, who feared "a similar descent upon the Hawaiian group." In fact, the prince had become alarmed to the extent, Gregg thought, that he might prove receptive to proposals that the United States annex the islands in order to guarantee their safety. Though Hawaiian annexation would not occur for decades, Hawaiian officials remained worried about the filibusters over the months following Gregg's dispatch. In November, Gregg reported that prejudice was being "constantly engendered against Americans ... by the frequent rumor of filibustering expeditions from California."[12]

American filibusters never did mount an attack on Hawaii, but they might have done so had Louisiana's US Senator John Slidell had his way. In May 1854, in order to assist the Quitman plot, Slidell had formally but unsuccessfully moved that Congress temporarily legalize such private attacks by suspending America's neutrality laws. Although Slidell rationalized his measure by saying that he wanted to facilitate filibustering in support of Cuban revolutionary activity against Spain, his initiative had the potential to unleash thousands of filibusters against all sorts of places, since surprising numbers of Americans throughout the decade considered becoming filibusters despite its illegality. Some such talk was obviously not intended to be taken literally, as when the African-American intellectual James McCune Smith told Frederick Douglass that American free blacks would encounter less racial discrimination if they could prove to whites their capacity for vigorous action. "We must," Smith exclaimed, "do something to take away this reproach of imbecility; it does not matter so much what we do, whether we overrun Sonora, or create an Industrial School." But much of the "chatter" was serious indeed. Had filibustering been legalized as Slidell wished, there is no telling how many such expeditions would have been launched.[13]

What to make of so much US belligerence against other countries within one compact time frame? Not much, were the happenings of 1854 an aberration from the American narrative. But one could make a similar case using alternate events for virtually any year before the Civil War. Such persistent aggressions confirm recent historiography showing the United States as a more imperialist nation than its leaders, for the most part, have been willing to concede, or the public believe. As one scholar puts it, Americans mistakenly tend to take for granted that since their nation was founded in warfare against an empire, its citizenry had "little appetite or interest in foreign conquest." Such comforting assumptions distort America's origins, since the true pre-Revolutionary imperialists of British North America and the instigators of the war that cleared the continent of French colonies were Pennsylvania fur traders rather than colonial officials in London. The stereotype of US innocence certainly becomes problematic regarding the mid- and late nineteenth century.[14]

The standard rationale for anti-imperial interpretations of US nineteenth-century history rests on the partial fiction that, although the United States experienced dramatic territorial growth, it eschewed imperialism by incorporating annexed territory into its body politic and relatively quickly conferring citizenship on the inhabitants of acquired lands. European imperial powers, in contrast, ruled conquered peoples as colonial subjects. That is, as Thomas Hietala points out in his discussion of US territorial rhetoric in the 1840s (a decade when the United States added some 800,000,000 acres to the national domain), although American expansionists actually invoked the term "empire" to paint their nation's future, they simultaneously claimed exemption from imperial stigmas since their system supposedly was based on consent. For a long time, many scholars too uncritically accepted this self-congratulatory perspective, and their presumptions became enshrined as textbook truths. Elementary and secondary school history textbooks of the 1940s, Frances Fitzgerald tells us, typically emphasized Franklin D. Roosevelt's Good Neighbor policy respecting Latin America while treating imperialism as a "European affair." US restraint culminated, according to this American myth, at the turn of the twentieth century in China – with the United States pursuing a supposedly benign "open door" policy at the very time that the European powers and Japan were carving out spheres of influence there. True, America annexed its Spanish–American War prize of the Philippine Islands around the same time and attempted to rule Filipinos as conquered subjects, but this, according to the traditional view, was such a deviation from established American policy that the US eventually conferred independence on the islands. As Frederick Merk put it in a pathbreaking work on Manifest Destiny, imperialist doctrines misrepresented America's "national spirit." Rather, Americans anticipated that their nation might best improve the world by providing a model for representative government elsewhere.[15]

Newer interpretations often disagree. Richard W. Van Alstyne's 1960 synthesis, *The Rising American Empire*, argued that America's ambitions from the beginning were global rather than limited continentally, and recent scholars have almost made it trendy to apply terms like "empire" and "imperial" to the nation's nineteenth-century expansionist record, often incorporating the words within their book titles. Consider, for instance, Amy S. Greenberg's *Manifest Manhood and the Antebellum American Empire*, Fred Anderson and Andrew Cayton's *The Dominion of War: Empire and Liberty in North America*, and Eric T. Love's *Race over Empire: Racism and US Imperialism.* Anderson and Cayton extend this discussion by applying such an understanding to American military history, arguing that Americans generally memorialize some of their wars rather than all of them, and that American memory obscures those conflicts, including Indian wars, suggestive of American aggression and imperialism. Such chapters in our past evoke unpleasant dissonance that we seek to avoid confronting, since Americans typically would rather believe their country "peace-loving" and anti-imperial.[16]

Can we utilize such constructs to address the aggressions of 1854? Yes, especially in light of Anderson and Cayton's provocative finding that a persistent Jacksonian strain of borderland warfare – by which people, not governments, become the best judges of means to their own security – infected America's foreign relations. According to this perspective, the mission of the US government "was to facilitate, not obstruct, local wishes." Certainly the Cuba filibusters felt this way. Feeling threatened by rumors that Spanish authorities intended to emancipate Cuba's slaves, which the filibusters stigmatized as the "Africanization" of the island, they believed that they had every right to seize the law into their own hands and bitterly resented it when federal legal and military authorities dared to interfere with their operations. Not surprisingly, Anderson and Cayton reference both filibustering and the defensively defiant language of the Ostend Manifesto within their short treatment of the 1850s in *The Dominion of War*.[17]

But let us go further than Anderson and Cayton, and consider the contemporary ramifications of US overseas aggressions in the 1850s. From the viewpoint of some foreign observers and victims, US gunboat aggressions were unwarranted, an infringement of codes of civilized national behavior. Commander Boutwell's tactics in Fiji, for example, provoked remonstrations from natives as well as missionaries in the islands. One chief wrongly victimized by Boutwell's heavy-handed tactics condemned the officer's behavior as "unworthy of the Government of America." British Foreign Secretary Lord Clarendon, during an interview about the Greytown affair with US minister James Buchanan, angrily complained that England's "American cousins" seemed to have concluded that force provided "the right mode" of resolving diplomatic differences between the two nations. The US government's publication in early 1855 of documents concerning the Ostend Conference led to similarly phrased recriminations abroad, with the London *Times* suggesting that George Washington would never have tolerated such "dishonourable" diplomacy. During the American Civil War, an Englishman explained to his American cousin that the Ostend Conference had so offended the English that many people in his country now were taking comfort in seeing the "lawless" citizens of the United States enmeshed in bloodshed within their own borders. Now the US, a country more "over-bearing in its diplomacy" than any in the history of humanity, would be distracted by war from its customary aggressive course abroad.[18]

But foreign observers, especially the European Great Powers, could only say so much about US gunboat diplomacy, given the heavy-handed methods of their own overseas military establishments in the recent past. From the late 1830s through the late 1840s, for instance, French naval commanders had used threats of bombardment during a series of visits to Tahiti in order to wring concessions about Catholic missionary activity there from the island's queen. Eventually, in 1847, France converted the island into a protectorate. Meanwhile, between 1837 and 1842, French gunboats intimidated Hawaii's king into a series of concessions about missionaries and trading rights in those islands. During its Opium Wars with China in the late 1830s and early 1840s, and then again in the late 1850s (the second time in alliance with France), Britain protected its merchants' lucrative drug trade in the Far East, gained Hong Kong, opened other Chinese ports to British trade, and extracted additional concessions from Chinese imperial officials. In 1843, the British had temporarily seized Hawaii; six years later, that nation temporarily took possession of Tigre Island off the coast of Honduras. The island had strategic significance because it overlooked a possible Pacific outlet for a contemplated canal across Central America. Greytown, most relevantly, might never have become Hollins' target had not a considerable naval flotilla from Britain's Jamaican colony in 1848 driven Nicaraguan authorities from the port, attacked and destroyed a Nicaraguan fort upriver, and compelled Nicaragua's government to agree to a treaty recognizing Britain's de facto occupation of San Juan del Norte. President Pierce, therefore, had a legitimate basis for observing that there had been "repeated instances in the history of states standing in the very front of modern civilization where communities far less offending and more defenseless than Greytown have been chastised with much greater severity," in his exculpatory message to Congress about Hollins' bombardment.[19]

Foreigners had better cause for umbrage at US filibustering since no other nation matched the United States when it came to popular support for private expeditions and the number of such plots. One Nicaraguan diplomat in Washington characterized US filibustering as the "scandal of the age," and many foreigners were so bewildered by the amount of filibustering that Americans engaged in that they could only assume that virtually all Americans were filibusters, if not in practice, at least in spirit. The British traveler, Charles Mackay, for example, hardly saw William Walker as indispensable to America's filibuster movement. Rather, Mackay viewed the US's most important filibuster as only a "straw upon the wind" – totally expendable since literally "hundreds of others" would "supply his place" if fate should "give him the pirate's death, instead of the victor's laurel, and a high gibbet instead of Nicaragua." A British diplomat used similar logic when characterizing the entire American population as gun-toting, reckless, and desperate people who, along with their government, shared Walker's ambitions.[20]

Mackay's allusion to Walker's "pirate's death," a rather accurate prognosis given the filibuster's execution without trial by a Honduran firing squad not long after Mackay's travel account was published, deserves rumination. Filibusters, from the perspective of many observers abroad, passed so far beyond the pale of decent human behavior, as one British official in Belize phrased it, that "no civilized being" could approve of them. Repeatedly, foreign commentators condemned filibusters as pirates, though there were plenty of other synonyms in play, such as "vipers" and "freebooters." Thus, an English newspaper cautioned readers against sympathy for filibusters executed by Spanish authorities in Cuba because there was "nothing to distinguish the sufferers from ordinary pirates or murderers," and the commander of a British steam war vessel cautioned some of Henry Kinney's associates that if Kinney's force landed at Punta Arenas without authorization from the US government, he would "seize and treat them as pirates." Spain's captain general in Cuba, the island's governing official, issued a proclamation at the time of the first major US-based filibuster to Cuban soil in 1850, warning that "foreign pirates" had arrived; and, around the same time, Spain's minister to the United States, Angel Calderón de la Barca, denounced the invaders as pirates in official correspondence with the State Department. The next year, Calderón's wife, Fanny, in a letter to the American magazine editor Orestes Brownson outlining her husband's views about the second expedition, observed that had the minister the time to write a full article for Brownson's journal, he "would speak to the *impunity* of the pirates who attacked Cardenas" and the robbery and murder that they committed. Fanny included with her letter a translation of instructions from Spain's government to her husband arguing that hostile acts against a country at peace with one's own country was tantamount to piracy under international law. Ultimately, Brownson published an anti-filibustering article entitled "Piratical Expeditions against Cuba" in the January 1852 *Brownson's Quarterly Review* that elaborated the Calderons' arguments.[21]

The governments and peoples of Mexico and the Central American states, with as much cause to resent US filibusters as the British and Spanish, railed against them with similar phrasing. Walker's force, from the perspective of Mexican officials, committed "piratical depredations." To Luis Molina, Costa Rica's chargé d'Affaires in Washington, Nicaragua's nationality and independence had been obliterated by "pirates who sailed from the coasts of the United States." Perhaps the most telling language came from the Mexican physician who claimed to have been the one to execute Henry Crabb after that filibuster surrendered his force to Mexican troops at Caborca, Sonora, during an 1857 filibuster. "I had the opportunity to cut Crabb's head off and I have got it in a preserve to remember the piraticle [*sic*] action of Crabbism," exulted the filibuster's professed executioner.[22]

Perhaps more importantly, the overwhelming majority of foreign commentators assumed that the US government tolerated the expeditions. America's minister in France, William C. Rives, reported to the State Department at the time of the Cuba filibuster of 1850 that it was becoming common for the French press to insinuate that the filibuster had been "winked at" by the US government. Rives' counterpart in Mexico, James Gadsden, reported in 1853 that he encountered a prevailing suspicion "that the Government in Washington secretly favored these movements." The British publication, *Blackwood's Magazine*, hypothesized that American leaders were unwilling to put the filibusters down because filibustering was so popular in the United States that politicians feared they would lose office should they truly exert themselves to interrupt the attacks. Some overseas commentators reversed the common wisdom and even argued that instead of the filibusters manipulating the US government, federal leaders were pulling the filibusters' wires. British Foreign Secretary, Lord Clarendon, believed that Washington was implicated in both the Kinney and Walker affairs in Central America, telling the British Prime Minister, Lord Palmerston, that Kinney was "of course acting under secret instruction from the United States government." None other than Karl Marx, in a public letter dated from London not long after the Civil War commenced, bluntly claimed that the White House had "directed" all of America's filibuster attacks on Central America.[23]

Further, foreign critics believed, even if US authorities were innocent of complicity in the launching of expeditions, they betrayed their obligations under international law to punish filibustering perpetrators after the fact. Although US leaders arrested several filibuster leaders, including Walker, following their reappearance on US soil after failed invasions, federal authorities only won a handful of convictions in those cases. The low conviction rate was incomprehensible to many foreign governments, especially that of monarchical Spain. As one scholar put it, Spaniards found it difficult to fathom what transpired in American courts since in their own country "the outcome of a trial could be influenced by the regime in Madrid." Foreign governments had relatively little understanding of how legal technicalities, American presumptions of innocence, and public opinion thwarted conscientious efforts by US officials to prosecute the invaders.[24]

Instead, foreigners commonly jumped to the conclusion that US leaders must be complicit in the expeditions. That many American leaders of the period, in both the Congress and the White House, were, indeed, confirmed believers in Manifest Destiny and uninhibited about rhetorically proclaiming its precepts seemed to validate such assumptions, as did American major party platforms, especially those of the Democrats, which sometimes boldly endorsed programs of territorial expansion. President Franklin Pierce, though perhaps not quite as stridently expansionist as some congressional leaders of his Democratic party, provides a useful example of the alarming rhetoric emanating from Washington. Pierce announced in his March 1853 inaugural address that his administration would pursue new territorial annexations because such acquisitions were essential to the nation's national security and commercial interests. In his first annual message to Congress the following December, Pierce affirmed that, although some critics had formerly challenged America's steady expansion "through acquisitions of territory," these additions were "now universally seen and admitted to have been wise in policy" – a step "in the advancement ... of the human race, in freedom, in prosperity, and in happiness." True, Pierce also slipped language into both messages indicating his intolerance of filibustering as a means to such ends – "no apparent advantage can be purchased at a price so dear as that of national wrong or dishonor" – and all presidents of the period released a minimum of one formal proclamation to the American people denouncing filibustering and warning US citizens about their criminality. But, from the perspective of foreign complainants, it was unfathomable that filibuster leaders could go about their illicit planning day after day, attract widespread publicity, and still avoid imprisonment. Rather, it made sense to read filibustering intent into all US expansionist behavior. Thus, when in 1854 US Secretary of State William L. Marcy told the British minister to the United States in an obviously joking manner that the United States would expect Anglo-French toleration for its plans to annex Cuba in return for US neutrality in the Crimean War (which pitted Britain and France against Russia), the minister seriously predicted to his government that Marcy would eventually propose a US alliance with Britain and France "if we only wink very hard at a little filibustering" against Cuba. And the Parisian banker, Baron Salomon de Rothschild, learning during a sojourn to the United States that the Democratic Party's 1860 national platform included a plank for the acquisition of Cuba, instinctively reacted that it "smells of a filibuster." He jumped to this conclusion even though the platform, which endorsed Cuba's annexation on "honorable" terms, said nothing of the sort.[25]

How could William Walker have ever commenced his "scandalous" attack on Baja California from San Francisco, one Mexican minister to the United States wondered in a complaint to the State Department, when it "had been announced" beforehand that Walker's expedition was about to leave the port? Obviously, federal officials there were grossly incompetent in carrying out their preventive responsibilities. Perhaps such authorities were even so implicated in the plot that they never had any intention of exercising proper vigilance. As another Mexican representative in Washington put it when discussing an earlier filibuster, it was "beyond doubt ... that the authorities of the United States on the frontier, witness, dissemble and tolerate this iniquitous invasion." Washington needed to do something differently, if it really wished to prevent such affairs. Yet a third exasperated Mexican minister remonstrated that presidential proclamations of good intent were nice, but they would only forestall future expeditions if the government made an example of past culprits by seeing to it that they were "tried and punished." Contrasting the failure in San Francisco with anti-filibustering passages in Pierce's recent message, Mexican diplomats could only inquire pointedly what Washington was doing to ensure the prevention of such attacks in the future.[26]

Similarly, a London newspaper applied circumstantial evidence and logic to discredit arguments that America's governing officials made a conscious effort to prevent an 1851 expedition against Cuba from leaving US soil:

> We cannot ... excuse the Americans for having, either by supineness or want of   due vigilance, allowed such expeditions to leave their shores. It will be said that they eluded the vigilance of the authorities; this will never be accepted as an excuse, because it is impossible. Armaments of that magnitude, organization so complete, the vast amount of arms, munition and provisions, the hiring of vessels, all these demands, indeed, require an amount of publicity: even when the transactions are attempted as quietly as possible, they could not escape the notice of Government officers at the place of departure. There must have been ... great remissness, if not connivance ... [by US port authorities].[27]

Spanish leaders agreed, highlighting particular evidence that they felt proved conclusively the complicity of US officials with the filibusters. For instance, Calderón, in reference to an incident after the 1850 filibuster to Cuba, when a Spanish war vessel had chased a fleeing filibuster vessel from Cuban waters back to Key West, Florida, expressed astonishment that the customs collector at Key West had taken no steps to prevent the filibusters debarking there with their arms. This lapse occurred, he observed, even though the pursuing Spanish admirals had alerted US vessels in the area to the crimes that the "pirates" had just committed.

Foreign governments felt so besieged by filibustering, that they sometimes simply assumed that filibusters even influenced US foreign policy initiatives that ostensibly had nothing to do with such plots. Spanish officials, for example, suspected that an attempt in 1854 by the US commissioner to the Dominican Republic to negotiate the lease of part or the whole of Samaná Bay for an American coaling station and naval base was evidence that Americans intended turning the bay into "an immense den of filibusters." Foreign observers, in fact, were so paranoid about filibustering that they became vulnerable to elaborate conspiracy theories about the US government. Perhaps the most revealing evidence of such thinking came in the dispatch of one British diplomat in Washington who instinctively discounted documents that seemingly indicated that William Walker operated entirely independently of Washington in his conquest of

Nicaragua and had absolutely no intentions of annexing the country to the United States after he pacified it. The documents consisted of correspondence between Walker and his régime's minister to England, the Cuban exile Domingo de Goicouria, which was released to the *New York Herald* in the fall of 1856. One of Walker's letters emphasized that Goicouria was to convince the British that, rather than being the agent of US expansion, Walker hoped to help Britain forestall the move southward of the US North's "expansive democracy." Rather than take Walker's missives at face value, Britain's chargé d'affaires in Washington, John S. Lumley, hypothesized: "As to Walker's pretended hostility against the US government, no one believes in it." Obviously Walker's show of antagonism to the US represented

> a blind put forward to induce H.M.'s government [Great Britain] to give up Greytown to Walker (that is to the United States) as a convenient harbour for the naval force which will be required in the Caribbean Sea when Central America shall have been conquered by lawless citizens of the US.

Today, we know from a number of sources that Lumley got it completely wrong, and that the documents were quite valid, at least the parts indicating Walker's independence from the US government. But Lumley was hardly unique in misreading Washington's intentions. Two years later, William Gore Ouseley, Britain's envoy to resolve disputes with the United States and several Central American states over British holdings and claims in Central America, reached the conclusion while passing through Washington, DC that President Buchanan was conniving at Walker's machinations as a means of enabling the United States to gain complete control of transit routes across Central America, and perhaps even possession of the entire isthmus. Ouseley claimed that a reliable, private source had intimated to him that US Secretary of State Lewis Cass regularly appeared at the "low ale and wine houses where the adventurers meet," reassuring them that, although the president intended to keep up the pretense in public of opposing filibustering, he would do nothing to stop Walker from a new invasion. Surprisingly, Cass, a notorious territorial expansionist, was not one of the three members of Buchanan's cabinet falsely accused in a French liberal's 1861 travel account as having been members of the Knights of the Golden Circle, a Mexico filibustering group.[28]

Some foreign observers explained, additionally, that if US leaders coddled filibusters, it was understandably because as leaders of a democratic country with elected officials, they were obliged if they wanted to remain in office to carry out the wishes of American public opinion, which from a foreign vantage point appeared to be highly pro-filibustering. During the late antebellum period, there were many rallies and other public demonstrations for the filibusters, especially in America's port cities. Such rallies by no means indicated majority popular support for the expeditions. But to foreign observers who often ignored signs of anti-filibustering US opinion, and instead projected filibustering sentiments on the entire American populace, the complicity of the average American appeared obvious. Thus the Parisian correspondent of a Washington, DC newspaper reported in June 1850 that in reaction to the recent filibuster to Cuba, some papers in the French capital branded all Americans as buccaneers and pirates, rather than just those actually enlisted in the assault.

The British antislavery writer, Harriet Martineau, who interpreted the expeditions as attempts by Southern slaveholders to extend their labor system into the tropics, believed that the attacks had "depressed" America's "national character" and that filibustering, and other displays of America's territorial greed such as the Mexican–American War, had so "marred the peace and morals" of "civilized" society as to create "a world-wide distrust of the American republic, as the great buccaneering Power of the coming time." When Nicaragua's minister to the United States wished Pierce's administration to officially repudiate Henry Kinney's occu-pation of Greytown, he claimed that Kinney's men were affixing "a stain upon the good name of a noble, great and generous Nation." A group of merchants in a Honduran port petitioning in late 1858 for British military help, at a time when William Walker's forces had arrived in nearby waters in another effort against Central America, contended that filibusters, who reportedly had selected their town as a base, merited the "execration of civilized nations." Furthermore, they felt that America's government dis-honored itself by failing to stop their attacks.[29]

Particularly revealing was a diplomatic exchange occurring immediately prior to Secretary of State Cass resigning his office in the fall of 1860. Trying to deflect criticism by Luis Molina, who was then representing several Central American states in Washington, Cass conceded that the United States had its share of filibusters, but argued that so had many other countries throughout history. Apparently referring to Giuseppe Garibaldi's irregular campaigns that year on the Italian peninsula, Cass contended that Europeans were just then carrying on filibusters "upon a scale unknown in this hemisphere." Further, Cass suggested, European governments had no more success than the United States did in detecting and punishing such criminals, even though European leaders had more centralized power at their disposal than did his own administration, which had to operate within a limiting federal system of governance. By the time Molina responded, Cass had resigned from Buchanan's cabinet. But Molina told Cass's replacement, Jeremiah S. Black, that Cass had seriously erred in conflating America's invaders of Latin America, who deserved the "reprobation" of "all the civilized world," with Garibaldi's patriots, who were fighting for the "noble cause" of Italian unification.[30]

An element of hyperbole, of course, attached to foreign commentary on US filibusters. Foreign observers, especially diplomatic representatives, hoped to prod US officials into taking more energetic preventive measures than they seemed willing to adopt against filibustering, and naturally struck the most alarmist, overstated positions they could to induce this policy shift. However, many anti-filibustering Americans, of various political, sectional, and religious affiliations, conceded that the adventurers had significantly tarnished the national image of their country, making it into a veritable pariah within the world community. Thus, Congressman Abraham Venable of North Carolina warned his colleagues that filibustering amounted to a "national iniquity," and Pennsylvania native Josiah Gorgas, commanding the US arsenal in Augusta, Maine, in 1857, concluded that the expeditions represented "a stain on our national character." The next year, in his annual message to the New Jersey state legislature, Governor William Newell reminded his listeners that filibustering contradicted "international comity and law." And at the Washington Peace Conference in February 1861, a last-ditch effort to reach a sectional settlement that might preserve the Union, the Free Soil lawyer and Republican politician from New York, David Dudley Field, alluded to how the filibustering expeditions of the 1850s had already "disgraced this land." Many domestic critics, moreover, supported foreign arguments that the US government was actually in cahoots with the adventurers. *The Atlantic Monthly*, for example, accused officials of the Buchanan administration of having "very blind eyes and very slippery hands" regarding the "freebooters" because of "secret communications" from a hypocritical president whose public denunciations of filibusters were intended to cover his appeasement of them.[31]

Certainly, US commentators had no more compunctions than foreign critics about locating filibusters below the skull and crossbones. Virginia's Democratic congressman, John Letcher, for example, dismissed William Walker as "no better than a Pirate," and assumed that the American people knew better than to support a man out to plunder other countries. Many Yankees, such as the anti-abolitionist, conservative New England Whig John Park and the New York City lawyer George Templeton Strong, who both lambasted filibusters in their diaries, used similar phrasing. Strong conceded Spanish officials in Cuba the right to shoot such pirates immediately upon their capture.[32]

Some of the strongest commentary emanated from the press. A correspondent for a San Francisco paper pleaded with the citizenry of California to support US naval efforts to interdict reinforcements for William Walker's forces in Mexico so that Californians could prove themselves a "law-loving people" who cared about America's "faith and integrity." The Washington (DC) *Constitution* complained that, although filibuster apologists maintained the pretence that the adventurers were spreading liberty abroad, they were actually accomplishing the opposite by "creating a disgust for the institutions" of the United States. The *New-York Evangelist* contended that American freebooters had violated "principles of international propriety" by invading Cuba, even if Spanish rule there was as oppressive as the most "flaming" pro-filibuster stump orator described it. Orestes Brownson, in his magazine article about Cuban filibustering, suggested that if America wished to preserve its national honor and the credibility of its institutions, it must offer Spain formal apologies as well as reparations for damages resulting from the expeditions. The American government and people, Brownson argued, were deluded in thinking that their commitment to democracy gave them the license to "interfere to establish popular institutions wherever they please." Brownson's words resonate today, as Americans grapple with the fallout from their recent intervention in Iraq.[33]

The most perceptive American commentators took their concerns about filibustering beyond the abstractions of national honor, and worried that the expeditions might so affect the goodwill of foreign states toward their country that they might seriously jeopardize US interests abroad. Out in the Hawaiian Islands, for instance, Commissioner Gregg felt that his mission was compromised enough by the movement that he implored Hawaii's foreign minister not to judge all Americans by "such outlaws." But the injury to America's image was naturally most severe in Latin America, the target of virtually all of the immediate pre-Civil War filibustering attacks. Once, many Latin Americans had considered the United States a beacon of democratic resistance to European monarchies. In fact, the liberal founders of Central America's United Provinces, a transitory government including Honduras, Nicaragua, Guatemala, El Salvador, and Costa Rica that lasted for about a decade-and-a-half following the collapse of Spanish rule in the Isthmus, mined the US Constitution for ideas when developing their 1824 constitution. America's federal system of government, especially, drew attention as worth consideration. US travelers to Central America as late as the years immediately prior to the 1850s' filibuster attacks generally received extremely warm receptions from the native population on the Isthmus. Walker's advent, subsequently, destroyed America's benign image, especially since Yankee aggression contrasted with Britain's gradual withdrawal from its imperial Central American holdings during the same period. Central Americans, Thomas Leonard notes, were so traumatized by the filibustering onslaught that they remained wary of US designs on their territory well after Walker's execution. An 1856 editorial in the *Saturday Evening Post* shows that observant antebellum Americans, without Leonard's benefit of hindsight, already comprehended the blow dealt to America's image by the Walker–Kinney filibusters. This Philadelphia publication opined that, although in earlier times the peoples of the Western Hemisphere below America's southern borders had revered the United States as a "political ideal," they were now because of Walker's invasions "becoming averse to us" as a nation that put domination above what is right.[34]

Many of the US military, civil, and judicial officials whose responsibilities included stopping, arresting, and trying filibusters felt similarly about their adversaries. Thus, the US Navy's commander, V.M. Randolph, who rather boldly blockaded an island off the US Gulf coast in 1849 to prevent a filibuster exodus against Cuba, believed that he was obligated to stop "piratical" acts so as to preserve "untarnished the honor of the nation." Secretary of State William L. Marcy, who seems to have been by far the most determinedly anti-filibustering member of Franklin Pierce's cabinet, considered William Walker a "pirate" who needed to be "rooted up." US Supreme Court judge John A. Campbell, who proved to be the filibusters' nemesis on more than one occasion, derided them as "pirates" carrying out the schemes of "grocers & steamboat agents" to win an empire in the tropics. US diplomats abroad, who had ample opportunity to directly observe filibustering's impact upon other governments and populations, found no reason to demur. Rives, in France, reported that the filibusters had "compromised" the "honor of the country." James Gadsden, America's minister in Mexico at the time of Walker's intrusion, believed that conservative Mexican interests were not only using the attacks to foment anti-Americanism, but also more profoundly to undermine Mexican tendencies toward US-style liberalism, democracy, and capitalism. Affirming that the "American system is strong enough to propagate itself without inviting disguised auxiliaries to debase and abuse it," Gadsden told the State Department that the "private expeditions, which are charged with the encouraging sympathy of the U. States Government, are all made use of . . . to create a national dislike of the American and barbaric system of progress."[35]

By now, it should be obvious that this chapter is heading toward irony. At a time in the twenty-first century when US leaders are accustomed to renouncing other countries – most notably in recent years Iraq, Iran, and North Korea – as "rogue" states occupying an "axis of evil," it seems worth recalling that, in the late antebellum period, the United States was regarded throughout a large share of the world as a rogue state for both producing and failing to repress filibusters. More arrestingly, foreign critics occasionally attacked the filibusters in language suggesting behavior beyond the pale of comprehensible human behavior. Whereas George W. Bush has vilified contemporary terrorists as "thugs and assassins," Spain's minister to the US painted the American filibusters who invaded Cuba in 1850 as brigands bent on firing and pillaging Cuba's cities, murdering her population, and committing other excesses meriting the "execration of mankind." Mexico's ministers to the United States, similarly, lodged complaints with the State Department that America's filibusters bore responsibility for "scenes of horror and blood" and threatened the "extermination" of the inhabitants of Lower California and Tamaulipas. In July 1857, Nicaragua's dual presidents complained to James Buchanan, now US President, that the filibusters were "robbers and outlaws, who in the broad light of day, without the slightest restraint or shame, committed every kind of depredation and crime." That fall, Antonio José de Irisarri, in the capacity of minister from Guatemala and El Salvador to the United States, described Walker as "the burner of whole villages ... the plunderer of churches." Spanish and Latin American anti-filibustering rhetoric, in other words, represented Walker and his men in terms not all that different from the way modern terrorists have been condemned by the Bush administration and the American press. An American diplomat posted to Nicaragua and Costa Rica toward the end of the filibuster era reported back to Washington that there was, throughout all of Central America, a "dread" at the "bare mention" of William Walker's name.[36] Alexander Dimitry, the US minister who reported these fears, could have been describing Western reactions to Osama bin Laden's videotape releases after 9/11. Certainly such a language of detestation foreshadowed recent presidential declarations about modern terrorists.

Further, just as today's crisis in terrorism revolves partly around concerns of faith – the tension between Western Judeo-Christian values and Islamic Wahhabi fundamentalism emanating from mosques and madrassas – so too did the mid-nineteenth-century filibustering crisis reflect clashing religious cultures. In that case, the filibusters and the radical expansionists who supported them worshipped at the shrine of the superficially secular doctrine of Manifest Destiny. Although the phrase, by implying that the United States was obviously fated to grow territorially, seems religiously innocent, it was actually, as Anders Stephanson argues, "a sacred-secular project" coined at a time when "apocalyptic Protestantism and utopian mobilization" held considerable sway, and was profoundly fraught with Protestant undertones. The original two pronouncements of the ideology in John L. O'Sullivan's New York City publications, the *Democratic Review* and the *New York Morning News*, both cited "Providence" as the ultimate authority for America's destiny to expand. Although many American Catholics and Jews embraced their nation's expansionist projects (O'Sullivan himself was never particularly committed to his Episcopalian affiliation and eventually converted to Catholicism), most filibusters and their supporters attached to Manifest Destiny what we might label a Protestant endorsement. Virtually all the countries attacked by the filibusters immediately before the Civil War were Catholic; further, they experienced considerable political turmoil, and lagged behind the United States in terms of transportation networks, public education, and industrial development. Filibusters commonly attributed what they perceived as a lack of progress and democracy abroad to Catholicism's oppression, arguing that Catholic priests had so much autocratic control over their parishioners and governments as to stifle creativity, development, and republicanism.[37]

When a US diplomat in Central America reported to the State Department in 1859 that British diplomats had been going to considerable pains to convince Guatemalans that, without their protection, Central Americans would again be the "prey of buccaneering swarms of marauding filibusters," who would "desecrate their religion" and cause "devastation and annihilation," he spoke to the centrality of faith within Latin-American perceptions of US filibusters. In fact, Catholicism provided the inspiration for much of the pan-Central-American resistance to the invasions. Thus, as Costa Rican Catholic bishop Anselmo Llorente y Lafuente sought to inspire his republic's troops as they prepared to fight Walker, he called on them to rally in the defense of their "sacred religion." And, when the President of New Granada (today, Colombia) in 1857 applauded Costa Rica's "holiest of causes" as that state's army tried to bring down Walker's régime by war, he suggested that filibustering, by threatening South America's language and institutions, amounted to cultural as well as military warfare.[38]

In the minds of many domestic and foreign commentators, filibustering represented an attempt to impose American values on other peoples, which of course not only foreshadowed, in some ways, the Wilsonian diplomacy of World War I, but also President George W. Bush's post 9/11 crusade to implant American political institutions within autocratic Middle Eastern states. But we can take modern parallels further. During the filibuster era, peoples attacked or threatened by the filibusters considered their homeland security at stake.

When Bishop Llorente sent off Costa Rica's soldiery, for instance, he beseeched them to rally in defense of "our Homeland." To guarantee their homeland security in warring against what were perceived as US terrorist threats, threatened states responded with defensive precautions and sought the assistance of international coalitions. Reacting to the filibuster invasions of Cuba in 1850 and 1851, for example, Spanish leaders sought Anglo-French military protection for the colony. In 1852, a Spanish initiative even led to a formal proposal by the English and French to the United States (eventually rejected by the US government), by which Britain, France, and the United States would collectively act to "discountenance" all filibusters against Cuba, as well as disavow interest in annexing Cuba themselves, which theoretically would discourage American filibusters wanting to attack again. Similarly, Latin American countries seriously considered international alliances as means of warding off the American filibuster hordes. In a public speech in Paris in June 1856, at the height of Walker's power in Central America, for example, the exiled Chilean anti-clerical intellectual and social radical Francisco Barquín Bilbao argued that the United States, as one of the world's two empires (the other was Russia) was in the process of seeking "global domination" through proxy "predatory guerrillas" (read: filibusters) infiltrating the isthmus and threatening the Panama crossing. Bilbao argued the necessity for South American unification, in the form of an international court, the end of inter-American tariffs, and a congress with each South American republic sending an equal number of representatives. Such a "United States of the South," he predicted, could wage effective war against the Yankee "colossus." For "Walker is invasion, Walker is conquest, Walker is the United States." The very next month, in fact, Venezuela's foreign minister, citing occurrences in Central America that were "known everywhere," sent out a circular letter (based on a Chilean initiative) calling for such a conference in Panama, because of its centralized location. And in September, representatives from Chile, Ecuador, and Peru signed a draft treaty of union, along the lines of Bilbao's proposal. This document included articles that denounced filibustering expeditions as "piratical" and calling for mutual defensive efforts against them. Further, the draft treaty provided that upon ratification, all the other Spanish–American states and Brazil (formerly Portuguese) be invited into the union. In December, with that treaty pending, Costa Rica sent out invitations for the other Latin American republics to attend a congress at San José. Ultimately, although there was a lot of enthusiasm for the unification movement in Ecuador, which itself had been a filibustering target, and although Costa Rica, Guatemala, El Salvador, and the post-Walker government in Nicaragua agreed to the unification proposal, the treaty fell through before the end of 1857 for various reasons, including US opposition, arguments over technicalities in its provisions, and perhaps most important, the fall of Walker's régime. Walker's defeat undercut the sense of urgency that drove the unification movement.[39]

The important point, for our purposes, is how close other nations came to taking very drastic steps in their quest for homeland security against American citizens who were feared, in their day, every bit as much as the terrorists are today. Just how far the Central American states might be willing to compromise their own autonomy for security against filibustering was anybody's guess, especially prior to Walker's defeat in 1857. The US Minister to Great Britain, George Mifflin Dallas, believed in May 1856, at the height of Walker's power, after pondering recent debates in Parliament, that all the Central American states might feel compelled in self-defense to seek a formal British Protectorate over them. Dallas may have overstated the case, but not by much. A US diplomat reported in 1858 that Costa Rica's president told him that Costa Rica would have offered itself as a colony in 1856 to any nation willing to shield it from Walker. That May, at Rivas, Nicaragua, Costa Rica's president did sign a joint declaration with Nicaragua's president contending that William Walker's anticipated next invasion of Nicaragua already had US government patronage and inviting France, England, and Sardinia to make Nicaragua and Costa Rica into a protectorate under whatever conditions the European powers insisted upon. And, in 1860, in the wake of William Walker's final expedition to Central America, the government of Honduras expressed its preference that Britain maintain a protectorate over coastal territory (the Bay Islands off Honduras' coast and that part of the Mosquito Coast within Honduras) that Britain had previously agreed to transfer to Honduras, rather than leave the territory vulnerable to a future filibuster attack.[40]

Of course, one hesitates to take presentism too far. The tactics of modern terrorists, for example, bear little resemblance to those employed by

William Walker's filibuster gang. Most obviously, neither Walker nor any of his antebellum filibuster peers intended mass killings of civilians as a tactic to achieve their political objectives. Nor did filibusters commit suicide for their cause. Whereas antebellum filibusters tended to cross borders as part of formally organized military invasions prepared to immediately engage an enemy in traditional combat, modern terrorists tend to infiltrate individually or in small groups from one country to another in the hopes of avoiding open combat, at least initially. And, although the term terrorist, which originated in the beheadings of the French Revolution, was already in currency, the filibusters escaped its application to themselves.[41]

Still, filibustering had commonalities with modern terrorism. The filibusters, for instance, used secret codes, false identities, and other subterfuges to communicate with each other while avoiding arrest, and they manipulated the press every bit as much as al Qaeda has utilized Al Jazeera, sometimes even posting notices informing citizens how to sign up for pending expeditions. Most importantly, the filibusters committed acts of mass destruction during their campaigns. When the Texas Ranger James H. Callahan needed to cover his retreat from Mexican territory back across the Rio Grande into Texas during his October 1855 filibuster, for instance, he set the village of Piedras Negras on fire, burning it down. The most horrific operation of William Walker's army, moreover, evokes ever so slightly al Qaeda's destruction of the World Trade Center in 2001. What is most significant, from a modern perspective, is less that Walker's troops in November 1856 carried out his orders to burn Granada, a city more than 300 years old, than that Walker, much like Osama bin Laden's infamous post-9/11 tape, subsequently crowed publicly over the destruction and its psychological impact. In his autobiographical account of his Nicaraguan campaigns, Walker gloated over the meaning of the loss of this "cherished city" to his "Legitimist" enemies and defended its reduction as conforming with the laws of war:

> They [the Legitimists] had for their chief city a love like that of a woman; and even after years have passed tears come to their eyes when they speak of the loss of their beloved Granada.... The destruction of Granada was ... a long step toward the destruction of the Legitimist party; and thus the Americans of Nicaragua were able to cripple their most bitter and consistent foe.

Walker, thus, celebrated his elimination of Granada not merely for its military value to his adversaries, but also for its symbolic place in their culture, much as Osama bin Laden exulted about the collapse of that emblem of US capitalism, New York's World Trade Center.[42]

What is, perhaps, relevant concerning our current plight in Iraq and Afghanistan, however, has much less to do with the filibusters' superficial resemblance to modern terrorists than that foreign governments and populations conceptualized them as such and genuinely believed that the US government was fostering their warfare, either through substantive assistance or, minimally, by relaxing enforcement of the Neutrality Law against them.

In truth, at least three of the four US presidents between the end of the Mexican War and the beginning of the Civil War strongly opposed filibustering, and the fourth (Franklin Pierce) at worst wavered in his attitudes about the expeditions. More importantly, all four administrations adopted policies designed to curtail filibustering expeditions, and implemented them. Each one of the presidents issued proclamations to the American people reminding them of the illegality of filibustering and cautioning them against participating in such endeavors, often with the caveat that filibusters forfeited federal protection in the event of their capture and internment abroad, and that they faced prosecution at home for their crimes. Further, cabinet officials during all four presidencies sent out repeated orders from Washington to US officials posted at or near likely filibuster departure points – that is, customs, navy, army, and revenue cutter service officers, as well as US marshals and district attorneys – calling upon them to enforce the Neutrality Act by preventing the departure of expeditions and by arresting and prosecuting offenders. Additionally, the US government during these years, a time when there was no FBI or CIA, hired special agents and extra lawyers to gather evidence against filibusters and prosecute them effectively. If US presidents and their cabinets secretly got the word to federal officials that they did not really mean their own instructions, as foreigners and domestic critics alike suspected, they did a remarkably effective job of covering their tracks. The documentation simply does not exist to sustain such accusations, though there is ample evidence that many federal officials in the field were filibustering sympathizers and sometimes relaxed enforcement of America's neutrality on their own initiative. US presidents removed at least two federal officials from office for perceived derelictions in carrying out their anti-filibustering duties.[43]

A final return to our 1854 guidepost drives this point home. Although, upon taking office, President Pierce reportedly intimated to some of the filibuster leaders through third parties that his administration would not interfere with their schemes, and although Pierce's expansionist rhetoric and diplomatic initiatives such as the Gadsden Purchase clearly demonstrated his desire to supplement the national domain, the New Hampshire Democrat ultimately let the filibusters down, interfering in one way or another with virtually all the expeditions of his presidency. As Secretary of State Marcy put it in an explanatory message to the US minister to Spain, in response to "misapprehensions" about the government's policy: "The President has sedulously maintained these salutary provisions of law [the Neutrality Act] and repressed all unauthorized expeditions." Marcy explained that the President not only believed it his duty to enforce all US law, but also that he was determined to leave the decisions about war and peace with foreign nations in Washington's hands, rather than those of private individuals.[44]

Certainly, the administration was displeased by William Walker's invasion of Mexico, which was at about its midpoint as the year began. Consistent with Marcy's assertions, the president not only issued a proclamation against filibustering to Mexico on January 18 – at a time when Walker was desperately in need of reinforcements – but his cabinet also sent out a succession of orders to its enforcement personnel to stop criminal attacks across the border. In January, Secretary of War Jefferson Davis ordered the US army general in San Francisco to use his "utmost" ability to forestall any "unlawful expeditions against the territories of foreign powers." A few days later, Attorney General Caleb Cushing charged the United States District Attorney for California, S.W. Inge in San Francisco, to employ his "utmost vigilance" to discover and prosecute any violators of the Neutrality Law in his district. After Walker fled Mexico and crossed the US boundary in the spring of 1854, and surrendered to the US army following the failure of his recent invasion, Marcy instructed Inge to maintain his vigilance against filibusters. Inge should ensure that no more expeditions would get out, and he should prosecute Walker so that "Mexico will be convinced of the scrupulous fidelity of this government to its duties and obligations towards her as a neighbour and a friend." Around the same time, Marcy instructed Inge's counterpart in New Orleans (with copies going to US attorneys in New York City, Huntsville [Texas], Mobile, and Key West) to "exert all the power you possess" to "suppress" any filibuster from that port, and to "have judicial proceedings ... at once" instituted against anyone who had already violated the Neutrality Act.[45]

Not only did the administration position itself that year against filibustering to Mexico, but it took action against Quitman's Cuba plot. Pierce specifically condemned filibustering to Cuba in a May 31 presidential proclamation to the American people, a pronouncement that the filibusters considered a serious enough impediment to their scheme that one of Quitman's closest associates mailed a public protest to the press denouncing the edict as illegal and untimely. But the administration, rather than reconsider its position, followed up the proclamation with legal proceedings against Quitman and his collaborators. In June, a federal judge charged a grand jury in New Orleans to investigate Quitman's plot, and when the hearings failed to result in indictments, the judge compelled Quitman and two of his principal associates to post a $3,000 bond apiece as a guarantee that they would obey the Neutrality Act for the next nine months. The next month, Marcy sent E.W. Moise, the district attorney in New Orleans, a copy of a Cuba filibustering circular, hoping that the paper would prove "useful to you in discharging your official duties under ... the neutrality act of 1818." Apparently the administration conveyed similar desires to its district attorney for Mississippi, Horatio

Harris. One of Quitman's confidants informed him that Harris had thrown the filibuster community in Jackson, the state capital, "into a fog" by getting out the word "that he had heard very lately from Washington that ... 'Pierce was determined to prevent any expedition.'" That same month, another of Quitman's confidants traveled to Washington in an attempt to rouse support for the expedition, only to find that the very word "filibusterism" when spoken in the offices of the administration "puts them on nettles," and that hardly anyone in Washington understood the need for an invasion of Cuba. It is no wonder that the pro-filibustering Spanish-language sheet *El Filibustero*, a New York City publication, denounced the US government for refusing its aid to Cuban revolutionary elements.[46]

Over the next two years or so, the Pierce administration similarly took legal and military action against the Kinney and Walker movements to Central America, as well as rumored plots against Ecuador and Ireland. In one particularly revealing letter, Cushing told Inge in San Francisco and the US district attorney in Monterey, California, that the president would not let them relent in their anti-filibustering responsibilities even when the filibusters pretended to obey the Neutrality Act by posing as normal travelers and deferring all military organization until they left US territory. Conceding the difficulty of differentiating filibusters from genuine passengers on departing steamships, Cushing said sternly that Inge nonetheless should do his best to make that very distinction because Nicaragua was "entitled to the special good will of this government."

The point is not that Pierce's record on filibustering was perfect, that there were no lapses, or that another chief executive might have done even better in stopping these affairs. In fact, Durwood Ball, a close student of the army's record in San Francisco during this period, bluntly asserts that Pierce's "tacit acknowledgment of unsanctioned imperialism" subverted the anti-filibustering constabulary duties of soldiers at that post. Rather, my point is that Pierce was sufficiently anti-filibuster for the actual criminals to regard him as an obstruction. John Quitman, on the verge of canceling his Cuba plot partly because of the president's failure to cooperate, denounced Pierce's administration as "humbug" in February 1855. One of Walker's comrades in a letter home from Managua, Nicaragua, claimed that to appease John Bull "Pierce, Marcy and Co." had come "very much down on Walker and his *gang* simply to keep them *infernal* 'Neutrality Laws' inviolate." Another of Walker's associates, similarly exasperated, observed in October 1856 that, although the American people favored the filibuster cause, their government's "blind" policy left the filibusters isolated within the international community. Also revealing is a remark in a public letter from one of Kinney's subordinates, William Sydney Thayer, after Kinney's vessel grounded on a reef on its way to the Mosquito Coast and British officials in Jamaica assisted them in getting out of their predicament. Thayer reflected that "the paw of the British lion" had provided "a more safe refuge for Col. Kinney than the talons of the American eagle." Even Pierce's recognition in the spring of 1856 of Walker's Nicaraguan government is suspect as pro-filibustering policy. Pierce's gesture, as Cushing later explained in a public letter to a Boston newspaper, came at a time when Walker's régime was headed by a native Nicaraguan as president, and could legitimately present itself as the country's "*de facto* government" according to America's "settled policy" of recognizing established polities. After Walker appropriated the presidency for himself, as Cushing accurately recounted, Pierce quickly withdrew the recognition. There simply is no evidence that the administration's multiple anti-filibustering instructions to its civil and military agents were merely a charade to mask pro-filibustering intent. In an age when there was no Internet, telephone, radio, or television contact between Washington and its representatives in the field, the US mail and telegraph messages constituted the primary and often only ways that the federal government could get its policies implemented at the local level. Why should we assume, without substantive countervailing evidence, that Pierce and other chief executives of the pre-Civil War years did not intend their recipients to take them seriously?[47]

This 1854 story, perhaps, has some cautionary value today. Starting immediately after the attacks on the World Trade Center, in part because of the shocking subsequent discovery that almost all the 9/11 suicide hijackers were Saudis, and their leader Muhammad Atta was Egyptian, the US media has been full of accusations that many of our presumed allies in the war on terrorism have actually been guilty of secretly fostering it. Saudi Arabia has received the brunt of this criticism. Thus, for example, in an important *New Yorker* piece in October 2001, Seymour M. Hersh accused the Saudi royal family, starting in 1996, of channeling "hundreds of millions of dollars" to terrorist groups, including al Qaeda. Michael Moore's movie *Fahrenheit 9/11* implied that the Bush administration allowed Saudis in the United States, including members of the bin Laden family, who might well have been involved in the attacks, to fly out of the country in the immediate aftermath of the incident. Dore Gold, in his 2003 work *Hatred's Kingdom*, argued that prior to 9/11, a "generation of Saudis" had been brainwashed by the nation's establishment to hate Christians and Jews as infidels, and that the Saudi government was accustomed to using "international charitable networks to assist the most extreme Islamic organizations that accepted hard-line Wahhabi views," including bin Laden's network. But, for years, charges have circulated that other allied governments in the Middle East and Asia have also either channeled aid to terrorists or only gone through the motions of hunting them down. How could Osama bin Laden have escaped America's manhunt on the Afghan–Pakistani border, and how could the Taliban continue to operate in that region, many analysts wonder, without the tolerance of Pakistan's autocratic ruler, General Pervez Musharraf?[48]

History, of course, never really repeats itself. That foreign states misjudged the US government's filibustering policies in the 1850s has absolutely no bearing on whether modern commentators misrepresent US allies like Saudi Arabia or Pakistan. Further, we err seriously if we conclude that just because the United States could not stop filibusters from crossing borders in the 1850s, foreign states today lack the capacity, assuming that they have the will, to stop terrorists. Too many variables have changed dramatically since the 1850s, such as methods of communication and surveillance, weaponry, the ideologies at stake, and the size of national military establishments, for verdicts based on historical analogies, especially considering the autocratic, and therefore far less transparent, governments at issue today in comparison to the relatively open and democratic nature of the US government before the Civil War. Our retrospective look at the 1850s suggests something far more modest – simply that we hedge our bets until the evidence is definitive. It is as absurd for us today to assume that foreign despots – whose unpopular régimes are highly vulnerable to subversion – have no commitment to rooting out terrorists, as it was for foreign states in the 1850s to assume that a nation committed to territorial expansion allowed criminal adventurers to be its surrogates just a few years after the national domain had just been vastly extended by traditional methods of war and diplomacy.

Notes

The author would like to thank his wife, Jill May (Purdue University College of Education) and his colleague, Michael G. Smith (Purdue University Department of History) for their perceptive suggestions regarding this chapter.

1 George N. Hollins to Samuel Francis Du Pont, April 14, 1852, Samuel Francis Du Pont Papers, Hagley Museum and Library, Wilmington, DE; Edward M. Callahan (ed.), *List of Officers of the Navy of the United States and of the Marine Corps from 1775 to 1900* ... (1901; reprint edn, New York: Haskell House Publishers, 1969), 727; David F. Long, *Gold Braid and Foreign Relations: Diplomatic Activities of US Naval Officers, 1798–1883* (Annapolis: Naval Institute Press, 1988), 126–127; Robert A. Naylor, *Penny Ante Imperialism: the Mosquito Shore and the Bay of Honduras, 1600–1914:a Case Study in British Informal Empire* (Rutherford: Fairleigh Dickinson University Press, 1989), 46–48, 152–174; Allan Nevins, *Ordeal of the Union*, 2 vols (New York: Charles Scribner's Sons, 1947), 2: 366.
2 Bongos were vessels carved out of single tree trunks that could carry about fifty people. Craig L. Dozier, *Nicaragua's Mosquito Shore: the Years of British and American Presence* (Tuscaloosa: University of Alabama Press, 1985), 78.
3 William O. Scroggs, "William Walker and the Steamship Corporation in Nicaragua," *American Historical Review* 10 (July 1905): 793; James M. Woods, "Expansionism as Diplomacy: the Career of Solon Borland in Central America, 1853–1854," *The Americas* 40 (January 1984): 399–415; Long, *Gold Braid*, 122–126; Dozier, *Nicaragua's Mosquito Shore*, 79, 84–85, 87–89; James P. Delgado, *To California by Sea: a Maritime History of the California Gold Rush* (Columbia: University of South Carolina Press, 1990), 59; J.L. White to J.W. Fabens, June 16, 1854, quoted in Vicksburg *Weekly Whig*, September 26, 1855;

John F. Crampton to Lord Clarendon, August 22, 1853, and the editor's notes, in James J. Barnes and Patience P. Barnes, *Private and Confidential: Letters from British Ministers in Washington to The Foreign Secretaries in London, 1844–67* (Selinsgrove: Susquehanna University Press, 1993), 80–81. For the evolution of Britain's Mosquito protectorate (including its relationship to the ambiguously worded and controversial US–British Clayton–Bulwer Treaty of 1850), see Dozier, *Nicaragua's Mosquito Shore*, 1–75, 80; Karl Bermann, *Under the Big Stick: Nicaragua and the United States Since 1848* (Boston: South End Press, 1986), 39–43; Naylor, *Penny Ante Imperialism*, 179–181.

4 Samuel Francis Du Pont to Henry Winter Davis, August 7, 1854, Samuel Francis Du Pont Papers. John H. Schroeder, however, in *Shaping a Maritime Empire: the Commercial and Diplomatic Role of the American Navy, 1829–1861* (Westport: Greenwood Press, 1985), 128, minimizes the bombardment's significance, arguing that it represented a single attempt to safeguard American property abroad rather than being part of any overall policy to extend US influence.

5 David Potter, *The Impending Crisis, 1848–1861*, comp. and ed. Don E. Fehrenbacher (New York: Harper and Row, 1976), 7, 145, 177–180; Robert W. Johannsen, *To the Halls of the Montezumas: the Mexican War in the American Imagination* (New York: Oxford University Press, 1985), 302–310; Otis A. Singletary, *The Mexican War* (Chicago: University of Chicago Press, 1960), 20–21.

6 Samuel Eliot Morison, *"Old Bruin": Commodore Matthew C. Perry, 1794–1858* (Boston: Little, Brown and Company, 1967), 282–285, 290–382, 425, 427–429. Paul Varg, however, emphasizes that Perry's triumph had less to do with his intimidating force than that Japanese imperial officials were impressed by the examples of modern technology that Perry brought with him and a Japanese recognition that "the time had come for a change." Paul A. Varg, *United States Foreign Relations, 1820–1860* (East Lansing: Michigan State University Press, 1979), 283–284. Further, it should be noted that Morison contends (429) that Perry deserves remembrance as an "imperialist with a difference," because he did not want the forceful acquisition of overseas concessions.

7 The meeting of the three ministers actually began at Ostend, Belgium, before being adjourned to Aix-la-Chapelle, and the document was generally identified with Ostend by commentators at the time. Frederick Moore Binder, *James Buchanan and the American Empire* (Selinsgrove: Susquehanna University Press, 1994), 200.

8 Amos A. Ettinger, *The Mission to Spain of Pierre Soulé, 1853–1855: a Study in the Cuban Diplomacy of the United States* (New Haven: Yale University Press, 1932), 339–364. By self-preservation, the US diplomats at Aix-la-Chapelle meant the danger that Spain's rumored emancipation of Cuba's slaves would actually occur, and that when news of the event reached the United States, it would trigger slave resistance or rebellion in the Southern states. The Australian paper is quoted in Long, *Gold Braid*, 303, with the word "Nicaragua" inserted in brackets after "Greytown." Long points out that Boutwell's destruction included the hamlet of a chief who had actually rescued some Americans from other natives who had taken them captive.

9 Robert E. May, *Manifest Destiny's Underworld: Filibustering in Antebellum America* (Chapel Hill: University of North Carolina Press, 2002), xi–xii, 1–4.

10 Isaac H. Trahue to John A. Quitman, July 1, 1854, John L. O'Sullivan to Quitman, July 10, 1854, William Mason to Quitman, July 15, 1854, John Marshall to Quitman, July 18, 1854, Samuel Walker to Quitman, July 31, 1854, John Quitman Papers, Houghton Library, Harvard University, Cambridge; Thomas P. Farrar to John S. Thrasher, July 6, 1854, John Quitman Papers, Mississippi Department of Archives and History, Jackson. For an extended account of Quitman's conspiracy, see Robert E. May, *John A. Quitman: Old South Crusader*

(Baton Rouge: Louisiana State University Press, 1985), 236–252, 270–295. The Quitman plot was aborted in early 1855. Quitman never actually set sail for Cuba.

11 José de Marcoleta to William L. Marcy, May 4, November 22, December 11, 1854, William R. Manning, comp., *Diplomatic Correspondence of the United States: Inter-American Affairs, 1831–1860*, 12 vols (Washington, DC: Carnegie Endowment for International Peace, 1932–1939), 4: 404, 425–427, 429–431; E. Bradford Burns, *Patriarch and Folk: the Emergence of Nicaragua, 1798–1858* (Cambridge: Harvard University Press, 1991), 194; Joseph A. Stout, Jr., *Schemers & Dreamers: Filibustering in Mexico, 1848–1921* (Fort Worth: Texas Christian University Press, 2002), 33–37; Charles H. Brown, *Agents of Manifest Destiny: the Lives and Times of the Filibusters* (Chapel Hill: The University of North Carolina Press, 1980), 257–457; Ralph Lee Woodward, Jr., *Rafael Carrera and the Emergence of the Republic of Guatemala, 1821–1871* (Athens: University of Georgia Press, 1993), 289–293. Kinney's company later changed its name. See Nicaraguan Land and Mining Company, *A Home in Nicaragua! The Kinney Expedition: its Character and Purposes* (New York: W.C. Bryant and Co., 1855). There is a copy of this pamphlet in the William Sidney Thayer Papers, Library of Congress, Washington, DC.

12 David L. Gregg to William L. Marcy, January 21, November 14, 1854, Records of the Department of State, Despatches from United States Commissioners in Hawaii, Microfilm Copies, T 30, Roll 5, National Archives, Washington, DC. Gregg's anticipations about the filibustering threat's potential for Hawaiian annexation may have been misplaced, but in 1860 Russia's minister endorsed Alaska's cession to the US in a dispatch to his government partly on the logic that were it not for Alaska's small value, it would "not be safe from American filibusterers." Edward de Stoeckl to Alexander Gorchakov, January 4, 1860, quoted in Howard I. Kushner, "Visions of the Northwest Coast: Gwin and Seward in the 1850s," *Western Historical Quarterly* 4 (July 1973): 303.

13 *Congressional Globe*, 33 Cong., 1 Sess., 1021–1024; James McCune Smith to Frederick Douglass, May 4, 1854, in *The Black Abolitionist Papers*, C. Peter Ripley (ed.), 5 vols (Chapel Hill: University of North Carolina Press, 1985–1992), 4: 223.

14 Edward G. Gray, "Visions of Another Empire: John Ledyard, an American Traveler Across the Russian Empire, 1787–1788," *Journal of the Early Republic* 24 (Fall 2004): 348; Matthew C. Ward, "Reluctant Imperialists? William Pitt, Pennsylvania, and the First Global War," *Pennsylvania Legacies* 5 (May 2005): 7.

15 Thomas R. Hietala, *Manifest Design: Anxious Aggrandizement in Late Jacksonian America* (Ithaca: Cornell University Press, 2, 191–193, 270; Frances Fitzgerald, *America Revised: History Schoolbooks in the Twentieth Century* (Boston: Little, Brown and Company, 1979), 56; Frederick Merk, *Manifest Destiny and Mission in American History* (New York: Alfred A. Knopf, 1963), 228–265.

16 Richard W. Van Alstyne, *The Rising American Empire* (1960; paperback edn, Chicago: Quadrangle Books, 1965), 6–7, 9, 100; Amy S. Greenberg, *Manifest Manhood and the Antebellum American Empire* (Cambridge: Cambridge University Press, 2005); Fred Anderson and Andrew R.L. Cayton, *The Dominion of War: Empire and Liberty in North America, 1500–2000* (New York: Viking, 2005); Eric T.L. Love, *Race over Empire: Racism and US Imperialism, 1865–1900* (Chapel Hill: University of North Carolina Press, 2004); Thomas Schoonover, *Uncle Sam's War of 1898 and the Origins of Globalization* (Lexington: University Press of Kentucky, 2003); Shelley Streeby, *American Sensations: Class, Empire, and the Production of Popular Culture* (Berkeley: University of California Press, 2002); Brady Harrison, *Agent of Empire: William Walker and the Imperial Self in American Literature* (Athens: University of Georgia Press, 2004); William Earl Weeks, *Building*

The United States as rogue state   59

the Continental Empire: American Expansion from the Revolution to the Civil War (Chicago: Ivan R. Dee, 1996). Much of this work was foreshadowed by Walter LaFeber, *The New Empire: an Interpretation of American Expansion, 1860–1898* (Ithaca: Cornell University Press, 1963). LaFeber explained (viii) that, although he avoided using the actual term "imperialism" in his narrative, because by then it had become so loosely applied to Cold War affairs that its application to nineteenth-century foreign policy would confuse readers, he found the term "colonialist" very appropriate for US policy in the period, which sought "both formal political and economic control" of overseas territory.

17 Anderson and Cayton, *Dominion of War*, x–xii, 209, 232, 279, 289–292; May, *John A. Quitman*, 277–279, 283–295.

18 Long, *Gold Braid*, 302–303; Binder, *James Buchanan*, 184; London *Times*, quoted in Ettinger, *Mission to Spain*, 407; Mitchell Henry to S. Weir Mitchell, January 20, 1862, in *Weir Mitchell: His Life and Letters*, Anna Robeson Burr (ed.) (New York: Duffield and Company, 1929), 100–104. President Pierce's Second Annual Message to Congress (December 4, 1854) played down the anger abroad concerning the Greytown affair by merely alluding to its having become "the subject of complaint on the part of some foreign powers." James D. Richardson, comp., *A Compilation of the Messages and Papers of the Presidents*, 20 vols (New York: Bureau of National Literature, 1897–1911), 284.

19 Robert Aldrich, *The French Presence in the South Pacific, 1842–1940* (Honolulu: University of Hawaii Press, 1990), 19–21, 51; Ernest S. Dodge, *Islands and Empires: Western Impact on the Pacific and East Asia* (Minneapolis: University of Minnesota Press, 1976), 168–169; Peter Ward Fay, *The Opium War, 1840–1842* (1975; paperback edn, New York: W.W. Norton, 1976), 362; Dozier, *Nicaragua's Mosquito Shore*, 56–57; 71–72; Richardson, comp., *Messages and Papers*, 5: 284.

20 Antonio José de Irisarri to Lewis Cass, October 8, 1857, Manning, *Diplomatic Correspondence*, 4: 609–610; Charles Mackay, *Life and Liberty in America: or, Sketches of a Tour in the United States and Canada, in 1857–8*, 2 vols (1859; reprint edn, New York: Johnson Reprint Corporation, 1971), 2: 77; John S. Lumley to Lord Clarendon, December 7, 1856, Barnes and Barnes, *Private and Confidential*, 167–169.

21 T. Price to (C.H.) Darling, July 21, 1860 (handwritten copy), Samuel Morrish to the Secretary of the Admiralty, September 24, 1860 ("vipers"), Great Britain, Foreign Office, Consular Despatches from Honduras, FO 39/10; the *Guardian*, September 10, 1851; British commodore quoted in John H. Wheeler to William L. Marcy, January 15, 1855, Manning, comp., *Diplomatic Correspondence*, 4: 436; Proclamation of Don Federico de Roncali, Count of Alcoy, May 19, 1850 (Havana, Cuba) *Diario de la Marina*, translation, enclosed in Robert B. Campbell to John M. Clayton, in *Senate Executive Documents*, 31 Cong., 1 Sess., #57, 38–39, 34–36; Angel Calderón de la Barca to Clayton, May 31, 1850, *Senate Executive Documents*, 2 Sess., #41, 41; Fanny Calderón de la Barca to Orestes Brownson, August 1, 1851 (with enclosure of undated instructions of the Spanish government, no addressor, to Angel Calderón de la Barca, translated by Fanny Calderón de la Barca), Angel Calderón de la Barca to Brownson, January 31, 1852, Orestes Brownson Papers, Microfilm Copy, Roll 3; "Piratical Expeditions Against Cuba," *Brownson's Quarterly Review*, New Series, 6 (January 1852): 66–95. In an exchange with the State Department about just how piracy should be defined, Calderón argued for broadly construing the term so as to include persons who committed acts "such as pirates are in the habit of committing ... that is to say, assaults, robberies, and acts of incendiarism." Angel Calderán de la Barca to John M. Clayton, July 2, 1850, Manning, comp., *Diplomatic Correspondence*, 11: 516–517. Rodrigo Lazo points out that because pirates

had a somewhat romantic image in some nineteenth-century literary circles, the term did not always carry negative baggage when applied to filibustering. Rodrigo Lazo, *Writing to Cuba: Filibustering and Cuban Exiles in the United States* (Chapel Hill: University of North Carolina Press, 2005), 27–28.

22 Juan N. Almonte to William L. Marcy, December 21, 1853, Luis Molina to William L. Marcy, April 8, 1856, Manning, comp., *Diplomatic Correspondence*, 9: 685–686, 4: 512; Dr. J.C. Hernandez to Dr. George Hammond, April 15, 1857, reprinted from the *San Francisco Herald* in *San Joaquin Republican* (Stockton, CA), May 30, 1857.

23 William C. Rives to John M. Clayton, June 13, 1850, James Gadsden to William L. Marcy, November 19, 1853, Manning, comp., *Diplomatic Correspondence*, 4: 609, 9: 666; "Nicaragua and the Filibusters," *Blackwood's Edinburgh Magazine*, American edition, 42 (March 1856): 314; Kenneth Bourne, *Britain and the Balance of Power in North America, 1815–1908* (Berkeley: University of California Press, 1967), 187 (Clarendon quotation), 190; Karl Marx, "The North American Civil War," letter dated October 20, 1861 and published in *Die Presse*, October 25, 1861, in *Marx and Engels on the United States* (Moscow: Progress Publishers, 1979), 88.

24 James W. Cortada, *Spain and the American Civil War: Relations at Mid-Century, 1855–1868* (Philadelphia: American Philosophical Society, 1980), 9; May, *Manifest Destiny's Underworld*, 123–127, 133–167.

25 Richardson, comp., *Messages and Papers*, 5: 198–199, 208–209, 212; May, *Manifest Destiny's Underworld*, 123–124; John F. Crampton to Lord Clarendon, March 2, 1854, in Barnes and Barnes (eds), *Private and Confidential*, 94; Baron Salomon de Rothschild to ?, May 1, 1860, in *A Casual View of America: the Home Letters of Salomon de Rothschild, 1859–1861* (Stanford: Stanford University Press, 1961), 42; Thomas Hudson McKee (ed.), *The National Conventions and Platforms of All Political Parties, 1789–1905*, 6th rev. edn (Baltimore: Friedenwald Company, 1906), 108–109.

26 Juan N. Almonte to William L. Marcy, December 21, 1853, Luis de la Rosa to John J. Crittenden, October 23, 1851, Manning, comp., *Diplomatic Correspondence*, 9: 685, 415–417.

27 *Nautical Standard and Steam Navigation Gazette* (London), September 13, 1851.

28 Angel Calderón de la Barca to John M. Clayton, May 31, 1850, *Senate Executive Documents*, 31 Cong., 2 Sess., #41, 41; Luis Martínez-Fernández, *Torn Between Empires: Economy, Society, and Patterns of Political Thought in the Hispanic Caribbean, 1840–1878* (Athens: University of Georgia Press, 1994), 48; John S. Lumley to Lord Clarendon, November 30, 1856, William Gore Ouseley to Lord Malmesbury, September 26, 1858, in Barnes and Barnes (eds), *Private and Confidential*, 164–165, 203; William Gore Ouseley to the Earl of Malmesbury, July 6, 1858, *British Documents on Foreign Affairs: Reports and Papers from the Foreign Office Confidential Print*, Part I, Series D, 9 vols, vol. 7: *Central America, 1856–1886* (Washington, DC: University Press of America, 1992), 71–72; Serge Gavronsky, *The French Liberal Opposition and the American Civil War* (New York: Humanities Press, 1968), 75. A good account of the Goicouria documents is Brown, *Agents of Manifest Destiny*, 355–358. So far as I know, there is no credible evidence that Buchanan's Secretary of War, John B. Floyd, Secretary of the Treasury, Howell Cobb, or Secretary of the Navy, Isaac Toucey, were members of the "KGC."

29 Paris correspondent letter, June 13, 1850, in *Daily National Intelligencer* (Washington, DC), June 29, 1850; Harriet Martineau, "The Slave Trade in 1858," *Edinburgh Review* 120 (October 1858): 550; Martineau, "American Domestic Policy at the Centre and Circumference," *The Spectator*, May 15, 1858, in *Writings on Slavery and the American Civil War: Harriet Martineau*, Deborah Anna Logan (ed.) (DeKalb: Northern Illinois University Press, 2002), 138–139; José

de Marcoleta to William L. Marcy, October 8, 1855, Manning, comp., *Diplomatic Correspondence*, 4: 481; letter of eleven merchants to the British Superintendent of Belize, December 27, 1858, Great Britain, Foreign Office, Consular Despatches from Honduras, FO 39/7; Brown, *Agents of Manifest Destiny*, 430–431. It was common for anti-filibustering British and French observers to assert that Southern pro-slavery extremists bent on spreading their labor system into the tropics spearheaded the US filibustering movement. See, for example, the comments of British diplomat John Lumley, also reporting the views of France's minister to the United States, John S. Lumley to Lord Clarendon, November 30, 1856, Barnes and Barnes (eds), *Private and Confidential*, 165. For public displays of pro-filibustering sentiment in the United States, and the relationship of filibustering to slavery and America's sectional crisis, see May, *Manifest Destiny's Underworld*, 65–79, 111, 249–279.

30 Lewis Cass to Luis Molina, November 26, 1860, Molina to Jeremiah S. Black, December 26, 1860, in Manning, comp., 4: 176–184, 953–963.

31 *Cong. Globe*, 32 Cong., 2 Sess., 190; Josiah Gorgas Journal, June 7, 1857, *The Journals of Josiah Gorgas*, Sarah Woolfolk Wiggins (ed.) (Tuscaloosa: University of Alabama Press, 1995), 11; William A. Newell's message quoted in *New York Herald*, January 16, 1858; David Dudley Field remarks, February 20, 1861, in *Debates and Proceedings in the Secret Sessions of the Conference Convention*, L.E. Chittenden (ed.) (New York: D. Appleton, 1864), 168; *Cong. Globe*, 32 Cong., 2 Sess., 190; *The Atlantic Monthly* 1 (April 1858): 749–750.

32 John Letcher to James D. Davidson, January 2, 1858, in F.N. Boney, *John Letcher of Virginia: the Story of Virginia's Civil War Governor* (Tuscaloosa: University of Alabama Press, 1966), 72; John Park Diary, May 23, 1850, Boston Public Library, Boston; George Templeton Strong Diary, August 24, 1851, *The Diary of George Templeton Strong*, 4 vols (New York: Macmillan Company, 1952), 2: 62.

33 Correspondent of the *San Francisco Herald*, letter from San Diego dated March 11, 1854, quoted in *New York Daily Times*, April 10, 1854; *The Constitution* (Washington, DC), October 8, 1859; *New York Evangelist*, September 11, 1851; Brownson, "Piratical Expeditions," 70.

34 David L. Gregg to R.C. Wyllie, November 13, 1854, Despatches from United States Commissioners in Hawaii, Roll 5; Thomas M. Leonard, *Central America and the United States: the Search for Stability* (Athens: University of Georgia Press, 1991), 7–8, 30–31; Greenberg, *Manifest Manhood*, 83–86; *Saturday Evening Post* (Philadelphia), May 17, 1856.

35 V.M. Randolph to William B. Preston, September 1, 1849, in *Senate Executive Documents*, 31 Cong., 1 Sess., 87–89; Marcy, quoted in Ivor Spencer, *The Victor and the Spoils: a Life of William L. Marcy* (Providence: Brown University Press, 1959), 370–371; John A. Campbell to Jeremiah S. Black, November 22, 1838, in Jeremiah S. Black Papers, Library of Congress, Washington, DC; William C. Rives to John M. Clayton, June 13, 1850, James Gadsden to William L. Marcy, September 2, 1854, Manning, comp., *Diplomatic Correspondence*, 6: 609–610; 9: 728–729.

36 "Bush Vows to Fight Until Terrorists' Defeat," *New York Times*, July 12, 2005, A10; Angel Calderón de la Barca to John M. Clayton, June 7, 1850; Manuel Larrainzar to Daniel Webster, June 16, 1852, Juan N. Almonte to William L. Marcy, December 12, 1854, Tomás Martínez and Máximo Jerez to James Buchanan, July 27, Antonio José de Irisarri to Lewis Cass, November 10, 1857, Alexander Dimitry to William H. Trescot, August 6, 1860, Manning, comp., *Diplomatic Correspondence*, 9: 509, 736; 4: 587–589, 628, 913–914. Dámaso Rivera, captain of native opposition troops opposed to Walker's rule in Nicaragua, claimed in August 1856 that a detachment of Walker's men on a reconnaissance mission had not only plundered haciendas and ranchos but also harassed and executed

civilians. Alejandro Bolaños-Geyer, *William Walker: the Gray-Eyed Man of Destiny*, vol. 4: *War of Liberation* (Lake St. Louis: Privately published, 1990), 88–89.

37 Anders Stephanson, *Manifest Destiny: American Expansion and the Empire of Right* (1995; paperback edn, New York: Hill and Wang, 1996), 28, 5; Merk, *Manifest Destiny*, 31–32; Hietala, *Manifest Design*, 255; Edward L. Widmer, *Young America: the Flowering of Democracy in New York City* (New York: Oxford University Press, 1999), 46; May, *Manifest Destiny's Underworld*, 115.

38 Beverly L. Clarke to Lewis Cass, October 15, 1859, in Manning, comp., *Diplomatic Correspondence*, 4: 783–786; Message of the President of New Granada, February 1, 1857, translation, enclosed in Philip Griffith to Earl of Clarendon, February 5, 1857, Great Britain, Foreign Office, General Correspondence, Colombia and New Granada, FO 55/131; Bishop Llorente, quoted in Lowell Gudmundson and Héctor Lindo-Fuentes, *Central America, 1821–1871: Liberalism Before Liberal Reform* (Tuscaloosa: University of Alabama Press, 1995), 110.

39 A. Ettinger, "The Proposed Anglo-Franco-American Treaty of 1852 to Guarantee Cuba to Spain," *Royal Historical Society Transactions*, 4th series, 13 (1930): 149–186; Norman Graebner (ed.), *Manifest Destiny* (Indianapolis: Bobbs-Merrill, 1968), 253–265; Llorente address in Gudmundson and Lindo-Fuentes, *Central America*, 110; Francisco Bilbao, "The Model American Congress," Paris, June 22, 1856, Treaty of Union, Santiago de Chile, September 15, 1856, in *Documents on Inter-American Cooperation*, Robert N. Burr and Roland D. Hussey, (eds), 2 vols (Philadelphia: University of Pennsylvania Press, 1955), 1: 129–138; Gustave A. Nuermberger, "The Continental Treaties of 1856: an American Union 'Exclusive of the United States'," *Hispanic American Historical Review* 20 (February 1940): 32–55.

40 George Mifflin Dallas to William L. Marcy, May 27, 1856, Mirabeau B. Lamar to Lewis Cass, September 29, 1858, "Declaration of Tomás Martínez and Juan Rafael Mora" (translation), May 1, 1858, Manning, comp., *Diplomatic Correspondence*, 7: 645–647, 4: 714–716, 692n–693n; Carlos Gutierrez to Lord John Russell, translation, in Great Britain, Foreign Office, Consular Despatches from Honduras, FO 39/8.

41 Robert A. Friedlander, *Terrorism: Documents of International and Local Control*, 41 vols (Dobbs Ferry: Oceana Publications, 1979–2003), 1: 6. The logic of the presidents in seeking British, French, and Sardinian intervention rested on the knowledge that these particular powers had recently performed a similar function in assisting the Ottoman Empire against Russia in the Crimean War.

42 May, *Manifest Destiny's Underworld*, 70, 151–156, James H. Callahan to Elisha M. Pease, October 13, 1855, Elisha M. Pease Papers, Austin History Center, Austin Public Library; Ronnie C. Tyler, "The Callahan Expedition of 1855: Indians or Negroes?," *Southwestern Historical Quarterly* 70 (April 1967), 581; Alejandro Bolaños Geyer, *Favored of the Gods: Biography of William Walker* (Masaya, Nicaragua: Privately Printed, 2002),126–127; William Walker, *The War in Nicaragua* (1860; reprint edn, Tucson: University of Arizona Press, 1985), 340–341. When a post-Civil War claims commission tried to resolve all US–Mexican claims disputes, it made 186 awards to Mexican citizens. A striking 150 of these came from the single incident of Callahan's burning of Piedras Negras. J. Fred Rippy, *The United States and Mexico* (New York: F.S. Crofts & Co., 1931), 279n–280n. Walker, on one occasion, employed an assassin in an attempt to kill two Costa Rican generals waging war against his forces. The agent, who was to pretend to be a deserter from the filibuster side to get access to his targets, instead went over to the Costa Ricans and confessed his assignment. Bolaños-Geyer, *War of Liberation*, 246–247.

43 May, *Manifest Destiny's Underworld*, 119–143.

44 William L. Marcy to Augustus C. Dodge, May 1, 1855, Manning, comp., *Diplomatic Correspondence*, 11: 211–213.

45 Franklin Pierce Proclamations of January 18, May 31, 1854, in Richardson, comp., *Messages and Papers*, 5: 271–272; Jefferson Davis to John Wool, January 12, 1843, *House Exec. Docs.*, #88, 35 Cong., 1 Sess., 6; Caleb Cushing to S.W. Inge, January 16, 1854, *Sen. Exec. Doc.*, 34 Cong., 1 Sess., #68, 7–8; Marcy to S.W. Inge, June 13, William L. Marcy to E.W. Moise, June 5, July 7, 1854, RG 59, Domestic Letters of the Department of State, M40, Roll 40, National Archives.

46 Franklin Pierce Proclamation of May 31, 1854, in Richardson, comp., *Messages and Papers*, 5: 272–273; John Henderson letter, June 10, 1854, in *New York Herald*, July 4, 1854; William L. Marcy to E.W. Moise, June 5, July 7, 1854, RG 59, Domestic Letters of the Department of State, M40, Roll 41, National Archives; May, *John A. Quitman*, 285–287; F. Jones to John A. Quitman, June 10, 1854, John Quitman Papers, Mississippi Department of Archives and History; Samuel Walker to Quitman, July 31, 1854, John Quitman Papers, Harvard University; Lazo, *Writing to Cuba*, 36.

47 Durwood Ball, *Army Regulars on the Western Frontier, 1848–1861* (Norman: University of Oklahoma Press, 2001), 89, 94, 96–101; John Quitman to Exander McClung, February 4, 1855, John Quitman Papers, Houghton Library; Caleb Cushing to S.W. Inge and Pacificus Ord, December 14, 1855, Cushing Circular to "District Attorneys in principal ports of the United States," December 8, 1855, Cushing to G.S. Cannon, January 14, 1856, *Sen. Exec. Docs.*, 34 Cong., 1 Sess., #68, 11, 10, 15; William L. Marcy to E. Warren Moise, February 15, 1855, Domestic Letters of the Department of State, roll 41; Robert E. May, "The Slave Power Conspiracy Revisited: United States Presidents and Filibustering, 1848–1861," in David W. Blight and Brooks D. Simpson (ed.), *Union & Emancipation: Essays on Politics and Race in the Civil War Era* (Kent: Kent State University Press, 1997), 16–22, 27; Mark J. Van Aken, *King of the Night: Juan José Flores and Ecuador, 1824–1864* (Berkeley: University of California Press, 1989), 246–247; Cushing to J. McKeon, December 12, 1855, quoted in London *Times*, February 1, 1856; John S. Brenizer to "Dear Brother in Law," July 24, 1856, John S. Brenizer Papers, Tennessee State Library and Archives, Nashville; Appleton Oaksmith to William Walker, October 13, 1856, Appleton Oaksmith Papers, William R. Perkins Library, Duke University, Durham, North Carolina; W.S.T. to the *New York Evening Post*, July 12, 1855, in *New York Evening Post*, August 7, 1855; Caleb Cushing to the Editors of the *Boston Daily Advertiser*, reprinted in *New York Times*, October 23, 1857. See also US army Captain B.R. Alden's letter to General Ethan A. Hitchcock, January 17, 1854, Ethan A. Hitchcock Papers, Library of Congress, reporting Alden's recent interview with Marcy. Alden records his delight at Marcy's obvious approval of Hitchcock's recent efforts to stop filibustering from San Francisco, as well as Marcy's disgust with Inge, who had recently dropped the government's libel on a filibuster ship. B.R. Alden to Ethan A. Hitchcock, January 17, 1854, Ethan A. Hitchcock Papers, LC; May, *Manifest Destiny's Underworld*, 158–159. My interpretation on Pierce's filibustering policies correlates with that of the primary scholarly work on the Pierce presidency. See Larry Gara, *The Presidency of Franklin Pierce* (Lawrence: University Press of Kansas, 1991), 143–144, 150–154.

48 Seymour M. Hersh, "King's Ransom: How Vulnerable are the Saudi Royals?," *The New Yorker*, October 22, 2001, 35–40; "Factual Back-Up for Fahrenheit 9/11: Section Two," Online, available at: www.michaelmoore.com/books-films/f911reader/index.php?id=17 (accessed June 30, 2005); Dore Gold, *Hatred's Kingdom: How Saudi Arabia Supports the New Global Terrorism* (Washington, DC: Regnery Publishing, 2003), 183–193; "Pakistan Changes the Subject," "To Many, Talk of a Crackdown in Pakistan Seems Hollow," *New York Times*, March 20, 2004, A12, July 20, 2005, A10.

3 Billy Yank and Johnny Reb take on the world

Civil War veterans' views of war, liberty, and empire

Carol Reardon

Editor's introduction

> After the Civil War, Union and Confederate veterans alike showed little interest in or support for US global activism. Eventually Northern veterans supported action abroad, including the Spanish American War in 1898, while Southerners were less enthusiastic and remained bitter over sectional differences. Although they united to support US entry into World War I, the Civil War veterans divided again after the armistice. Challenging the traditional interpretation, the author argues that sectional reconciliation did not come with the creation of an American empire.

In the late 1880s, as Civil War veterans celebrated the conflict's silver anniversary with monument dedications and reunions on their old battlefields, Billy Yank and Johnny Reb seemed to embrace a common vision for a peaceful future. The old soldiers planned to live out their lives enjoying social and civic progress in a nation united and at peace. Thousands who wore the Blue and Gray had cheered former Confederate Colonel William R. Aylett, who, at a reunion at Gettysburg in 1887, averred that "we have come forth from the baptism of blood and fire in which we were consumed," and "over the tomb of secession and African slavery we have created a new empire, and have built a temple to American liberty." Never forgetting that war's exaction in life and treasure, when Union veteran Thomas Barr pondered a simple question – "What has been gained?" – he concluded: "Everything." He then enumerated the compensations that had accrued to the nation since 1865:

> slavery gone, labor dignified ... the Republic accepted at home and abroad as a demonstration of man's capacity for self-government; and a people filled with an earnest purpose to build strongly and for all time upon the foundations laid by the fathers a nation to serve as a beacon-light to all the peoples of the earth.[1]

In their more mature years, Johnny Reb and Billy Yank used their status as veterans to contribute frequently to national debates on the use of American military power, at home or abroad. They believed they possessed incontrovertible authority to do so. As a Union veteran explained, the unique commitment he and his comrades in both Blue and Gray had accepted during the war years granted them special privilege in this regard, noting "there can be no naturalized citizen in our soldier world."[2] Indeed, many survivors of both great armies continued to identify themselves as soldiers long after war's end, symbolically re-enlisting in quasi-military organizations that protected their interests, preserved their history, and promoted their continued corporate identity as soldiers. Former commissioned officers in the Union Army might be elected into membership in the Military Order of the Loyal Legion of the United States (MOLLUS), established in 1865, while Northern veterans of all ranks gravitated toward the Grand Army of the Republic (GAR), founded in 1866. An Army of Northern Virginia Association and similar groups for Confederate veterans flourished briefly in the 1870s, then foundered until the organization of the United Confederate Veterans in 1889.

Despite the common bond they shared as "those who had borne the battle," however, when Civil War veterans considered the multiplicity of issues relating to war, empire, liberty, and national character that emerged by century's end – and despite Colonel Aylett's comments that won applause from both Union and Confederate veterans – Billy Yank and Johnny Reb did not always march in step with each other or with the nation at large. Stuart McConnell, the most accomplished scholar of Civil War veterans organizations, has posited that, unlike other patriotic groups of their time, the old soldiers seldom demonstrated a "simple, undifferentiated patriotism," but responded instead to "a complex mix of loyalties."[3] As the nineteenth-century Age of Empire and Revolutions ended and the first three decades of the twentieth-century Age of Intervention brought the United States to the eve of World War II, Civil War veterans infrequently supported the use of American armed forces to resolve international questions. Moreover, even when the veterans' voice offered support, often enough only Billy Yank spoke up. In marked contrast, Confederate veterans, when they spoke with a corporate voice, became only occasional interventionists, and their reasons for their stand invariably demonstrated the persistence of a significant sectional – and not national – identity that extended well past the war's golden anniversary that, by tradition, sealed post-war reconciliation.

During the Civil War's silver anniversary years, many former Union and Confederate soldiers active in veterans' affairs expressed a common vision about American exceptionalism. In 1894, a Union veteran described liberty as "the exemption from all restraint save that of the laws of justice and order; the exemption from submission to other men, except as they represent and enforce those laws." Moreover, he noted, only "one republic is liberty's native home – America." Even while acknowledging that "the

God-given mission of the republic of America" to extend such blessings "to all the peoples of the earth, before whose eyes it is the symbol of human rights and human liberty," he did not suggest that the United States actively intervene by force of arms to do so. Indeed, he believed that, first and foremost, the nation had an obligation to protect the fires of liberty against all those who sought to extinguish them. "O, for her sake, guard well thyself!" – the veteran intoned – "Sail thou on, peerless ship, safe from shoals and malign winds, ever strong in keel, ever beauteous in prow and canvas, ever guided by heaven's polar star."[4]

Exceptionalism did not equate to support for international interventionism to extend its blessings beyond national boundaries. Veterans remained satisfied to portray the United States simply as the world's shining role model. Former Captain Henry Castle of Illinois expressed delight that he lived long enough to know that "in mud hovels in the deepest heart of Africa, in thatched huts on the banks of Ganges, in cabins buried among Siberian snows, portraits of Lincoln are found," and that the spirit of liberty resulting from four years of hard war paved the way for a "horizon strewn with wrecks of stricken dynasties – crowns crumbling, thrones trembling ... hoary despotism shriveling."[5] He made no plea for the United States to take any action to accelerate the process.

Not surprisingly, both Northern and Southern veterans watched on with distaste as the world's major powers sought to expand their empires and extend their global reach. Faraway land grabs, such as that occurring in China and Korea, did not win favor with Civil War veterans. About the effect to carve up China, one Northerner noted:

> It is one that we can very well afford to be entirely neutral in. While we can reprobate the inexcusable robbery of a weak people, yet there is no difference in the robbers, and we need not prefer any one to the others. Our business is to confine ourselves to a vigorous assertion of the Monroe Doctrine, and make sure that there shall be no grabbing this side of the Atlantic.[6]

A fiercely isolationistic Carl Adae, former captain in the 4th Ohio Infantry, bragged to his MOLLUS chapter in 1885 about the nation's recent progress and asserted, "We have, one and all of us, long since come to the conclusion that our country is quite as large as we want it." Desiring to protect it from outside forces that might undermine liberty's blessings, Adae rejected any effort to reach out even to the world's most desperate seekers of liberty, noting that "instead of a desire for annexation on our part, I think any of our neighbors wishing to join us would have to beg pretty hard to be let in."[7]

Well into the mid-1890s, in the absence of a direct foreign threat, Civil War veterans – mostly citizen-soldiers who returned home when the conflict ended – rarely endorsed legislation designed to increase the size of

the American military establishment or to modernize its arms and equipment, at least in part to prevent political leaders from taking up a more
aggressive posture in an increasingly dangerous world. When faced with
an affront to national honor, certainly Civil War veterans might demand
satisfaction and even facetiously an acceptably proportionate military
response to right a perceived wrong. During a dispute with Italy in 1891,
for instance, a Georgian requested War Department permission to "raise a
company of unterrified georgia rebels to invade rome[,] disperse the
mafia and plant the stars and stripes on the dome of St. Peters."[8] But, in
general, the veterans viewed any long-term military build-up as unwise.
Reuben C. Benton, a former Vermont artillery officer, addressing his
MOLLUS chapter during the debates over increased naval appropriations
in the mid-1890s, asked, "Shall This Country Build More Battleships?" –
and answered his own question with a resounding "no." Beyond the
expense of untried new technology, he simply saw no need for a fleet with
offensive capabilities. "What is most needed is an intelligent adaptation of
our defenses," he concluded.[9]

Billy Yank's isolationistic tendencies, at least, slowly began to dissolve in
the mid-1890s. At first, their nascent support for greater activism in hemi-
spheric and global affairs required a case-by-case evaluation based on a
single criterion only: national security. Protection or expansion of liberty
played little role in their deliberations. For example, the possibility of
annexing the Hawaiian Islands inspired heated debate in the pages of the
GAR's weekly newspaper, the *National Tribune*, in the late 1890s. Union
veterans quickly condemned the economic arguments offered up by
potential allies in the sugar trust, decrying the businessmen's love of "pelf"
over "patriotism." To the men who once wore Union blue, support for
annexation rested solely on their concerns about the ambitions of Great
Britain, for whom Hawaii represented "the missing link" in its "chain of
island fortresses" surrounding the United States.[10] They did not see in
Hawaii's annexation an opportunity to extend the blessings of liberty to its
indigenous peoples. "There is no reason why if we annex a country, we
should take it immediately into our political bosom, and give its people all
the rights and privileges of American citizens," wrote a Northern veteran,
preferring the British system, which "has all varieties and shades of
Government for her various colonies, each being what she thinks is the
best for their peculiar condition."[11]

Ultimately, a threat only ninety miles south of the Florida peninsula
finally changed the world view of Northern veterans toward a more active
and wide-ranging acceptance of interventionism. Since the late 1880s, for
reasons of both security and morality, GAR members occasionally had
raised concerns about Spanish rule in Cuba. When the Cubans took up
arms in the mid-1890s to throw off Spanish control, Union veterans joined
with many other Americans to express their admiration for the freedom
fighters and compared their situation to that faced by American colonists

in the 1770s. Well before the sinking of the *Maine* in Havana Harbor, Union veterans expressed interest in taking up arms to help the Cubans achieve their freedom. As Ziba Graham, a Michigan veteran who once fought on the slopes of Little Round Top exclaimed, "Boys of 1861, how I wish we were boys of 1895!"[12]

By February 1898, many Northern veterans could look beyond national defense posture to voice encouragement for the Cubans seeking self-government, democracy, or liberty. They seldom touted the security of American investments as a reason to back the Cubans. Nor, as a general rule, did they employ the kind of martial rhetoric designed to inspire American manhood, as Kristen L. Hoganson has demonstrated as common among other Americans with strong interventionist tendencies.[13] Interestingly, however, Union veterans did not consider a resort to armed force as the only, or even the most likely, way to help the Cubans or to end Spanish mis-rule. "Let timid souls pull in the tremolo stop of their nerves," one wrote in late January 1898, adding, "There is going to be no war with Spain."[14] They expected the diplomats to resolve matters. Even though they found the sentiments expressed in the DeLome letter to be "rankling" and unappreciative of American forbearance, even the sinking of the *Maine* elicited few immediate calls by Northern veterans to use armed force against Spain; indeed, they seemed content to await the results of the investigation to determine the cause of the explosion. If it proved to be an accident, then, they argued, the remedies had to be sought in naval architecture and ship-building; but, if the explosion were no accident, then, as one veterans asserted, "no power can avert instant war with Spain, and the conquest of Cuba."[15]

During the two months between the *Maine* explosion and the formal declaration of war, many individual GAR chapters, following the example of the national organization, passed resolutions committing their members to support the president. The Department of Pennsylvania's commander announced that his members had "passed through the furnace of war, and knowing the evils, suffering, destitution, and horrors that are its unavoidable attendants, are for peace, but only when accompanied by honor to our flag and justice to our citizenship." The Far-ragut Association of Naval Veterans awaited the findings of the board of inquiry into the sinking of the *Maine,* but if it proved to be the result of Spanish treachery, then, offering their full support, "we feel there is but one course for our Government to pursue." The GAR post of Ellsworth, Michigan, resolved that "While opposed to war, except as a last resort, [we] are firm for maintaining National honor and offer [our] service in defense of [our] country's honor and freeing of Cuba."[16]

As the Michiganders' resolution suggested, ejecting the Spanish from Cuba presented an opportunity for the United States to do something noble, not merely protective of national security. As one Union veteran wrote:

we are now, and have been, living neighbor to a worthy, though help-less people, who are, and have long been, engaged in a life and death struggle for the "equal and inalienable rights of men," the rights of self government. Their heroic deeds and efforts in a noble cause have been calling long and loud to their neighbors across the Florida strait, and from whom they reasonably expect a helping hand.

He hoped to silence the ignominious cries of "commercial relations" and even "National policy" with the knowledge

> that this Nation in the morning of its existence stretched forth its hands and appealed for help in the hour of gloom and doubt, and but for the timely assistance of a friendly power the American Repub-lic must have died in its infancy.[17]

The formal declaration of war in April triggered an even greater outpour-ing of support from Union veterans, and a concern for national security played little part in it. The members of the GAR post of Wallace, Nebraska, resolved that "Cuba has been so misruled and the war carried on in such a barbarous manner as to bring disgrace on the United States of America, all other American republics, and liberty-loving people the world over." The post in Middletown, Missouri, completely sympathized with both "the Cubans struggling for liberty" and the families of the sailors lost on the *Maine*.[18] The editors of the *National Tribune* hoped that Presid-ent McKinley would send an army of "100,000 well-drilled, well-disciplined, intelligent American soldiers" as a force to do "missionary work," noting that their presence would bring "a flood of new and better ideas to the people who have been dwelling in the darkness of Spain." That army, which, as the editors noted, "is pretty thoroughly in the hands of the old volunteers of 1861," could help every Cuban start "a little ways at least toward a higher plane."[19]

As the liberating of Cuba expanded to include other Spanish holdings, the lure of empire – and the attendant positive social and political con-sequences that might follow – won more converts among Northern veter-ans. "Come to think of it," the editor of the *National Tribune* wrote in July 1898 concerning the question of annexing the Philippine Islands, "we are in very good shape to set up business as 'a world power.'" With few dis-senting comments, the *National Tribune* recorded strengthening support among Union veterans for taking possession of the entire archipelago. But the United States should proceed only from the noblest of motives. The American army deployed there must be "a redeeming, peacemaking, civi-lizing force." No longer merely an instrument of national power, the army would become "the symbol of the highest civilization of to-day," to bring to peoples who have "groaned under the blackest and most rapacious tyranny for three centuries," the very "blessings of 'life, liberty and the pursuit of happiness'" to eight million people. The "sublime missionary work" of the American Army of Occupation "will bring about a startling transition from the darkness, ignorance and brutal oppression of Spain, to the good Government, enlightenment, peace and order of the United States." The United States had to hold on to the entire island chain, since handing them over to another power "without their wish and consent, is opposed to all American ideas," and leaving them vulnerable to conquest by an imperial power less enlightened than the United States could not be tolerated either.[20]

The Northern veterans' press also suggested another positive change to follow from the declaration of war against Spain. The response of former Confederate soldiers and their sons to McKinley's call to arms – invariably portrayed in the Northern press as enthusiastic and widespread – convinced many former Union soldiers to declare an end to sectional divisiveness. In Charleston, South Carolina, when a US Army band ended a concert with "The Star-Spangled Banner," the entire audience sang enthusiastically. "If the war with Spain had produced no other result than this revival of national spirit," an observer wrote, "it was not fought in vain."[21] Former Confederate Generals Fitzhugh Lee and Joe Wheeler made national news for trading in their gray uniforms for blue. One northern publication noted that Lee was "the grandson of Gen. Henry Lee, 'Light Horse Harry,' of revolutionary fame," and added that his father was an officer in the United States Navy; the account made no mention, however, of a far more famous uncle: Robert E. Lee.[22] Former Union General Oliver O. Howard waxed eloquently about Wheeler, his West Point classmate, noting how the old Confederate cavalrymen "blushed like a youth" as he donned once again a blue uniform, showing plainly "how glad he was to come back to the army which he had formerly left, and to the old comradeship of early days," proof positive that all sectional ill-will "was to be forever a thing of the past."[23] A Northern publication, the *Army and Navy Journal*, featured a letter written by sixteen former Confederates from Clarksville, Tennessee, who had witnessed the destruction of the USS *Mississippi* at Port Hudson in March 1863. Now, in 1898, they congratulated the sunken ship's former executive officer, Admiral George Dewey. They felt they knew

> better than anyone, except yourself, why you punished the Spaniards so severely at Manila. It was because you had been in ill-humor for more than thirty-five years over the loss of the *Mississippi*, and this was the first favorable opportunity you had found for giving full vent to your wrath.[24]

A New York publication described events in Chester, South Carolina, where the community came out to see off their local militia company, "the Lee Light Infantry – mark the name! – for the campaign for American honor."[25]

But descriptions of such events are somewhat misleading. Although many historians accept the Spanish–American War as the termination point of sectional ill-will, the spirit of national reconciliation had not taken hold quite so strongly as often suggested. Yes, some former Confederates mirrored the position of the Union counterparts on the Cuba question, well in advance of the sinking of the *Maine*. As early as the start of the Cuban revolution, former Confederate General Clement A. Evans, addressing a meeting of the Association of the Army of Northern Virginia, asked: "Why shall all America be free and the beautiful Queen of the Antilles be alone a slave?"[26] Some individual UCV chapters – just as their GAR counterparts – passed resolutions in support of the war effort.[27] But, most often, when former Southern soldiers addressed the key issues of the day as members of the United Confederate Veterans, they expressed views significantly at variance with those held by their Union counterparts. In so doing, they revealed the persistence of distinctly sectional interests and values that suggest the prematurity of any declaration of the end of the Civil War's divisiveness.

In sharp contrast with the *National Tribune*, whose editors filled columns every week with the most recent military news from Cuba and the Philippines, and Union veterans' encouraging reactions to it, readers of *Confederate Veteran* – the most widely circulating publication for and by Southern soldiers – read little in its pages about the conflict. Both the editor and many subscribers considered themselves to be "unreconstructed" rebels. *Confederate Veteran*'s readers responded to the editor's call to preserve the truth of Southern history, to honor the Confederate dead, and to teach the next generation of their fathers' heroism in defense of home, hearth, and liberty. The issues that fired the interests of the readers and inspired soldier correspondence concerned demands for the Federal government to return captured Confederate battleflags, the granting of pensions and the opening of "old soldier homes" for Southern soldiers, and the writing of "true" history books for Southern school children that did not denigrate the Confederate cause or the gallantry of the soldiers who once donned the Gray. They did not yet trust the federal government – or even their fellow Southerners of the "New South" stripe – to protect, let alone respect, their interests.

A thorough examination of *Confederate Veteran*'s 1898 and 1899 production run reveals only a handful of comments about the causes, conduct, or consequences of the Spanish–American War. Unlike the editorials that filled the pages of *National Tribune*, no *Confederate Veteran* correspondent commented much on the interrelated issues of imperialism, race, the extension of liberty, or even redeeming national honor from Spain's insults. About the sinking of the USS *Maine*, the editor included only a single column, an interview with former Confederate General Bradley T. Johnson, who, after returning from Cuba as a special correspondent for a New York paper, advised caution. "I have no opinion as to the 'Maine' explosion," Johnson had said. Willing to await official findings concerning the cause of the sinking, he praised the deliberateness of American actions:

> In the midst of events that would have thrown France into revolution, that would have lighted the fires of jingoism all over Great Britain and Germany, the great magnanimous, self-contained American people are holding their breath and gritting their teeth until they know.[28]

"The horror of war to the Southern mind is unmitigated," the journal's editor wrote as he endorsed Johnson's counsel, making clear that, even among his largely Democratic readership, "there was general accord with President McKinley in his strenuous efforts to avoid it." While he resented any "outrage upon their nation's flag in the destruction of the 'Maine' and so many of its crew," and even expressed a word of sympathy for the Cuban people, he launched instead into a condemnation of the "ultra actions" of the "young Congressmen from the South" and others "who advocated war without volunteering to go themselves."[29] Moreover, they considered Union veterans who supported the declaration of war to be hypocrites. As one Alabamian noted, they "fought us four years to prevent our doing just what they want the Cubans to accomplish to-day."[30]

Instead of extending support to the national war effort and the positive results that might follow from victory, readers of *Confederate Veteran* complained about the cultural insensitivity of Northerners in dealing with their Southern countrymen. If the Federal government really wanted the South's full support, the journal's editor offered a reminder: "From across the old line there should be careful deference until old prejudices are dead."[31] Interestingly, neither the editor nor the readers of *Confederate Veteran* believed that the South bore the blame for permitting sectional ill-will to continue to fester. Instead, they blamed Northerners for perpetuating the divisiveness of the 1860s. When it came right down to it, many Southerners felt that, by the 1890s, they had no need to go to any unusual lengths to "prove" their loyalty to the United States. As the editor of *Confederate Veteran* asserted, "it seems that home recognition – recognition of the South's patriotic integrity through the years of the past – is in order." For the past thirty years and more, he noted,

> we have in vain sought recognition for patriotism by the northern section of the Union. We have declared it and lived it, and our comrades by scores of thousands have gone down to death demonstrating its truth, and all in vain.

They recounted all manner of recent evidence that revealed the North's guilt in keeping alive a spirit of sectional hostility. When President Grover Cleveland had called for a return of Confederate battleflags just a few years previous – when there was no war, and no need for Southern men to help fill the ranks – the "howl was so great that his independence quailed and the project of their return was abandoned." As recently as 1896, a plan for a joint reunion for Union and Confederate soldiers in New York City fell apart when Northerners refused to allow Southerners to wear simple gray coats. "Such is the predominating sentiment of victors in the war that ended a third of a century ago. Such is the odium that a large element of Northern people have deliberately subjected the South to all these years."[32]

Southern veterans hoped a significant public display of loyalty to the United States might right these wrongs. Thus, after considering a call to change the site for the 1898 United Confederate Veterans reunion slated for Atlanta, a city already busy with war-related activities, the leadership of the organization decided, "The presence of actual war will tend to increase rather than diminish the interest of war veterans in our great annual convention." It also would provide a way to tell the entire nation that "The bond of our allegiance to the restored Union is sealed by our devotion and reverence for our living and dead, and it is this God-given virtue which challenges and compels the respect of our former foes."[33]

The results of that meeting did not produce the desired results. Thus, at local gatherings, large and small, Southerners pressed their demands for the nation's respect for its fighting men of 1861–1865 as the cost of obtaining their active support for the aims and conduct of the war of 1898. They did not think they asked too much. At the dedication of a monument to Confederate soldiers in Shelbyville, Tennessee, in October 1899, the orator noted that "Above all and beyond all other political loyalties, we are Americans and children of the great republic now known and honored throughout the earth." The North need make no special effort to praise the South; it only had to acknowledge the section's natural inclinations. After all, he pointed out:

> The South gave the world the Declaration of Independence; the South won the war of the Revolution; the South gained the victory of New Orleans; the South acquired the great State of Texas; the South, through her sons, did more than all the other sections of the country put together to create our government and establish our institution – and it is with just and proper pride that the people of the South are glad and grateful for the ever-increasing power and renown of these United States.[34]

Especially early in the conflict, Southerners' demand for respect almost entirely quashed discussion among themselves and with the rest of the nation on issues concerning the growth of empire or other potential consequences of the war with Spain. As the rest of the nation faced the world, the South continued to look inwardly. When Northern newspapers and journals began to label all American troops fighting in Cuba and the

Philippines as "Yankees," adopting the name the Spanish used, an outraged Georgian wrote nothing about the military operations but, instead, warned Southern newspaper editors not to apply the hated name to soldiers from the former Confederate states. "We are not more Yankees than Chinese or Hottentots," the author wrote, "and I hope the Southern people will reject the appellation."[35] Indeed, some Southerners went so far as to argue that, if "Yankee" was abhorrent to them, being included as part of a reunited "nation" appalled them even more. "We are not a nation," declared Adelia A. Dunovant, the historian of the Texas Division of the United Daughters of the Confederacy, who explained how the Founding Fathers – Northern and Southern alike – eliminated "that objectionable term 'nation'" in their deliberations over the constitution and "proclaimed that this government is a federative system of free, sovereign, and independent States – not a nation." To claim nationhood now, she argued, would "endanger our correct conception of the nature of the defense of the men whom we represent" and deter them from their stated object – "the vindication of the men of the Confederacy who fought and died in defense of the constitutional right of State sovereignty."[36]

Southerners did not receive the respect they believed the nation owed their section. Instead, they found only evidence of continuing disrespect. Southerners found insults in the Army's command assignments and in the deployment of Southern regiments. They resented unflattering parallels offered up by Northern veterans that compared Spain's quick efforts to reach a peace settlement to the "late, unlamented Southern Confederacy, which only wanted 'to be left alone.'"[37] Worse, since troops heading for Cuba or Puerto Rico trained at camps in Southern states and embarked from Southern ports, many Southerners found themselves confronting once again the inflammatory sight of blue army uniforms on Southern soil. "Many Southerners don't admire blue uniforms still," a *Confederate Veteran* columnist averred, and he suggested that some former Confederates who might have enlisted decided against it because they could not "feel as comfortable" in a uniform of that color. He joined a number of Southerners, who, in 1898 – for reasons entirely unconnected to practical utility in tropical environments – called for a switch in the color of US Army field uniforms to khaki, a change formalized in 1902.[38]

On those rare occasions when a Northerner "got it right" in his consideration of the South, the *Confederate Veteran*'s editor gave his words space in his columns. At the decoration of the graves of Confederate prisoners at Camp Chase, Ohio – part of the effort to extend the kind of respect Southerners demanded – Colonel W.D. Hamilton, former commanding officer of the 9th Ohio Cavalry, ennobled the wartime efforts of both sides and gave them equal roles in the nation's future:

> We can now see that God was preparing the nation through a sacrifice of blood to become his consistent agent in the difficult task of advancing

civilization in the dark places of earth and in extending Christian liberty among the islands of the sea. It was the training of the civil war that made the unparalleled achievements of the past year possible

He praised the "sons of the blue and the gray" who "fulfilled the promise of their fathers when they fell into the line side by side to test the power of Spain" and divided the honors equally between them.[39]

Such an appeal resonated well among Southerners, since, as the war continued and extended into the early twentieth century, former Confederates found they could not entirely ignore the course of global events. Southern veterans increasingly addressed national issues relating to the war, the extension of liberty, and the growth of empire. But they did so on their own terms, continuing to use language that reflected their strong sectional – not national – loyalties. "The blending of the old spirit of 1861 with the new of 1898 makes the soldier of the present a manly man, a soldierly soldier. He is a creature of interest everywhere; he wears a halo no other can hope to gain," wrote a Tennessee woman about Southerners who enlisted for overseas service:

> Tho he wears the blue and march to the tune of "Yankee Doodle," if a Southern, a true Southerner he will be forever. In Manila he is an American volunteer soldier, but he is more; he is a Southern American volunteer soldier.[40]

Nonetheless, several months after the conclusion of a treaty of peace, the editor of *Confederate Veteran* admitted that his journal "has not had much to say of the Spanish War." The root of his silence lay not with the cause, conduct, or consequences of the war. He cared little about a humanitarian war, an anti-imperial war, or the creation of a new American empire that opened up new opportunities and challenges for the future. The basis for his continuing resentment lay rooted deeply in the past. "The fraternism so emphasized by our fellow citizens of the North causes those who did not know so before to imagine that the Southern people have suddenly become loyal to the flag and to the Union." They simply failed to "realize just what has been the fact all the while." Indeed, he continued, Southerners "do not feel honored in the gush of Northern people in exultation over these evidences of restored fraternity to the Union."[41]

Clearly, the Spanish–American War did not terminate all sectional ill-will, and unresolved issues from the past distracted many Southerners from participating fully in national discourse on empire, liberty, and war. In the end, when Northern and Southern veterans finally shared a common vision for the nation's place in global affairs – although still promulgated with two separate voices through Union and Confederate veterans publications – it came nearly two decades after the war with Spain. During the first decade of the twentieth century, Northern and Southern veterans seemed to reach concurrence once again on a preference for a non-interventionist stance. They viewed the consequences of Spanish–American War more as an aberration than as a sea change in American foreign policy, and generally opposed the deployment of American troops abroad, for any reason, including the extension and protection of oppressed peoples. Only military efforts within the hemisphere, especially those with a clear connection to national security, drew the positive support of Civil War veterans.

Indeed, the *National Tribune* covered the Punitive Expedition into Mexico with genuine enthusiasm. Some Union veterans in 1916 dismissed the qualms of a few comrades who sought a resolution short of annexation, even suggesting that the United States should just take over that chaotic country. "Are we going to do any worse to Mexico than we did to Cuba and the Philippines?" asked one Union veteran, and, assuming no challenge, wondered, "Then why all this wailing?"[42] When William Jennings Bryan protested certain seemingly provocative actions against Mexico, the *Tribune*'s editor sarcastically wondered why the Secretary of State "had not yet gone to the length of recommending that we evacuate Texas, Arizona and New Mexico to preserve the peace. Possibly no one has suggested this to him yet."[43] At least one Union veteran, T.A. Higgins from Pennsylvania, went to Washington, DC, to enlist to go to Mexico; he was seventy-three, but "he does not look much past 60."[44]

Even former Confederates evinced open enthusiasm for military operations against Mexico. The passage of time softened sectional sentiments, and such successful golden anniversary ceremonies as that held at Gettysburg in July 1913 to salute veterans of both armies contributed to a genuine national reconciliation. In Pensacola, Florida, people flew the American flag during the Mexican crisis. A local editor admitted,

> That's right. We once thought that we could never again respect nor love it, but those days are past and gone.... If we were to have a war with any other nation – which God forbid – in no section would that Flag be waved more proudly.... Massachusetts and South Carolina, Florida and California would march side by side and the Flag would again be baptized in the blood of brothers, and the nation united as one man.

They would do so willingly because the Flag "is the symbol of a nation with the greatest aims that ever animated the human breast, and may it ever be a beacon light to all the world leading upward along the heights of freedom and the pursuit of happiness."[45]

But enthusiasm for military intervention in Mexico did not extend to possible American involvement in the Great European War. Until early 1917, both Union and Confederate veterans concurred wholeheartedly with Wilson's pledge to stay out of it. "The only feeling that true Americanism permits for the horrible European war," wrote a Union veteran, "is admiration for the courage of brave young soldiers, sympathy with the awful suffering of innocent millions and detestation of crimes against neutrals, especially Americans."[46] They damned the munitions makers, steel companies, and other Americans making "fortunes so large that even the old Roman looters of provinces would have felt like pikers in comparison."[47] They even criticized the Wilson administration for failing to protest the sowing of mines in the ocean, denying the rights of neutrals to free passage on this "common highway."[48]

Confederate veterans concurred with their Northern counterparts on the wisdom of staying out of Europe's war. But, rather than reach back to antiquity for a point of comparison, they chose to look back only as far as 1864. The *New York World* editorialized that "Europe has wasted blood and treasure on a scale never before approached, but none of the principal belligerents has experienced war as the South knew it in the last year of the Confederacy." A correspondent for the *Nashville Banner* lauded the Northern editor's perceptiveness. He noted that "What is said of the South's suffering, its endurance and its pluck, is a tribute to the defenders of the Confederacy, the more to be appreciated because it is all true." The United States did not need to become involved in this war, even though the record of "the Huns" in Belgium "was no worse than that of the soldiers of Sherman or Sheridan."[49]

Civil War veterans' sentiments changed dramatically with the German pledge to begin unrestricted submarine warfare. The *Tribune*'s editor immediately counseled,

> If we endure further insult and injury, we will slink back into the situation of a nation incapable of defending itself or asserting its right, and become the prey of any other nation that chooses to assault us. If we stand up solidly now behind the President and assert the rights of American, with all our physical, moral and pecuniary strength behind him, we will take our place as the foremost nation of the earth and the greatest factor of peace. The whole world will look to us as the might agency through which justice, right and the peace of the world can be secured and permanently maintained.

Once again, Union veterans passed a resolution of support for the president. The Farragut Naval Post in New York City voted to stand by Wilson's "demand for the cause of humanity and freedom of the seas." The Civil War and Spanish–American War veterans of Cook County, Illinois, assured Wilson that:

> Every veteran who wore the blue, every veteran who wore the gray, should be pleased and proud to show the world that the sprit of '76

and the spirit of '61 still burns fervently in his heart inspiring him to protect his fireside and the homes on the mountains, and hills, on the plains and valleys, to safeguard the rights of the American sailor whose home is the American ship flying the American Flag.[50]

The Lucius Fairchild GAR Post resolved, that, "As we stood by Abraham Lincoln in 1861, we now stand by Woodrow Wilson in 1917.... We will rally round the Flag, boys; rally once again, shouting the battle cry of freedom."[51] During the 1917 inaugural parade, the GAR contingent won wild applause for its banner "Ready for duty."[52]

When Congress approved a declaration of war in April 1917, Northern veterans reaffirmed their support. They justified their stand based on a need to redress grievous affronts to national honor. As one Union veteran wrote:

> While suffering greatly on account of a war which we had no partici-pation in bringing about, in which we had no hand, and in the results of which we shall have no share, we have maintained a most extra-ordinary patience under injuries inflicted by all the belligerent.[53]

As General Nelson A. Miles, one of the last Union officers still on active duty, told a MOLLUS meeting in Washington, DC, "Whenever humanity reached a higher order of intelligence, a love of liberty was manifested, progress and enlightenment were developed and a higher degree of civil government created," but now, "at this hour when civilization has reached its highest degree of excellence, selfish ambition – lust for unjustifiable con-quest – has brought the welfare of the race to its severest crisis." He con-sidered the World War "the most unjustifiable, appalling and colossal of all wars" because the Germans planned "to restore a despotism" by "attempting supreme control, not by right and justice, reason and humanity, but by the force of arms."[54] "We are not going to fight the German people," a Union veteran made clear. The real enemy was "Hohenzollernism," the influence of the military caste guilty of immense crimes and barbarities who proved to be "treacherous, faithless, regardless of treaties and rights, and aggressive wherever there was an opportunity to strike."

At a GAR banquet in Maryland in April 1917, *Tribune* editor John McElroy described American armies as models worth the emulation of those from all the warring powers:

> The difference between these armies and American soldiers and sailors is as great as between a breezy mountaintop and venom-laded swamp. Americans have never sacked towns, outraged women, mur-dered the innocent and unoffending, carried off young men and women into worse than slavery, and come back laden with booty, torn from the hands of humble toil.[55]

A few weeks later, after further reflection, he wrote:

> Never did any nation enter into war with more exalted ideals. There is absolutely no revenge, no hope of any material advantage to be gained. We do not want territory; we do not want German trade or colonies. There is absolutely nothing that we desire from the Germans except strict obedience to the recognized laws of humanity.

The greatest benefit the nation could gain would be "the general benefit which will accrue to humanity from the crushing of the soulless and utterly unscrupulous band of vandals who have inflicted immeasurable injuries and cruelties upon the world in their hunger for wealth and territory." He described American entrance into the war as "chivalrous, as knightly, as the expedition of some of the old mailed heroes of Romance against a devouring dragon that was devastating the country and consuming the people."[56] As the first troop ships prepared to leave for Europe, he described this war "as righteous a cause as ever called men to arms. It is one of those sublime emergencies which alone can move our peace-loving people to appeal to the dread arbitrament of the sword" to maintain "some high and holy principle" through "a concentrated moral, spiritual and physical might." Ultimately "it comes back to the old question upon which this Nation was founded. Whether the people shall rule themselves or be ruled by organized murderers and robbers."[57] His comments drew praise, not criticism, from his fellow Union veterans.

Unlike the case in 1898, Southern veterans and their children embraced views similar to their Northern counterparts and voiced them openly. One of the first individual testaments printed in *Confederate Veteran* came from John Shishmania, whose grandfather had emigrated from Armenia, settled in Kentucky, and fought for the Confederacy. The family still treasured a Confederate flag their soldier–ancestor carried back home after the war. When the United States declared war on Germany, John's mother pulled out the banner, handed it to her son, and said:

> It's the flag of your Kentucky grandfather. He fought for the right of a sovereign State to make its own laws. It's the flag of Lee and of Jackson and Beauregard. Johnny boy, if Uncle Sam ever calls you to fight, remember that it will only be in the same old cause of your Armenian ancestors and of your Confederate grandfather, who was made a prisoner twice. It's the cause of the Stars and Bars fought again under the banner of a world's democracy, under our flag, yours and mine, Johnny Boy, the Stars and Stripes. And remember, Johnny boy, if ever Uncle Sam calls you, your Southern mother wants you to go.

Shishmania concluded with, "And Johnny boy is going."[58] In Little Rock,

Arkansas, a company of Northern and Southern veterans, aged from seventy to eighty-five, mustered together for service to the State. They doubted they could do hard service, but, they admitted, "if they could get one of those long-range guns that the Germans are using on Paris, they might handle that with some effect."[59] In Texas, Captain J. A. Cummins, age seventy-five, reported that "I have done my best to get to go to France with the volunteers," and while his services were not accepted, he declared that if the younger men could not "put the fixin's on old Germany before they return," all "Uncle Sam will have to do is to call for the Confederate veterans. We can still give them the Rebel yell."[60] A fellow Texan agreed: "our boys . . . are called to defend democracy against autocracy. We are in it to win." Even at age seventy-four, he was "willing to do anything that I can that is honorable to help gain the victory and free the world from Kaiser, Sultan, or Czar, even if it is to take up a gun. . . . So on with the battle until the Kaiser cries 'Enough!'"[61] Confederate veterans taught Marine recruits the rebel yell, but some wanted to take a more active role, hoping that "the blending of a cowman's 'ee-yah' with the blood-curdling whoop of the Seminole will put 'pep' in the Marine Corps charges suffi- cient to dislodge the Boches from their trenches."[62]

Confederate Veteran printed in full the Confederate Memorial Day speech given at Arlington National Cemetery by former Southern soldier Bennett H. Young. After saluting the Southern dead, he addressed President Woodrow Wilson directly to promise him the full support of all Confeder- ate veterans. Noting that the new Selective Service process would draw from a pool of men aged twenty-one to thirty, Young suggested that if the selection did not pull in sufficient numbers, the President should consider drafting men between the ages of seventy and eighty. "I may confidently state that you will get some really very great soldiers," Young assured Wilson. The veterans of Shiloh, Antietam, Gettysburg, Chickamauga, Spot- sylvania, and Cold Harbor

> will be ready, if need be, to follow the Stars and Stripes on the plains of Belgium and the valleys of France, where they will contend for liberty and for humanity as they did for what they believed to be right in the great struggle of 1861–65.[63]

Throughout the war, both Northern and Southern veterans – and their Sons groups and associated women's groups, as well – sustained organized efforts to support it. The women's auxiliaries of both Northern and South- ern veterans groups sponsored hospital beds in Army hospitals in France, worked with the Red Cross, contributed to the Soldiers' Library Fund, and knitted socks for ambulance boys and Belgian civilians. The United Daughters of the Confederacy made war work a high priority for all its chapters. The first patriotic organization of any kind to purchase a liberty bond in Louisiana during the First Liberty Loan drive was the Ladies Confederate Memorial Association of New Orleans.[64] The UDC chapter in Denver, Colorado, served meals to soldiers passing through their city on the way to training camps. "The Southern women are not slackers," one noted.[65]

Confederate veterans committed more completely to support the causes, conduct, and consequences of American military intervention during World War I, at least in part because the federal government had taken pains to address the sectional issues that prevented true national cooperation in 1898. When the Army established camps of instruction for new recruits, many of them located in the South to support year-round training activity, it named a number of them for Confederate generals. A Richmond editor exalted that "for the first time since the War between the States the United States government officially paid a tribute to the military genius of noted war chieftains" in naming camps for Generals Robert E. Lee, John Gordon, P.G.T. Beauregard, and others.[66] Signs of respect such as these made it more palatable when Northern veterans asked attendees at the United Confederate Veterans meeting in Washington, DC, in 1917, to march with their battle flags furled, making clear that the they made the request not to insult them, but to emphasize "to the weak and uncertain and fearful and disloyal that we are all for our country first, last and all the time." The old Confederates complied, most wearing "a bowknot of the United States flag, and [a] little bronze Southern cross" instead of the Stars and Bars. One pleased Union veteran noticed that even "the twin abortion" – an entwined American and Confederate flag emblem – seemed in short supply.[67] In 1918, the United Confederate Veterans officially reaffirmed its support for President Wilson "in his faithful execution of the most gigantic trust ever placed upon the heart and brain of a human being" to obtain "the full and glorious fruitage of our nation's struggles and sacrifices in behalf of democratic liberty for all mankind."[68]

Other legacies of the Civil War revived to underpin the moral dimension of American involvement in the Great European War. Northern veterans resurrected the label of "copperhead" for all those, regardless of section, who opposed the war effort and rejected fundamental American values, describing the name as "the mildest term" that could be "applied to the spineless, mud-slinging, de-nationalized bush haunters, who look with unconcern on the starving children, the outraged women, the murdered boys and men, famine, pestilence, and red ruin caused by imperialism, and would rather rot in ease and peace than follow the precept of the Prince of Peace and wage righteous war that lasting peace may come."[69] A Confederate veteran encouraged his fellow Southerners to remember "the grand spiritual forces and achievements of their past" as they took up "the concerns of the present." Failure to do so would make Southerners "sordid, selfish, degenerate and incapable of great things." He further intoned, "It is almost the only thing that can be said in favor of war, that it arouses men from the lusts of flesh and sense and shows them things worth dying for."[70]

During World War I, Southern complaints of their section's second-rate treatment nearly disappeared. The South finally had become an equal partner in the nation's cause. Now, only two nagging issues could not be ignored. When the *New York Times* published "The Hohenzollerns and the Slave Power," the article's author declared "the spirit of the Old South" to be "essentially analogous to that of Germany," and the "arbitrary, aggressive, oppressive" slave power brought on the war "in the true Hohenzollern temper." Stung by the moral opprobrium of such a charge against his section, no less a personage than the president of The College of William and Mary complained vehemently that, "The fact is, there was never anything in common between the system of Germany and the system of the South.... There was no likeness whatever between Calhoun and Davis and Bismarck and Von Moltke."[71] Another southerner wondered "what brand of psychology is that which is horrified with German atrocities and proud of those of Sherman and Sheridan and their ilk, including thieving and murderous John Brown?"[72] The second nagging problem? US Army soldiers from Southern states still took insult when the international press referred to all American soldiers as "Yankees" or "Yanks."[73]

Age caught up with Civil War generation after World War I, and new veterans groups – including the Spanish–American War Veterans, the American Legion and the Veterans of Foreign Wars – slowly appropriated the mantle as corporate representatives for those who had borne the battle. Still, Billy Yank and Johnny Reb did not leave the public stage quietly. Until the final grand veterans reunion at Gettysburg in 1938, the veterans still had their say about the application of American power on the world stage.

Neither Northern nor Southern veterans seemed willing to write off the American effort in the World War as fruitless and costly. If nothing else, wrote one Massachusetts veteran, "The Civil War has now taken on a new and high value, in the eyes of the world, because the World War has confirmed the lessons of the epoch-making four years of American warfare," including the crafting of grand strategy "on a sound basis." The making of such a strategy required the consideration not merely of political and military strength but also of moral force, he argued, and, during the Great War, just as in the Civil War, overwhelming moral force against autocracy – the enemy of liberty – made it possible for the United States to "accomplish its full strategic objectives, in the time set by a crisis and on the enormous scale demanded by the World War."[74] When an editorialist suggested that "few American begrudge the cost of the war of 1861, because such war 'saved' this country," a Floridian retorted that "The sacred right of self-determination is, or should be, the same to students of history and lovers of liberty whether found in the setting of 1776, 1861, or of 1914."[75] The arrival of American soldiers, fired "with every sense of compassion for humanity being ruthlessly tortured," won the war for the Allies, but the nation's true nobility was best demonstrated in the decision to erect near its cemeteries on foreign soil "no monument that may appear to vaunt America's wealth or cause envy by those who are unable to cope with such expenditure of money."[76] Perhaps because of Wilson's Southern birth and loyalty to the Democratic Party, Southern veterans found it especially difficult to blame him for the emptiness of the Versailles agreements. Even three years after his death, a South Carolinian eulogized his ideals:

> The other statesmen were playing the game of diplomacy, Woodrow Wilson was playing the game of unselfish humanity; he was the wonderful intellect of the "Big Four," a great lighthouse of hope on a shore of jealousies. American wanted nothing but justice – an extended territory, no money remunerations – can you wonder why small countries looked to Woodrow Wilson, the President of the greatest government on earth?[77]

A powerful antiwar sentiment swept through much of the nation during the 1920s and 1930s. Many Union veterans refused to give in to it. Indeed, GAR leaders actively took on those who called for an end to war. "Some of our young men in these days are denouncing war under every circumstance telling us from the platform how horrible war is," averred Hosea Rood of the GAR's Department of Wisconsin in 1927. "But," he asked,

> who of us that have stood in the battle line have need to be told all this, for we know from experience just how terrible it is. Had we in our young manhood been extreme pacifists what would now be the condition of our country?[78]

Among those aging veterans who had witnessed war several times over the course of their long lives, former Confederate soldiers seemed far less likely than their Northern counterparts to support any resort to force of arms without clear justification. They admired the seriousness of Armistice Day ceremonies in England, which convinced them that the British would never start another war "because they have forgotten or never knew what war was like." The poppies in every buttonhole meant "They will not forget."[79] *Confederate Veteran* filled columns with quotations from the likes of Mahatma Gandhi – "Every problem would lend itself to solution if we determined to make the law of truth and non-violence the law of life" – and David Lloyd George – "The chariot of peace cannot advance along a road cluttered with cannon."[80] The Great Depression hit the South hard, leaving fertile ground for reminders of the high cost of war; a Tennessee newspaper determined that two-thirds of the Federal government's expenses in 1932, nearly $3 billion, would be needed to pay for war debts, the expenses of keeping up the army and navy, and payments to veterans of previous wars, expenditures "looking back to hatred and hostility between the nations of the world."[81] Southerners read with alarm that 1930 statistics showed that twelve years after "the war to end all wars," armaments in all but two of the major nations of the world had increased beyond pre-1914 levels. A Virginia newspaper noted in 1931 that, "Reading the news from France and Central Europe, one gets the impression that the plowshares beaten out of the late swords are about as shaky as all other kinds of shares these days."[82] In the final issue of *Confederate Veteran* in December 1932, the editor opined, that, "The world cries for peace, yet world peace is never with us." Americans had to take the lead and make the world's nations understood that the United States "will tolerate no more war by furnishing supplies of any kind – arms, money, food, clothing," he argued, even if it meant economic hardship at home. Interestingly, the Southerner concluded with a quotation usually connected with Ulysses S. Grant: "Let us have peace!"[83]

In July 1938 nearly 2,000 Civil War veterans – average age, ninety-four – gathered for one final reunion of the Blue and Gray at Gettysburg. The reunion's theme: peace. In keeping with the theme, organizers permitted "no re-enactment of any battle scene." An observer described the spectacle "planned and guided by a nation in peace and unity," recalling days of "the thin whispering of breezes blowing over flat fields and the memories of old men." It was "symbolic – of time, of the fading old passions and the coming of a new way of life." National Guardsmen showed off the new weapons of war, far more lethal than those carried by the soldiers in Blue and Gray, but mostly the old men "heard President Roosevelt call upon the nation to struggle eternally for peace and democracy." Perhaps most impressive of all to the old men in faded blue and gray, the president unveiled a new monument on Oak Hill, the Eternal Peace Light Memorial, where "henceforth a flame will burn above the battlefield as a symbol of the nation's peace and unity."[84] Shortly thereafter, as the old veterans boarded trains for all corners of the United States, the last great reunion of the occasional interventionists in Blue and Gray came to an end. And with their departure ended an era. Fifteen months later, German tanks and aircraft stormed across the Polish border to launch World War II.

Notes

1 Quoted in Carol Reardon, *Pickett's Charge in History and Memory* (Chapel Hill: University of North Carolina Press, 1997), 98; Thomas F. Barr, "Costs and Compensations of the War," in *Military Essays and Recollections: Papers Read Before the Commandery of the State of Illinois, Military Order of the Loyal Legion of the United States*, Volume 1 (Chicago: A.C. McClurg and Company, 1891), 524, 527.

2 S.C. Ayres, "The Vanishing Minority of the Loyal Legion with a Brief Sketch of the Order," in *Sketches of War History 1861–1865: a Compilation of Miscellaneous Papers Read Before the Ohio Commandery of the Loyal Legion, April 1912–April 1916* (reprint edn, Wilmington: Broadfoot Publishing Company, 1993), 161–162.

3 Stuart McConnell, "Reading the Flag: a Reconsideration of the Patriotic Cults of the 1890s," in John Bodnar (ed.), *Bonds of Affection: Americans Define Their Patriotism* (Princeton: Princeton University Press, 1996), 104.

4 "The Duty and Value of Patriotism," in A. Noel Blakeman (ed.), *Personal Recollections of the War of the Rebellion: Addresses Delivered before the Commandery of the State of New York, Military Order of the Loyal Legion of the United States* (New York: G.P. Putnam's, 1897): 202–203, 212.

5 Captain Henry A. Castle, "The Boys in Blue Turned Gray," in ibid., 477.

6 *National Tribune*, December 30, 1897; January 6, 1898.

7 Carl A.G. Adae, "Our Military Future," *Sketches of War History 1861–1865: Papers Read Before the Ohio Commandery of the Military Order of the Loyal Legion of the United States, 1883–1886* (Cincinnati: Robert Clarke & Co., 1888), 320–321.

8 Quoted in Gaines M. Foster, *Ghosts of the Confederacy: Defeat, the Lost Cause, and the Emergence of the New South* (New York: Oxford, 1987), 145.

9 Lieutenant Colonel Reuben C. Benton, "Shall This Country Build More Battleships?" in *Glimpses of the Nation's Struggle. Fourth Series. Papers Read Before the Minnesota Commandery of the Military Order of the Loyal Legion of the United States, 1892–1897* (Minneapolis: H.L. Collins, 1898), 214.

10 *National Tribune*, January 27, 1898.

11 *National Tribune*, November 4, 1897.

12 Ziba B. Graham, "Some of the Wrongs of Cuba," in *War Papers: Being Papers Read Before the Commandery of the State of Michigan, Military Order of the Loyal Legion of the United States*, vol. II (Detroit: By the Commandery, 1898), 93.

13 Kristin L. Hoganson, *Fighting for American Manhood: How Gender Politics Provoked the Spanish–American and Philippine–American Wars* (New Haven: Yale University Press, 1997), 93–99.

14 *National Tribune*, January 27, 1898.

15 *National Tribune*, February 24, 1898.

16 *National Tribune*, March 31, 1898.

17 *National Tribune*, March 3, 1898.

18 *National Tribune*, April 7 and 14, 1898.

19 *National Tribune*, April 21 and May 5, 1898.

20 *National Tribune*, May 12 and 19, 1898.

21 *Army and Navy Journal*, December 17, 1898.

22 *America's War for Humanity Related in Story and Picture Embracing a Complete History of Cuba's Struggle for Liberty and the Glorious Heroism of America's Soldiers and Sailors* (Boston: J.Q. Adams & Co., 1898), 169.

23 General Oliver Otis Howard, *Fighting for Humanity, or Camp and Quarterdeck* (New York: F. Tennyson Neely, 1898), 41.

24 *Army and Navy Journal*, June 25, 1898.

25 *America's War for Humanity*, 166.

26 Quoted in Foster, *Ghosts of the Confederacy*, 145–146.

27 See, for example, the resolution of the Winchester, VA, Turner Ashby UCV Camp, passed on March 21, 1898, in Robert Mallin and Richard Radi, *Ashby Camp Revisited* (Winchester: privately published, 1995), 51.

28 "Gen. Bradley T. Johnson on the 'Maine' Disaster," *Confederate Veteran* 6 (1898): 111.

29 *Confederate Veteran* 6 (1898): 304.

30 Quoted in Foster, *Ghosts of the Confederacy*, 146.

31 *Confederate Veteran* 6 (1898): 304.

32 "Serious Words with Veterans," *Confederate Veteran* 6 (1898): 146.

33 "Why Atlanta Reunion Should Be Held," *Confederate Veteran* 6 (1898): 242.

34 "Confederate Monument, Shelbyville, Tennessee," *Confederate Veterans* 7 (1899): 497.

35 *Confederate Veteran* 6 (1898): 256.
36 "The Term 'Nation,'" *Confederate Veteran* 9 (1901): 111.
37 *National Tribune,* July 28, 1898.
38 Ibid.
39 "Union and Confederate Veterans Assembled to Honor Confederate Dead," *Confederate Veteran* 7 (1899): 401–402.
40 "The Soldier of 1861–1898," *Confederate Veteran* 9 (1901): 311.
41 *Confederate Veteran* 6 (1898): 519.
42 *National Tribune,* June 29, 1916.
43 *National Tribune,* June 29, 1916.
44 *National Tribune,* July 13, 1916.
45 *National Tribune,* July 20, 1916.
46 *National Tribune,* June 29, 1916.
47 *National Tribune,* August 3, 1916.
48 *National Tribune,* August 10, 1916.
49 "The South's Suffering," *Confederate Veteran* 25 (1917): 5.
50 *National Tribune,* March 15, 1917.
51 *National Tribune,* April 19, 1917.
52 *National Tribune,* February 8, 1917.
53 *National Tribune,* February 8, 1917.
54 Nelson A. Miles, "An Address," in Military Order of the Loyal Legion of the United States, Commandery of the District of Columbia, *War Papers*, vol. 4 (reprint edn, Wilmington: Broadfoot Publishing Company, 1993), 502–503.
55 *National Tribune,* April 19, 1917.
56 *National Tribune,* May 10, 1917.
57 *National Tribune,* June 7, 1917.
58 "To Fight for Southern Principles," *Confederate Veteran* 25 (1917): 344.
59 "A Unique Military Company," *Confederate Veteran* 26 (1918): 237.
60 *Confederate Veteran* 26 (1918): 43.
61 *Confederate Veteran* 26 (1918): 189.
62 Undated article from *National Tribune,* reprinted in *Confederate Veteran* 26 (1918): 46.
63 "Memorial Day at Arlington," *Confederate Veteran* 25 (1917): 397.
64 *Confederate Veteran* 25 (1917): 428.
65 "The Colorado U.D.C.," *Confederate Veteran* 26 (1918): 39; "The Washington Division," ibid., 88.
66 Undated article from the Richmond *Times-Dispatch,* reprinted in *Confederate Veteran* 25 (1917): 343.
67 *National Tribune,* May 3 and June 14, 1917.
68 "Standing Behind the President," *Confederate Veteran* 26 (1918): 427.
69 *National Tribune,* April 19, 1917.
70 "An Appeal and a Suggestion," *Confederate Veteran* 26 (1918): 7.
71 Lyon G. Tyler, "The South and Germany," *Confederate Veteran* 25 (1917): 506. For similar sentiments, but with an interesting twist, see Dr. Henry E. Shepherd, "Historic Ironies – Sherman and German," *Confederate Veteran* 26 (1918): 17–19; "A Friendly Challenge," ibid., 508; "The World War: a Comparative and Historical Study," ibid., 526–527. For a continuation of the discussion, see Wolf A. Lederer, "Secession or Revolution," *Confederate Veteran* 39 (1931): 418–420.
72 Will T. Hale, "Historic Exposures Commended," *Confederate Veteran* (1918): 91.
73 "Americans or Yankees?" *Confederate Veteran* 26 (1918): 428; "Northern Propaganda," ibid., 469.
74 Captain Thomas G. Frothingham, "The Peninsula Campaign of 1862," in *Massachusetts Historical Society Proceedings* 57 (1923): 88; and "The Effect of the Effort of the United States upon the World War," in ibid., 55 (1921): 166.

75 "1776, 1861, 1914," *Confederate Veteran* 35 (1927): 77.
76 Cassie Moncure Lyne, "The Care of the American Dead Overseas," *Confederate Veteran* 35 (1927): 418.
77 "Virginia's Own," *Confederate Veteran* 35 (1927): 405.
78 Quoted in Thomas J. McCrory, *Grand Army of the Republic: Department of Wisconsin* (Black Earth: Trail Books, 2005), 54.
79 "London's Two-Minute Silence," *Confederate Veteran* 40 (1932): 45.
80 "Sayings of Noted Britons," *Confederate Veteran* 40 (1932): 319, 410.
81 "Where Tax Money Goes," reprinted in *Confederate Veteran* 40 (1932): 119.
82 "Present War Armament," *Confederate Veteran* 39 (1931): 125; ibid., 239.
83 "For International Peace," *Confederate Veteran* 40 (1932): 412.
84 Extracts from the Elizabeth, NJ, *Daily Journal*, quoted in Harry George Woodworth, *Civil War Veterans in the 20th Century* (Bowie: Heritage Books, 2003), 255–256, 259.

4 Defining Eisenhower's America
War, power, and race relations, 1941–1961

Edward O. Frantz

Editor's introduction

> Though personally comfortable with the racially divided military in which
> he had spent his entire adult life, Eisenhower during World War II recog-
> nized the contradiction in fighting the "Great Crusade" against the Axis
> powers with segregated US armed forces. Running for president during
> the Korean War, Eisenhower's military experience and iconic stature were
> his most significant political assets. Yet his military background left him
> poorly equipped to deal with the civil rights issues he faced after his elec-
> tion. This chapter illustrates how the heroic mind behind D-Day failed to
> become the heroic heart behind new civil rights policies. Eisenhower the
> general did more to advance liberty for the peoples of Western Europe
> than Eisenhower the president did for people of color in the United
> States.

Immersed in the tenacious fighting during the Battle of the Bulge,
Supreme Allied Commander Dwight D. Eisenhower huddled with Communication Zone Commander J.C.H. Lee to forge a solution to the critical
manpower shortage that they confronted during the last winter of World
War II. Recognizing that African-American soldiers were an underutilized
resource at their disposal, Eisenhower and Lee reached out to them in
their appeal for non-combat troops to go to the front: "This opportunity
to volunteer will be extended to all soldiers without regard to color or
race but preference will normally be given to individuals who have had
some basic training in Infantry."[1] By February 1945, 4,562 African-
American soldiers seized this opportunity, providing a much needed jolt
in the arm to the Allied war effort.[2]

Although this vignette illustrates a number of vital trends regarding the
intertwined themes of war and power, its primary purpose is to serve as an
introduction to Dwight Eisenhower's complicated relationship with civil
rights. Most historians agree that Eisenhower was a gradualist on civil
rights issues, known for his careful statements and skepticism about the
power of law to change popular prejudice. Many of these same historians
have observed that Eisenhower's army career had made him comfortable

with segregation and provided the lens through which he viewed all racial issues. Few studies, however, have probed Eisenhower's army experiences and his presidential leadership to demonstrate a clear understanding of his lukewarm approach to civil rights leadership. By exploring the ways in which military service influenced his attitudes toward civil rights as president, this chapter demonstrates how Eisenhower's army experiences manifested themselves in domestic policy contexts while he was president. Moreover, the exploration of this topic enables us to contemplate one of the intriguing unasked questions in Fred Anderson and Andrew Cayton's *The Dominion of War*: what can we learn about individuals who choose not to wield power that they have accrued as a result of their military reputation?

Dwight Eisenhower's vital role in grappling with civil rights issues epitomizes one of Anderson and Cayton's central claims: "that the quest for liberty and the pursuit of power together have created an American historical dialectic catalyzed and made dynamic by war."[3] In countless ways, the Eisenhower presidency characterized the tension between liberty and the pursuit of power. Indeed, Eisenhower's political career was made possible and necessary by his pursuit of power; Americans looked to Eisenhower to lead them during the Cold War because of his World War II battlefield success. Civil rights, while important to some Americans in 1952, simply was not what a majority of Americans placed as their top priority as they looked for a president. Security and leadership were priorities, and no-one seemed better suited to offer those two qualities to the American people than Eisenhower. Precisely because of his leadership and his ability to offer security to so many Americans, Dwight Eisenhower was perfectly situated to make major strides on civil rights issues while president. His caution and passivity in this realm would therefore prove to be that much more disappointing.

Segregated army life provided the normative atmosphere of Eisenhower's adult life, but biographies make apparent that even before his education at West Point, he was unlikely to challenge societal conventions. The product of traditional education and strict Mennonite parents, Eisenhower was encouraged to memorize, not to think critically or creatively. His boyhood home of Abilene, Kansas, was distinctly white, with about 150 African-Americans out of a population of just over 3,500 in 1900.[4] Like many Midwesterners who grew up in relatively racially homogeneous backgrounds, Eisenhower never seems to have questioned segregation, but rather accepted it as part of the natural order.[5]

Eisenhower likely lacked awareness of the considerable losses of power that people of color had been experiencing since the year of his birth in 1890. In that year, Mississippi became the first Southern state to disenfranchise its black citizens through its state constitution. By 1911, when Eisenhower entered West Point, every Southern state, along with Oklahoma, had found a way to eliminate a majority of its African-American voting-age population. Combine the loss of political rights with the legalized sanction of Jim Crow segregation in the 1896 *Plessy* v. *Ferguson* case and the systematic racial terror campaigns that peaked during the last decade of the nineteenth century and the result was an era that some have labeled "the nadir" of post-slavery life for African-Americans.[6] Like most young adults, Eisenhower lacked the comparative perspective necessary to contemplate the state of American race relations when he began his studies of West Point. Unfortunately, West Point's curriculum and its student body would only serve to reinforce Eisenhower's tendency to see racial segregation as a natural phenomenon. The academy had not always been exclusively white, but was practically so, as only three African-Americans graduated West Point between the end of the Civil War and World War I.[7]

The West Point years (1911–1915)

The experiences of blacks at West Point on the eve of Eisenhower's birth illustrate the alarming acceptance of anti-black sentiments within the American military establishment. The third graduate of West Point, Charles Young, graduated from the academy in the year before Eisenhower's birth, in 1889. Although he performed ably in both the Spanish–American War and the Mexican expedition in 1916, Young's career was fraught with difficulty. Throughout his years at West Point, hazing rituals and the individual racism of a number of classmates resulted in an atmosphere even less inviting to Young than to his fellow cadets. Indeed, after a fellow African-American graduated from the academy in 1887, no white classmate would room with Young. Even after graduating West Point, Young faced hostility and skepticism throughout the entirety of his career. By 1917, Young had risen to the rank of lieutenant colonel and expected to command American troops during World I. Against his wishes, Young was placed on the retired list before he got the chance, much to the outrage of the African-American press. Some Southern officers, it seems, found it offensive to receive orders from an African-American superior. The intervention of arch segregationist Senator John Bell Williams of Mississippi in the matter helped tip the scales against Young, and with the approval of President Woodrow Wilson, Young was forced to retire. The order had no direct influence on Dwight Eisenhower's career, but it demonstrates that in 1917, as they would throughout the remainder of Eisenhower's public life, political considerations outweighed efficiency and justice on matters involving race and the military.[8]

Because Charles Young would prove to be the last African-American to graduate from the academy until 1936, during his years at West Point (1911–1915), Dwight Eisenhower did not have the opportunity to interact with a single African-American cadet. Having left Kansas for West Point, Eisenhower had somehow found a place with even fewer people of color.

Surrounded by people who looked and were encouraged to think the same, young Eisenhower could not help but reach the conclusion that African-Americans lacked the capacity to lead troops into battle. Other stereotypical assumptions may have followed as well; given the era and the location in which he operated, there is little to suggest that Dwight Eisenhower had any reason to challenge notions of white supremacy. To its critics, West Point was particularly removed from the world around it. Encased in tradition, the academy had embraced few of the educational reforms sweeping America at the time. In a particularly pointed critique, Douglas MacArthur claimed that at West Point, cadets "had no opportunity to familiarize themselves with the mores and standards of people in the world without. . . . They were thrust into the world a man in age, but as experienced as a high school boy."[9] At best, West Point was in a transitionary stage during Eisenhower's years there.

At home and abroad (1915–1940)

Having come of age in racially segregated America and received an education at a predominantly white institution, Eisenhower embarked on a professional life in a segregated army. Some of Eisenhower's posts were located throughout former slave states where African-Americans were second-class citizens. Most notably, Eisenhower was posted at Fort Sam Houston for the better part of the period between 1915 and 1917. He was also briefly stationed at Forts Oglethorpe and Benning, Georgia. The Eisenhowers moved considerably, spending time in Pennsylvania, Panama, the Philippines, and the Washington, DC area, as well as many places in between. Although the names of the bases changed, the racial practices on most did not. Racial segregation would be the norm even at a place like Fort Leavenworth, Kansas, where Eisenhower studied as part of the Command and General Staff school during 1925–1926. More than a decade after Eisenhower left Leavenworth, it was still a bastion of Jim Crow segregation.[10] Segregationist practices in Eisenhower's home state were not notable in and of themselves (indeed the most famous defendant in the 1954 *Brown* v. *Board of Education* suit was the school board of Topeka), but they were particularly lamentable given the importance that officers placed on their training at the Command and General staff school. Eisenhower called his year there a "watershed in my life."[11] It is that much more regrettable that this vital year reaffirmed the segregationist practices that Eisenhower had already learned to internalize. Although the United States changed dramatically between 1917 and 1940, the army's racial policies did not. Eisenhower therefore remained aloof from the slowly rising tide of civil rights protest.

Much to his disappointment, Eisenhower remained stateside throughout the duration of World War I. Eisenhower was more than likely oblivious to it at the time, but World War I proved to an even greater disappointment to African-Americans eager to use the war as a catalyst to greater rights both within the army and American society in general. The army trained only two African-American combat divisions of volunteers, while the remaining black troops were assigned non-combat duties.[12] Facing not only the horrors of trench warfare, but also suffering from poor training and haphazard deployment, African-American infantrymen compiled a fighting record that allies thought was admirable while adversaries thought was underwhelming. As was becoming customary, army brass refused to make any difficult decisions regarding the future of African-American troops, and hoped that after the war they could simply resume the peacetime tradition of four black regiments. Consciously or not, Dwight Eisenhower took notice, because he would pursue a similar path of leadership when he became president.[13]

World War II and its aftermath (1940–1951)

By the time the next World War had broken out, the army had not appreciably changed its plans for black troop employment. The army's policy was to utilize African-Americans in proportion to their composition of society. The goal was therefore to have African-Americans comprise roughly 10 percent of the troops. Those troops were trained and ultimately deployed in entirely segregated units. The War Department insisted, however, that such employment was not discriminatory. As historian Ulysses Lee noted, "the distinction between discrimination and segregation was not always clear."[14] The distinction, however, is a telling window into the army's policy regarding race relations. A product of that system, Eisenhower never seems to have considered whether segregation was, in and of itself, discriminatory. As black Americans submitted themselves to the draft, they were keenly aware that, although they were being asked to fight for the liberties of others, they would not enjoy the liberties given to white soldiers while doing so.

Even before Pearl Harbor, black Americans knew that the army's policy for recruiting and employing troops would be a sticking point. Judge William Hastie, civilian aide to Secretary of War Henry Stimson, proposed that the army gradually changed its implementation policy. He was direct in his criticism of the practice, writing: "the Military authorities do not comprehend the amount of resentment among soldiers and civilians, white as well as black, over the rigid pattern of racial separation imposed by the army."[15] African-American advocates, including the National Association for the Advancement of Colored People (NAACP) leader Walter White and Brotherhood of Sleeping Car Porters chief A. Philip Randolph, urged Army Chief-of-Staff George Marshall to seize the opportunity to use black troops more effectively than they had been used during previous American wars. Marshall resolutely resisted using the army as an agent of change, however:

A solution of many of the issues presented by Judge Hastie ... would be tantamount to solving a social problem which has perplexed the American people throughout the history of this nation. The army cannot accomplish such a solution and should not be charged with such an undertaking.[16]

This expression is noteworthy not only for its frankness, but also because it mirrors attitudes that Eisenhower himself would embody throughout the most important years of his leadership. Marshall, moreover, was one of Eisenhower's three most important mentors. Marshall's probing military intellect and his organizational genius apparently could not overcome societal conventions. Although it was less efficient to do so, the army would continue to segregate its troops throughout the duration of World War II.

After Pearl Harbor, Eisenhower soon found himself assisting Army Chief-of-Staff George Marshall in implementing the American war effort. Eisenhower appreciated the difficulties involved in maximizing American manpower. Eisenhower faced severe challenges, however, not only because the army restricted the duties that African-Americans could perform, but also because many American allies were hesitant to house black troops in their midst. In a memorandum to Marshall dated March 25, 1942, Eisenhower explored various strategic positions where the army had troops. Army generals, diplomats, or local officials offered resistance to the presence of black troops in all of the areas that he surveyed, including Alaska, Australia, Hawaii, Panama, Bermuda, Iceland, Trinidad, Chile, Venezuela, and even Liberia. The problem with black troops in Liberia, according to Colonel Harry Alexander McBride, was that "their rate of pay placed them in a preferred status with reference to the native population." Eisenhower evidently learned that when asked, most localities expressed a strong preference against black troops. Consequently, American strategists simply decided that they would not disclose the racial composition of units. Because he was writing a memorandum for the Chief-of-Staff, Eisenhower did not disclose any of his personal views on the subject. The army seems to have been aware at this early date, however, that its policy created difficulty. The subject line of Eisenhower's memorandum reads "The Colored Troop Problem."[17] At issue was not only the treatment of African-Americans within the military, but also their acceptance in the larger world.

Although Eisenhower's position could not be gleaned from the memorandum he prepared for George Marshall in March of 1942, a letter he wrote to John C.H. Lee in September of the same year is more revealing. Now in charge of the American efforts in the entire European theater, Eisenhower had to reflect on the presence of African-Americans stationed in the United Kingdom. As with so many of the issues that he had to confront during the war years, this required acute diplomatic sensibilities.

Because the British were unaccustomed to large numbers of blacks in their midst, Eisenhower asserted, racial policies would have to be different than in the United States. Rather than segregate black troops away from local people, Eisenhower encouraged intermingling "on a basis mutually acceptable to the individuals concerned." Eisenhower took an even stronger stance regarding any prejudicial statements issued by officers or soldiers toward any particular racial group, stating: "The spreading of derogatory statements concerning the character of any group of United States troops, either white or colored, must be considered as conduct prejudicial to good order and military discipline and offenders must be promptly punished."[18] To be sure, Eisenhower couched his argument on the basis of military discipline, as opposed to morality, but the order nevertheless demonstrates that, at this stage of his career, Eisenhower was capable of taking strong, unambiguous stands on issues involving the rights of African-Americans. He may have been more concerned about public relations or diplomatic relations than about abstract issues of rights, but the order indicates that Eisenhower recognized that the status of African-Americans in the military required delicate handling.

Eisenhower had banned derogatory statements among his soldiers, but until the Battle of the Bulge he did little to challenge the ways in which black soldiers were deployed under his command. Those positions, which were almost entirely subservient, had the reputation of being derogatory in and of themselves. Black troops most often found themselves in support units, including transportation, service, and construction. They rarely, if ever, saw the front lines of battle. Thus, it might have made little difference if British citizens did not hear white soldiers degrading their black counterparts. Seeing black troops perform little more than menial labor would convey a strong sense of the continued second-class citizenship for black soldiers in the American army during World War II.[19]

Practical considerations during the last winter of the war made Eisenhower re-evaluate the use of African-American troops under his command. Casualty rates among infantry riflemen had been particularly high and immediate replacements of new recruits were not forthcoming. This practical manpower dilemma led Eisenhower to propose his appeal to black troops willing to serve. Retrained, these troops were organized as platoons that were plugged into the needs of existing army groups. Forming some forty-five platoons, the soldiers who volunteered for service played a critical role in the final Allied push during the spring of 1945.[20]

It is entirely plausible to assume that Eisenhower and other American military strategists would have emerged from the end of World War II convinced that, when given greater opportunities, African-American soldiers would respond accordingly. The deployment of black infantrymen during the final months of the war had not been a universal success, but given the restraints under which they operated, black soldiers had accorded themselves quite well. Thus, blacks were disappointed by a report prepared by

General Alvan Gillem during the final months of 1945. Gillem advocated continuing the cautious program of racial quotas that the military had followed throughout most of the war. In the short term, which he labeled "Initial Objectives," Gillem advocated the continued use of quotas to achieve American military goals. In the long term, however, the report envisioned the use of all manpower, without regard to race, in future military engagements.[21] A leading scholar of army desegregation has called the Gillem Report "a progressive step in the history of American race relations."[22] Given the report's extreme caution, however, the assessment from the Pittsburgh *Courier* seems more appropriate: "the Army command had undergone no real change of heart."[23] Because more widespread change was not immediately forthcoming, like all previous wars in American history, World War II illustrated to African-Americans both the opportunities and the limits of those opportunities in the American military.

Eisenhower did not comment on the Gillem Report directly, but his actions as Army Chief-of-Staff indicate his sympathy to the extreme conservatism and evasiveness that had characterized race relations in the military. Upon receiving the Gillem Report, Eisenhower sent it on to Secretary of War Robert Patterson for acceptance, with the proviso that it be approved "subject to such adjustment as experience shows is necessary."[24] Both the report itself and Eisenhower's reaction to it demonstrate the delicate, deliberate approach that would continue to characterize Eisenhower's approach to civil rights issues for the remainder of his life. Nothing about the report was glaringly objectionable to any particular camp. It made conventional assumptions and devised conventional solutions to the perceived problems. Above all, the report, like Eisenhower himself, hoped that by maintaining the status quo, it could pass the obvious problems on to someone else.

In the interlude between the Gillem Report and the 1952 presidential election, Eisenhower, as Chief-of-Staff between 1945 and 1948, witnessed President Harry Truman's decision to integrate the American armed forces. Truman did so after Senate hearings about universal conscription, which had taken place in April 1948. During these hearings, African-American leader A. Philip Randolph made headlines by declaring that a proposal for universal military service, which was being debated by Congress, would be hamstrung if the military continued to pursue its Jim Crow policies. Using Mahatma Gandhi as his inspiration, Randolph threatened that he would lead a massive campaign of passive resistance. "Negroes are in no mood," Randolph told the Senate Armed Services Committee, "to shoulder a gun for democracy abroad so long as they are denied democracy here at home."[25] Two days later, Eisenhower appeared before the same committee. His testimony there indicates that, despite his order during the Battle of the Bulge, he had not progressed significantly beyond the position on segregation that George Marshall had taken in 1941. Eisenhower rejected the notion that the army played any role in perpetuating racial inferiority, stating that it was merely a mirror of society. As reported in the Chicago *Tribune*, he also offered a disingenuous defense of perpetuating the quota system. On average, Eisenhower said, black soldiers did not score as well on military intelligence tests, and therefore abandoning the quota system might also jeopardize the ability of blacks to achieve promotions.[26] Most enticingly, Eisenhower also offered a preview of the stance he would take during his presidency by holding up hope for the eventual improvement of race relations, but opining "if we attempt merely by passing a lot of laws to force someone to like someone else, we are just going to get into trouble."[27]

One must keep in mind Eisenhower's unparalleled reputation to appreciate the weight of his testimony. Although he had recently retired from the army, his plainspoken demeanor, humility, and winning smile had made him a candidate much in demand by both political parties. His stint as Chief-of-Staff had only increased his gravitas and reputation. Therefore, his testimony was that much more disappointing. It indicated that Eisenhower either did not appreciate the power of his position, or, if he did, that he did not believe that desegregation was a policy that would help American manpower in future conflicts. He did not even appear to consider the paradox that A. Philip Randolph had raised a day earlier about second-class citizens fighting for the liberty of others. At this point in his public career, he did not have to think of himself as a steward for all Americans, but even from the standpoint of improving the army, his decision lacked foresight.

It is worthwhile to contrast Eisenhower's 1948 testimony about racial prejudices in the army with his determined effort to "denazify" Germany at the conclusion of World War II. In the first case, and later as president, Eisenhower insisted that personal prejudices could not be retrained by societal institutions. Yet during the occupation of Germany at the end of the war, Eisenhower had been an ardent champion of denazification. As he argued with General George Patton about the scope of the process, Eisenhower made it apparent that his view of denazification was thorough: "victory is not complete until we have eliminated from positions of responsibility and, in appropriate cases, properly punished, every active adherent to the Nazi party."[28] In pursing such a policy, he was not only ensuring that victory was complete, he was also sending a strong message to the German people that the Nazi mindset was no longer acceptable. A vital component of that mindset, of course, was Aryan supremacy. Although many African-Americans during World War II made specific comparisons between the Southern champions of white supremacy and Nazis, Eisenhower must not have seen a compelling parallel. Did Eisenhower think there was something about German racial ideology that made it more susceptible to change? If so, how could this be explained? Eisenhower's pursuit of power blinded him to Army policies that limited liberty for 10 percent of its soldiers. What was worse, he did so under the paternalistic guise of keeping promotion opportunities open for African-Americans.

The soldier as president

Eisenhower's 1952 election over Democratic candidate Adlai Stevenson ushered in a new chapter in American history. The first Republican elected in nearly a quarter-of-a-century, Eisenhower attempted to refashion his party into something that he called "modern Republicanism." He sought new recruits for the party and one of the regions from which he believed he could draw those recruits was the South. Solidly Democratic in nearly all presidential elections since 1876, the South was still home to Jim Crow segregation, disfranchisement, and racial terror. Eisenhower's quest to refashion the Republican Party and the quest of African-Americans to achieve the liberties that many of them had fought for during World War II came to a head during the eight years of his presidency. Throughout the administration, Eisenhower displayed extreme caution whenever civil rights issues came up, thereby missing a key opportunity to exercise the power of his position fully. His experiences in the army provided the atmosphere and basis on which to crawl forward.

Plainly Eisenhower's military background was his primary asset as he inherited the presidency. The United States was immersed in war on at least two major fronts: the "hot" war in Korea and the Cold War against the Soviet Union. No American seemed better qualified to lead American foreign policy during such treacherous times than the former Supreme Allied and NATO commander. Famous for his modesty, Eisenhower was more willing to play on his military celebrity that many Americans recognized. Indeed, as historians Chester Pach and Elmo Richardson have commented, during the 1952 election Eisenhower successfully sold himself "as a hero whose most notable qualities were the perfect antidote for the nation's ills."[29]

At times heroes are unwilling to tarnish their image. Eisenhower was by and large successful in most of the undertakings of his presidency, particularly in contrast to many of his successors. Yet his leadership on civil rights issues was sorely lacking. There were those who had hoped that Eisenhower's apparent appreciation of equality of opportunity during the Battle of the Bulge would coincide with the Republican Party's history as the Party of Emancipation to embark upon an aggressive era that some would label "The Second Reconstruction." Indeed, if the Republican Party had been founded on stopping the spread of slavery, Eisenhower had an ideal chance to modernize the party by reinvigorating its civil rights commitment in the atomic age. The NAACP's Roy Wilkins was not so sanguine, however. After meeting with the presidential candidate in 1952, Wilkins pronounced Eisenhower to be "West Point and Old Guard." Neither characterization, it was clear, was meant as a compliment.[30]

Although a number of the traditional civil rights movement landmarks occurred under Eisenhower's presidency, his reaction and involvement in three areas warrant closer attention. The 1954 *Brown* v. *Board of Education* ruling and the 1957 Central High School confrontation were the most important tests of his civil rights leadership.[31] The unanimous 9–0 Brown decision offered Eisenhower a unique mandate to embark upon the aggressive era of federal civil rights advocacy for which black Americans had long clamored. Instead, Eisenhower appeared to treat the ruling as if it were an infectious disease. Although he rarely commented directly about the ruling in public, in later years he would call the appointment of former California governor Earl Warren the "biggest damn fool mistake" of his life.[32] Publicly, Eisenhower demonstrated how a chief executive could create the appearance of faithfully upholding the law while doing the least amount possible to achieve the spirit behind said law. During regularly scheduled press conferences Eisenhower continually expressed the opinion that change in the field of civil rights was a long, torturous process. Americans should not expect major change overnight, he warned. After a few of Eisenhower's measured speeches, white Southern extremists got the message: they could resist *Brown* and not expect Eisenhower to respond aggressively. Eisenhower denounced extremists on both sides, but just as he failed to attack red baiting Senator Joseph McCarthy, whose tactics he abhorred, so did he refuse to use the apparatus of the presidency to topple White Citizens' Councils.

Moreover, Eisenhower had the unfortunate facility for seeming to side with the white Southern perspective when fielding questions during his press conferences relating to civil rights. When asked in 1956 about his reaction to the Southern Manifesto, a document opposing the engagement of the federal government in civil rights issues signed by 101 Congressman (including all but three Southern senators), Eisenhower seemed to defend his critics. "If ever there was a time when we must be patient without being complacent, when we must be understanding of other people's deep emotions as well as our own," the president said, "this is it." His caution in dealing with Southern critics might be less surprising when one remembers that it was an election year and Eisenhower still had dreams about reinventing the Republican Party. Nevertheless, Eisenhower went even further in trying to sympathize with the white Southern perspective by reminding the press corps "the people who have this deep emotional reaction on the other side were not acting over the past three generations in defiance of the law." Instead, Eisenhower claimed, they were "in compliance with the law as interpreted by the Supreme Court of the United Sates under the decision of 1896."[33]

This statement to the press was quite revealing. It was a moment where Eisenhower appeared to step beyond a simple answer during a press conference. Ike was doing more than just defending white Southerners who were having trouble reconciling themselves with the *Brown* decision. In fact, he seemed to be defending *his own* reaction to the sweeping change of constitutional interpretation that the decision appeared to offer. In other words, he was still trying to comprehend how a system that he had grown up with and known his entire professional life in the army was suddenly both outdated and unlawful.

Eisenhower's statement about *Plessy* v. *Ferguson* was accurate; his optimism with respect to desegregation in saying that the "American people ... will approach it intelligently and with patience and with understanding" demonstrated that he believed in progress.[34] Nevertheless, one searches in vain for Eisenhower's identification with the African-American perspective on the issue of civil rights legislation. Eisenhower could have taken his pick from a number of individuals and organizations itching to use the president's visibility and popularity to offer guidance on civil rights leadership, ranging from the NAACP to the Brotherhood of Sleeping Car Porters, the Urban League, to the recently formed Montgomery Improvement Association. Even though he was facing a frontal assault from many white Southern politicians, the old soldier preferred to avoid the battle at all costs.

Eisenhower's timidity in confronting the Southern Manifesto was one manifestation of his hesitancy to use his powers as Commander in Chief during 1956, but an action that he took later in that year was an even more revealing blow to the civil rights agenda. A draft of the Republican Party platform had read that the "Eisenhower administration and the Republican Party supports the *Brown* decision." Through his Attorney General Herbert Brownell, Eisenhower worked behind the scenes to revise the platform so that it read "the Republican Party accepts the *Brown* decision."[35] Not only had Eisenhower worked to remove his administration's name from the ruling, he had also changed the verb that accompanied the ruling. To say, as the revised platform did, that the party accepted the ruling was merely to admit that the party recognized the Constitutional power granted to the court. Thus, Eisenhower succeeded in changing a very mild endorsement of a ruling with no definitive timetable to a complete dodge of the issue. With the pace of civil rights protest increasing, such a position demonstrated that Eisenhower was, at the very least, behind the cutting edge, even within the party that he claimed he was interested in modernizing.

Even the most careful generals cannot always pick all of their battles, which explains the active stance that Eisenhower took when he sent army paratroopers into Little Rock, Arkansas, in September 1957. The Little Rock episode stands out as a dramatic example of the power that the president could use to enforce civil rights legislation. Although in the end it was the type of action that many civil rights leaders had advocated, Eisenhower had not had a moment of racial awakening. Indeed, as both contemporary and historical critics have noted, Eisenhower only acted at the last second, and although in the end he acted decisively, his unwillingness to confront demagogic Governor Orval Faubus contributed to the crisis.[36] On September 4, 1957, Faubus had dared the president to take a stand by deploying the Arkansas National Guard to prevent court-ordered desegregation. Called to Eisenhower's vacation spot in Newport, Rhode Island on September 14, Faubus gave the impression in a private meeting with the president that he would comply with the order to desegregate. Afterward, Faubus almost immediately backtracked, enraging the president in the process. To make matters worse, Faubus' action provided inspiration for other Southern governors down the road, including Mississippi's Ross Barnett and Alabama's George Wallace, who realized that, like Faubus, they could use the federal government as a pawn in their bids to galvanize their support within the various white Southern electorates. There was something to be said for Eisenhower's opinion that true leadership in the atomic age was crisis management, as opposed to crisis elimination, but even the presence of troops in Little Rock's Central High school for the remainder of the school year did not solve many long-term problems; the next year, rather than carry out its program of desegregation, Little Rock simply shut down its public schools.[37]

Such decisions by local school boards seemed to validate Eisenhower's opinion that government action or Supreme Court decree could not change people's personal prejudices. Instead, it might be more appropriate to consider how Eisenhower's frequent statements in sympathy with white Southerners likely exacerbated the situation. If the president repeatedly stressed that change in the realm of civil rights would have to be gradual, rather than immediate, and he urged sympathy for those who were acting on their belief in the righteousness of outdated law, it was likely that change in the realm of civil rights would be gradual and that white Southerners would feel emboldened to act on their beliefs. As long as they did not directly challenge the president and renege on promises in the way that Faubus had, they knew they were likely to escape the former general's wrath. Imagine, instead, if Eisenhower had taken the time to repeatedly identify with African-Americans by reflecting on their bravery under his command at the Battle of the Bulge. He even might have been able to argue that he believed in gradualism, but that as blacks had been in the United States for centuries and yet had never known equality, perhaps the process had been gradual enough. Instead, civil rights protests persisted throughout the Eisenhower presidency.

In evaluating Eisenhower's failure to wield his power on the civil rights issue, one of the most damning critiques is that he did not seem to use the powers of the presidency to educate himself or the American people on civil rights matters. At the urging of Chief-of-Staff Sherman Adams, the administration brought E. Frederick Morrow, an African-American lawyer who had campaigned for Eisenhower in 1952, into the White House in 1955. Given the title of Administrative Officer for Special Projects, Morrow would soon find that few projects would make it his way. Morrow had trouble enough even finding a secretary who would agree to work for him, while many of his colleagues in the White House avoided him. Eisenhower also seems to have had little to do with his special assistant, which might partially be explained by a biographer's assertion that Eisenhower was personally uncomfortable around Jews and blacks.[38] Morrow proved to be convenient photo-op material for Eisenhower during the 1956 election as the two appeared watching a World Series game between the New York Yankees and the Brooklyn Dodgers, but Eisenhower otherwise missed the opportunity to learn from his assistant. Morrow was thus left to muse in his diary that "perhaps only a Negro could understand the black American's burning desire for complete recognition."[39]

Eisenhower's gradualism and his Southern sympathies undermined his civil rights record, but his choice of words frequently alienated potential allies, too. Eisenhower was a stickler for proper usage and clear communication, yet he never could seem to grasp that phrases such as "you people," and "patience" when directed at African-Americans grated severely. When meeting with the African-American National Newspaper Association's members in May 1958, for instance, Eisenhower told the group that they "must be patient" with respect to full citizenship rights.[40] In Morrow's charitable assessment, he thought that his boss had chosen "what might be considered an unfortunate term."[41]

The short-term importance for Eisenhower's unfortunate advice to the press association was that it finally caused the president to agree to a White House meeting with civil rights leaders. The delegation, which consisted of Roy Wilkins of the NAACP, A. Philip Randolph of the Brotherhood of Sleeping Car Porters, Lester Granger of the Urban League, and Martin Luther King, Jr., of the Southern Christian Leadership Council. Many thought that this meeting should have occurred years earlier, and, indeed, Eisenhower's statements during the meeting revealed that his attitude had not changed significantly since the 1940s.

The June meeting was Martin Luther King's first with the president and, like many African-Americans, King hoped that the meeting would signify more aggressive involvement on the part of the president. Yet King and the other civil rights leaders would emerge from the meeting feeling as though they had made little impression on the president's thought process. Their forty-five-minute meeting with the president included a nine-point program to encourage Eisenhower's increased involvement in civil rights enforcement. According to King chronicler Taylor Branch, King's main mission was "to try to lure Eisenhower into greater activity by summoning up feelings of duty and glory."[42] As with the World Series game, the meeting resulted in some nice photo opportunities for those involved, but Eisenhower did not emerge as an advocate for greater federal involvement in civil rights issues. If Branch was right about the delegation's attempt to appeal to the president's feeling of glory, they would have been well served to have remembered that the man who had successfully overseen D-Day and had helped to defeat Adolf Hitler needed little more glory in his life. Nevertheless, Eisenhower's reluctance to consider greater activity was supremely disappointing to the black community.

One other prominent African-American voiced his displeasure with Eisenhower's lukewarm civil rights leadership in 1958. Martin Luther King would eventually earn the reputation as the foremost champion of the civil rights movement, but in 1950s America, no black man commanded more respect and fame than Brooklyn Dodgers second baseman Jackie Robinson. A World War II veteran, Robinson had famously broken baseball's color barrier in 1947, a year before President Truman announced that he would integrate the military. Robinson retired in 1956, but remained a public figure and civil rights activist, as well as a visible Republican. Upon hearing Eisenhower's advice to African-Americans in 1958 "to be patient," Robinson wrote the president. Because of those words, Robinson claimed, he "felt like standing up and saying, 'Oh no! Not again.'" African-Americans, Robinson said, "have been the most patient of all people.... Seventeen million Negroes cannot do as you suggest and wait for the hearts of men to change." Robinson, for one, also thought that action by Eisenhower would dramatically improve the situation for black Americans. In the most damning sentence in the letter, Robinson indicted the president's caution: "I respectfully suggest that you unwittingly crush the spirit of freedom in Negroes by constantly urging forbearance and give hope to those pro-segregation leaders like Governor Faubus who would take from us even those freedoms we now enjoy."[43] Having demonstrated the same aggressiveness with the pen that he was known for on the baseball diamond, Robinson hoped that he would inspire a similar competitive flame in the president.

That competitive flame in the field of civil rights was imperceptible for the remainder of Eisenhower's presidency. Even those within the administration conceded that Eisenhower's civil rights record was one of the disappointments of the presidency. Speechwriter Arthur Larson, who otherwise thought that most Americans underestimated the strength of Eisenhower's leadership, thought the evidence pointed to "the inescapable conclusion that President Eisenhower, during his presidential tenure, was neither emotionally nor intellectually in favor of combating segregation in general."[44] Emmett John Hughes, in whom Eisenhower had confided "that the Supreme Court decision *set back* progress in the South *at least fifteen years*," meanwhile thought that Eisenhower displayed "basic insensitivity – or stubborn resolve – on the whole issues of civil rights."[45] E. Frederick Morrow, meanwhile, who was grateful for his opportunity but frustrated by the experience, tellingly wrote that the although

> the Administration has made more significant appointments than any other in recent history and that gestures have been made ... there is no strong, clarion commanding voice from the White House, right-

eously indignant over the plight of 18,000,000 Negroes in the United States . . .[46]

Most historians have concurred with the evaluation of Eisenhower's associates. Stephen Ambrose, generally known as an Eisenhower admirer, concludes that the area of civil rights was his "great weakness as a political leader."[47] Chester Pach and Elmo Richardson believe that Eisenhower uncharacteristically shirked his duty in this realm, because he "searched for a way to confine issues of civil rights to the courtroom, statehouse, or school board so he would not have to deal with them."[48] In the most exhaustive study of Eisenhower's civil rights record, Robert Burk concludes:

> Measured by how own standards, the President's leadership in the civil rights struggle had fallen short. His failure to commit himself unequivocally to racial justice, his willingness to settle for the political containment of racial problems rather than their solution, and his reluctance to intervene in matters of divided federal–state jurisdiction meant that white Southern resistance to black legal equality persisted as an immediate civil rights challenge to the Kennedy administration.[49]

In most respects, Dwight Eisenhower was the model citizen–soldier. His skill as both a general and a president during a critical era in American history was second only to George Washington's. Although Ike's military experience on the whole provided excellent training for his duties as president, it was sorely deficient in the field of civil rights. His presidency further underscores how struggles with foreign powers can and often have overshadowed struggles for domestic liberty. Had Eisenhower grabbed the opportunity to strike a bold path in civil rights leadership, he might well be remembered not only as the heroic brains behind D-Day, but also as the heroic heart behind new civil rights policies and the father of modern Republicanism. Instead, he reminds us that even great and powerful men will balk at opportunities to use their power to advance liberty.

Notes

1 Eisenhower Mss., J.C.H. Lee Correspondence, January 4, 1945, Draft of statement, in Alfred Chandler, Jr. (ed.), *The Papers of Dwight David Eisenhower: the War Years*, vol. 4 (Baltimore: Johns Hopkins Press, 1970), 2394.

2 The statistic of volunteers comes from Ulysses Lee, *The Employment of Negro Troops*, United States Army in World War II Special Studies, vol. 8 (Washington, DC: Office of the Chief of Military History United States Army, 1966), 693.

3 Fred Anderson and Andrew Cayton, *The Dominion of War: Empire and Liberty in North America, 1500–2000* (New York: Viking, 2005), xxiv.

4 United States Bureau of the Census, *Twelfth Census of the United States*, Volume

1: Population: Population of States and Territories, Chapter 10, Sex, General Nativity and Color Population, 617). Online, available at: www.census.gov/prod/www/abs/decennial/1900.htm.

5 Stephen Ambrose, *Eisenhower*, vol. 1: *Soldier, General of the Army, President-Elect 1890–1952* (New York: Simon and Schuster, 1983), 33.

6 The historian most associated with labeling the era the nadir for American race relations is Rayford Logan, *The Betrayal of the Negro: From Rutherford B. Hayes to Woodrow Wilson* (1954; New York: Collier, 1965).

7 Ambrose, *Eisenhower*, 1: 47.

8 For more on Young's life at West Point, see Brian Shellum, *Black Cadet in a White Bastion: Charles Young at West Point* (Lincoln: University of Nebraska Press, 2006). More on blacks in the military can be found in Bernard Nalty, *Strength for the Fight: a History of Black Americans in the Military* (New York: The Free Press, 1986). For the episode regarding Young's retirement, see Nalty, 109–111.

9 Quoted in Stephen Ambrose, *Duty, Honor, Country: a History of West Point* (Baltimore: Johns Hopkins Press, 1966), 271.

10 Nalty, *Strength for the Fight*, 131.

11 Dwight D. Eisenhower, *Stories I Tell to Friends* (1967; New York: Eastern Acorn Press, 1981), 200.

12 Nalty, *Strength for the Fight*, 109.

13 For more on African-Americans during World War I, see ibid., 107–142.

14 Lee, *The Employment of Negro Troops*, 83.

15 Quoted in ibid., 138.

16 Ibid., 140.

17 Dwight Eisenhower to George C. Marshall, March 25, 1942, in Alfred Chandler, Jr. (ed.), *The Papers of Dwight David Eisenhower, The War Years*, vol. 1 (Baltimore: Johns Hopkins University Press, 1970), 208–209.

18 Dwight Eisenhower to John C.H. Lee, September 5, 1942, in ibid., 1: 544–545.

19 For more on African-American service during World War II, see Nalty, *Strength for the Fight*, 162–183.

20 For more detail on this experience, see Lee, *The Employment of Negro Troops*, 688–706.

21 Morris J. MacGregor, Jr., *Integration of the Armed Forces, 1940–1965*, Defense Studies Series, vol. 1 (Washington, DC: Center of Military History United States Army, 1981), 161.

22 Ibid., 165.

23 Pittsburgh *Courier*, May 11, 1946, quoted in ibid., 164.

24 Ibid., 162.

25 C.P. Trussell, "Congress told UMT Racial Bars Would Unleash Civil Disobedience," *New York Times*, April 1, 1948.

26 "Ike Backs UMT Draft; Two Cardinals Split," Chicago *Tribune*, April 3, 1948.

27 Quoted in MacGregor, *Integration of the Armed Forces*, 229.

28 Ambrose, *Eisenhower*, 1: 423.

29 Chester J. Pach and Elmo Richardson, *The Presidency of Dwight D. Eisenhower*, revised edn (Lawrence: University Press of Kansas, 1991), 27.

30 Wilkins, quoted in Robert Burk, *The Eisenhower Administration and Black Civil Rights* (Knoxville: University of Tennessee Press), 28.

31 More on all of these episodes can be found in Burk.

32 Quoted in James Patterson, *Grand Expectations: the United States, 1945–1974* (New York: Oxford, 1996), 394.

33 News Conference of March 14, 1956, in *Public Papers of President Dwight D. Eisenhower, 1956* (Washington, DC: United States Government Printing Office, 1958), 304–305.

34 Ibid.

35 Stephen Ambrose, *Eisenhower*, vol. 2: *The President* (New York: Simon and Schuster, 1984), 337–338.

36 Patterson is one of the many historians to draw a similar conclusion. See *Grand Expectations*, 415.

37 For the fullest account of the Little Rock confrontation from Eisenhower's perspective, see Burk, *The Eisenhower Administration and Black Civil Rights*, 174–203. The statement about crisis management is from Arthur Larson, *Eisenhower: the President Nobody Knew* (New York: Scribner's, 1968), 194.

38 Ambrose, *Eisenhower*, 2: 387.

39 E. Frederick Morrow, *Black Man in the White House: a Diary of the Eisenhower Years by the Administrative Officer for Special Projects, The White House, 1955–1961* (New York: Coward-McCann, 1963), 248.

40 Burk, *The Eisenhower Administration and Black Civil Rights*, 238.

41 Morrow, *Black Man in the White House*, 218.

42 Taylor Branch, *Parting the Waters: America During the King Years, 1954–63* (New York: Simon and Schuster, 1988), 235.

43 Jackie Robinson to Dwight Eisenhower, May 13, 1958. Online, available at: archives.gov/education/lessons/jackie-robinson/images/letter-1958.htm.

44 Larson, *The President Nobody Knew*, 128.

45 Emmett John Hughes, *The Ordeal of Power: a Political Memoir of the Eisenhower Years* (New York: Atheneum, 1963), 201, 242.

46 Morrow, *Black Man in the White House*, 179.

47 Stephen Ambrose, *Eisenhower: Soldier and President* (New York: Touchstone, 1990), 336.

48 Pach and Richardson, *The Presidency of Dwight D. Eisenhower*, 149.

49 Burk, *The Eisenhower Administration and Black Civil Rights*, 263.

5 Cold War perceptions and the American experience of war

R. William Ayres

Editor's introduction

This chapter traces the development of enemy images in the early days of the Cold War and analyzes the effects those central images had on the perceptual judgments of US leaders concerning a broad range of issues facing them. These judgments drove US foreign policy throughout the 1950s and 1960s, creating new patterns of behavior in war and crisis consistent with the new ways in which American leaders saw the world. The result was not necessarily more American involvement in war or crisis than in pre-war periods, but different forms of involvement that would shape the US experience of war for a half-a-century.

World War II, it is widely understood, brought the United States into a new relationship with the rest of the world, opening an era of internationalism and ending permanently the isolationism of the past. While America had been consistently involved in wars throughout its history (as other chapters in this volume make clear), the postwar period brought the first sustained era of stable international engagement. As leaders of a self-acknowledged global power, American presidents and their advisors found themselves faced with a variety of questions and concerns that their predecessors could ignore, or deal with only sporadically. Thus, while the postwar period did not usher in a new era of American military interventionism (as some have argued), it did introduce new dimensions to America's relationship with war.

Being a global power made the US a permanent part of the international balance of power in ways that it had eschewed before. Whereas the post-World War I period, with its failed League of Nations and Kellogg–Briand treaties, had witnessed American attempts at global reformism, the aftermath of World War II brought a new dimension to US foreign policy – a stable adversary. In the past, America's enemies had been situational and fleeting; no lasting enmity developed after the War of 1812, or the Mexican–American War, or the Spanish–American War, at least for America's part. But the coming of the Cold War, with the prospect of a prolonged antagonism with the Soviet Union, introduced new ways of think-ing about and perceiving the world. The foreign policy perceptions of US leaders, more fluid in previous eras, became fixed around a set of images of the enemy and derivative perceptions linked to the central conflict with communism. This change, in turn, affected the ways in which US policy-makers thought and acted on issues of war and peace.

This chapter will trace the development of enemy images in the early years of the Cold War, and the effects those central images had on Amer-ican behavior, particularly with respect to American involvement in war. These images drove US foreign policy in the 1950s and 1960s, creating new patterns of behavior in war and crisis consistent with the new ways American leaders saw the world. The result was not necessarily more American involvement in war or crisis than in pre-war periods, but differ-ent forms of involvement that would shape the US experience of war for half-a-century.

Images of the other, foreign policy, and war

Foreign policy has always been about engagement with the other. Foreign affairs assumes an "us" and a "them," with the job of the policy-maker to made decisions regarding how we are going to act toward them, and how they might respond to us. This is particularly true in the arena of war, because war presumes an enemy and a set of (mostly military) tools with which to deal with that enemy. War presumes a relationship of antago-nism, although that antagonism – and the justifications for war – can take a number of different forms.

As a starting point, this chapter assumes that how we perceive others conditions how we behave toward them. At the interpersonal level, this is not at all controversial; we treat people we like differently from people we do not, even if we acknowledge universal rules calling for us to treat all people the same. In the 1950s, psychologist Fritz Heider wrote his *Psychol-ogy of Interpersonal Relations* based on this fundamental notion. Heider's central premise was that the basic building blocks of interpersonal percep-tion are not cognitive observations (facts we can see about others) but affective judgments (whether we like something or not). Thus, if we like the quality of bravery (affect) and perceive that someone is brave (cogni-tion), we will like that person (affective judgment) and respond to them accordingly. Conversely, if we dislike the quality of cowardice (affect) and perceive that someone is a coward (cognition), we will dislike that person (affective judgment). Heider further assumed that we will tend to cluster these judgments and observations, so that we associate positive traits with people we like and negative traits with people we do not like, while dis-counting or ignoring the negative qualities of liked people and the posit-ive qualities of disliked people.[1] He called this act of perceptional manipulation "balancing," since only by maintaining balanced images could people maintain psychological comfort and efficiency. Heider's essential insight is that people use affective judgments to simplify the processing of information about others, leading to balanced, integrated views that can easily form the basis for further judgment and action.

Starting with Heider, a literature has been built up on the psychological dynamics of images, combining strains of both affective and cognitive theories.[2] Building on these psychological theories, Richard Cottam and Richard Herrmann developed a theory of foreign policy images.[3] These images, each a stereotypical or ideal type, had one primary purpose – to help analysts to judge the motivations of a state (or of particular leaders), based on the assumption that if an analyst knows how a leader views another actor, the analyst will have a better idea of how the leader is likely to treat that actor. Some kinds of behavior – war, for instance – are perfectly justified (indeed, may be demanded) by some images but would be totally inappropriate for others. Images in Cottam and Herrmann's theory thus have both a type (Enemy, Colony, Ally, etc.) and an intensity, since some images will be held more strongly (and therefore motivate stronger behavior) than others. Drawing on Heider's theory, Cottam and Herrmann argued that images must be affectively balanced – that is, that they must be consistent, not necessarily in the logical, cognitive sense, but in terms of their associations of positive and negative traits with liked and disliked actors.

War has always been accompanied by strong images, because violence requires a strong psychological justification. In previous wars in American history, those images had been varied – Native Americans were frequently considered barbarians or even colonial subjects, while Spain was perceived as a degenerating empire.[4] As noted above, these images tended not to last, since the circumstances and power relationships on which they were based also didn't last. What the United States had not had in its history was a permanent adversary – an opponent of equal stature and power on the world stage that was, by its nature, hostile to fundamental US interests.

Cottam and Herrmann argue that this is the condition which calls for an Enemy image – an opponent of roughly equivalent power, hostile intent, perceived to be on the same cultural plane as one's own state. They described images in general as having three components: perceptions about the target's motivations, its capabilities, and its decision-making process. In the stereotypical Enemy image, the adversary's motives are described as "evil and unlimited," usually including some cluster of reasons for why it wants to dominate the world. The Enemy's capabilities are seen as strong on the surface, but if met with strong opposition, the Enemy will reveal itself as a "paper tiger" because it is domestically weak behind its armies and military strength. An Enemy's decision-making is described as unified and capable of creating and carrying out "complex and sinister plans."[5] This image is balanced, in Heider's sense, because it begins with a negative – the Enemy's evil motivations. The "paper tiger" capabilities allow for the acknowledgement that the Enemy appears strong (why else would it be a threat?), but that it is weak internally – since domestic cohesion and the support of the population are seen as positive qualities. Likewise, a sinister and highly organized decision-making style bolsters the overall perception of threat, since an Enemy divided against itself and ineffectual would be less imposing and (potentially) more sympathetic.

The overall motive behind the Enemy image is therefore derived from this integrated perception of threat. Leaders who hold a strong Enemy image desire first and foremost to defend their country against the threat, and tend to use that motivation to organize their foreign-policy preferences, not only towards the Enemy itself but across a range of issues that are potentially related. It is thus in the presence of Enemy images that foreign policy most closely resembles classic balance-of-power politics, with the threatened actor concerned with the zero-sum implications of its foreign policy actions.[6] While there is a long debate about whether images are causes, effects, or epiphenoma, these distinctions do not matter here. It may well be that the perception of threat comes first, and the image is constructed around it as justification for what the threatened actor wants to do anyway. It may also be true that images may be constructed based on feelings and perceptions, and then drive policy. It should also be noted that, although images are constructed stereotypes, image theory makes no particular distinction based on whether they are accurate or not. Some enemies may really be evil and trying to take over the world (although even in these cases, any "good" qualities would almost certainly be disregarded). Regardless, the key point for our purposes here is that images are *markers* – signs of the kinds of policy that can be expected. Images are generally not out of sync with policy, or else they would fail to provide justification (either beforehand or post hoc) for the decisions leaders make. The primary use here in tracking images, therefore, is to examine a sometimes hidden dimension to US policy, especially towards its enemies, in the Cold War, and explore the ways in which that altered the American experience of war in the postwar period.

Before the Cold War: Roosevelt and US images of enemies and allies

It certainly cannot be argued that the United States had never had enemies prior to the Cold War. During World War II, President Franklin Roosevelt's description of the Nazi regime in Germany, as well as Imperial Japan, fit most of the elements of the classic Enemy image quite well. He also described US allies in similarly stereotypical terms – including, interestingly enough, the Soviet Union, which helps to underscore the change in US thinking pre- and post-1945.[7]

Roosevelt's description of the Nazi regime invoked most of the elements of the Enemy image, even before the United States was officially at war. In his famous "Great Arsenal of Democracy" speech (December 29, 1940), he repeatedly accused the Nazis of plotting "world control" or of seeking to "dominat[e] or conquer[...] the world." He likewise explained that, "there can be no ultimate peace between their philosophy ... and our philosophy of government." He referred to the Axis as "war-makers" and talked about the "pious frauds" the Nazis used in justifying their aggression. He asserted that, "no nation can appease the Nazis.... There can be no appeasement with ruthlessness." These and many other phrases capture the stereotypical description of the enemy as having evil and unlimited aims.[8]

In the same vein, Roosevelt consistently described the Nazis as a unified entity, a monolithic force capable of executing "complex and sinister plans." Thus, in his 1940 speech, Roosevelt warned that the "evil forces" of the Nazi regime were "already within our own gates," "active in our own and in neighboring countries," "seek[ing] to stir up suspicion and dissension, to cause internal strife." He argued that "[t]hese trouble-breeders have but one purpose ... [i]t is to divide our people ... into hostile groups and to destroy our unity and shatter our will to defend ourselves."[9] In his 1945 State of the Union speech, with the war nearing its conclusion, Roosevelt also likened the Nazi regime and its Axis allies to "the strongest and most violently aggressive powers that ever have threatened civilization," while always evincing confidence that if the US put forth its maximum effort, it would win. These were likewise consistent with Enemy images – the Enemy is assumed to be unified, calculated and devious, and powerful – but its chief danger comes if the defending country fails to stand up for itself. If strong measures are taken, the Enemy can and will be overcome.[10]

Interestingly, Roosevelt's description of the Soviet Union, even late in the war, held close to the stereotypical Ally image, with no hint of the Red Scare of the 1920s or similar past problems with the Communist state. Thus, in his 1945 State of the Union speech, the President referred to the Soviet Union and Britain as our "two active and indomitable allies" in Europe. In the same speech he praised the "heroic defense of Moscow and Leningrad and Stalingrad" as well as the "tremendous Russian offensives" of 1943 and 1944. Grouping Russia together with England, China, France, and other US allies, he expressed confidence that in all of them "the peoples' hope is peace ... a peace that is durable and secure." And although he spoke in general terms of "differences among the victors," he argued that "[w]e must not let those differences divide us and blind us to our more important common and continuing interests in winning the war and building the peace." All these comments were delivered despite previous antagonism and tension with the USSR in the 1920s and 1930s, and clearly reflected the needs of the day. They also reflected stereotypical Ally image thinking, emphasizing commonalities of aims and motives and describing the Ally's capabilities in glowing and heroic terms, beyond the plain facts.[11]

World War II, being the largest and most exerting of America's wars to that point, clearly contained particular and even extreme circumstances. It is thus no surprise that American images of the key actors abroad contained strong stereotypes, nor that US actions should have been in accord with those stereotypes – total warfare against the Axis powers, substantial cooperation and diplomacy with its Allies, even those (like the USSR) with which it had not previously gotten along. This was a set of perceptions, and an experience of war, that America understood – a clearly evil enemy and valiant allies. In many ways, this image remains a prototypical American icon of "being at war" – although the subsequent decades were to introduce new forms of war, justified with new images.

The early Cold War: Truman and the new threat

US images of key countries abroad did not shift overnight with the ending of World War II. In the immediate aftermath of the war, though Nazism continued to be regarded as evil, it was a vanquished evil, no longer a threat to the world. The emphasis for new President Harry Truman was much the same as for Roosevelt: the establishment of a peaceful and stable world order, one in which there would be no war and therefore (by implication) no enemies.

Truman's 1946 State of the Union speech is a model of complex views and an emphasis on cooperation. Though the bulk of the speech was directed at domestic economic policy – Truman combined the annual State of the Union speech with the annual Budget Message – the President dealt first with foreign affairs and the role of the US in the postwar world. He talked extensively about the new United Nations Organization, and about how "concessions and adjustments will be required" in the "intricate, continuing business" of securing the peace. He spoke repeatedly of past agreements and the need for additional cooperation. Every specific reference to the Soviet Union was in terms of cooperative agreements – he recalled the "base of understanding" formed at Yalta, the agreements of Potsdam and Moscow, and the common interest of dealing with the "effective international control of atomic energy," in which cause were included the Soviet Union, France, and Great Britain. Unlike in wartime, Truman's rhetoric did not disavow differences or focus exclusively on commonalities; he recognized that there must be "active cooperation" and talked of the "challenging task" and "extensive complications" of the "accommodation of varying views of four governments [in administering Germany]."[12]

In retrospect, Truman's 1946 address is remarkable not so much for what was said, but for what he did *not* say. In discussing the future of US armed forces (then involved in a rapid and substantial demobilization from their wartime heights), he made no mention at all of any threat, specific or general, or any particular enemy for which US armed forces might be needed. Likewise, every reference to the Soviet Union was in the context of cooperation – challenging though it might be – and indeed, his rhetorical treatment of the USSR was scarcely different from his treatment of Great Britain, so often were they mentioned in the same breath. For a brief period, then, the US was a country without enemies, and its foreign policy – dedicated primarily to reconstruction and demobilization – reflected that view.

This view prevailed, interestingly, even in one of the speeches most commonly associated with the origins of the Cold War – George C. Marshall's address to Harvard University on June 5, 1947, commonly referred to as the "Marshall Plan speech." In it, Marshall makes no reference at all – not even a vague one – to any particular enemy. The problems of Europe he blames on structural economic forces, particularly the breakdown in the "division of labor" between rural countryside and city. There is only one veiled reference to other actors – a warning to "governments, political parties, or groups which seek to perpetuate human misery in order to profit there from." At the time and in retrospect, it is clear which parties and governments he was referring to – but to fail to name them at all maintained the possibility of cooperation, and certainly did not lay the groundwork for armed conflict, even of a proxy sort.[13]

Simultaneously, of course, new images *were* beginning to appear. President Truman's address to a joint session of Congress on March 12, 1947 showed some of the first outlines of the newly emerging, and very different, Enemy image, albeit in a very specific context. Like Marshall's address to Harvard three months later, Truman began with an appeal to the "gravity of the situation." Like Marshall, he spoke of economic difficulties and the destruction caused by the war – indeed, parts of the speech are remarkably similar to Marshall's economic analysis of the whole of Europe. But Truman also pinned the threat to Greece's freedom on "the terrorist activities of several thousand armed men, led by Communists." Interestingly, this was the sole reference to communism in the speech. Instead, he warned more generally about "totalitarian regimes imposed upon free peoples, by direct or indirect aggression, undermin[ing] the foundations of international peace, and hence the security of the United States." He argued that "every nation must choose between alternative ways of life" – one based on the "will of the majority" or one based on "the will of a minority forcibly imposed upon the majority." Some elements of the classic Enemy were here (the motive to take over, to dominate), but attributed not only to the enemy but also the surrounding conditions (the "evil soil of poverty"). He concluded by stating that "it must be the policy of the United States to support free peoples who are resisting attempted subjugation by armed minorities or by outside pressures" – a general claim that became the Truman Doctrine.[14]

Of course, it was well known to his audience which "outside pressures" and "totalitarian regimes" Truman was referring to. But the fact that this newly emergent statement of threat failed to specifically name the Enemy made it very different from the classic Enemy relationship with the Nazi regime during the war. Diplomatically, by not naming the enemy, Truman left open the door, if only a little, for continued dialogue, although he made clear that there was a binary choice to be made between freedom and totalitarianism – a classic component of Enemy stereotypes ("us" versus "them"). But this new, veiled Enemy image also called for a different kind of policy – not outright war, as was appropriate against the Nazi regime (or, in previous eras, against totalitarianism in Europe, or the Spanish, or Mexico). Rather, this new image was justification instead for involvement in the wars of others – in this case (with Greece and Turkey), by sending large amounts of money and small numbers of military personnel as advisors. By keeping to a vague, evil yet unspecified image, as much philosophical as tangible, Truman laid the groundwork for US involvement in "proxy struggles" as a new experience of warfare for the United States.

By 1949, this new image had taken a more solid and specified form. In his Inaugural Address on January 20, 1949, Truman again stated that "the United States and other like-minded nations find themselves directly opposed by a regime with contrary aims and a totally different concept of life." But again, rather than rhetorically pin the Enemy down to a specific state (though everyone must have known which state he would name), he chose to define the enemy in terms of a "false philosophy" – communism. He attributed to communism the same motives usually attributed in Enemy images – "deceit," "tyranny," "violence," and their belief that "war is inevitable." But he does not bring to bear the other, typical elements of the Enemy stereotype – strong capabilities that must be faced down, and a unified and rational decision-making force at the enemy's center. Communism, in Truman's terms, is thus a new kind of enemy – one defined by its motives but not attached to a particular political entity.[15]

This vagueness of form meant that communism could thus be everywhere or anywhere, and gave rise to general policy prescriptions like the determination to "resist armed attack from any quarter." In his speech, Truman sent a signal to the Senate regarding the upcoming NATO treaty – a form of permanent military alliance that the United States had hitherto avoided and even condemned as belonging to the politics of Europe only (recalling Washington's famous remark about avoiding "entangling alliances"). To sign a treaty of mutual defense with other significant powers outside the Western hemisphere would be to commit the United States, in advance, to fight a war abroad if the occasion arose. The previously foreseen war – even if by signing the treaty the members of NATO hoped to avoid it – was an entirely new experience for the United States. With this new kind of enemy came a new American relationship to war – one in which the United States would declare ahead of time its willingness to fight. The call to resist communism "from any quarter" also opened the US to involvement in wars in a wide range of theaters, something also never before considered. With the development of the early Enemy image of communism, therefore, the American government fundamentally altered the way it thought about war and the kinds of wars it would consider becoming involved with, laying the United States open (at least theoretically) to wars far and wide.

Cold War established: Eisenhower and the two enemies

The Eisenhower administration continued this trend begun by Truman and his advisors. Throughout the 1950s, statements about the enemy became increasingly two-tracked: those dealing with the Soviet Union as a specific state rival, and those dealing with International Communism as an ideological enemy. Unlike the World War II experience with Nazi Germany, in which the ideological enemy was synonymous with specific states in the international system, US statements in the 1950s suggested a more complex view of who the enemy was, requiring a more complex set of policies to deal with it.

Fitting for a former US Army General, Eisenhower's first inaugural address, delivered on January 20, 1953, was filled with foreign policy references. He began with a universal claim regarding the condition of the world in 1953: "The world and we have passed the midway point of a century of continuing challenge. We sense with all our faculties that forces of good and evil are massed and armed and opposed as rarely before in history." He continued his use of sweeping claims of moral conflict, arguing that the "enemies of [the United States] know no god but force, no devotion but its use. . . . Whatever defies them, they torture, especially the truth." He warned that the "conflict strikes directly at the faith of our fathers," adding that "nothing lies safely beyond the reach of this struggle. Freedom is pitted against slavery; lightness against the dark." As with most strong images of the enemy, we see the fundamental argument of Good vs. Evil, with no common ground and everything at stake.[16]

As with Truman, Eisenhower tended to connect this universal moral conflict not with a specific state-to-state relationship, but with a broader, more amorphous enemy. Thus in his second inaugural address (January 21, 1957), Eisenhower described a world that "stands tragically divided." But in explaining this division, he did not blame the Soviet Union; indeed, Russia is mentioned only once in the speech, and that near the end. Instead, he argued that the "divisive force is International Communism and the power that it controls."[17] In an address to the Associated Press on April 22, 1957, Secretary of State John Foster Dulles used much the same argument, decrying the "aggressive and devious designs of international communism" and arguing that "[i]nternational communism is on the prowl . . . [it] has proved to be oppressive, reactionary, unimaginative."[18] Even in Eisenhower's final speech, his Farewell Address of January 17, 1961, he spoke of "a hostile ideology global in scope, atheistic in character, ruthless in purpose, and insidious [*sic*] in method."[19] The primary source of evil in the world, for the Eisenhower administration, was thus not so much a specific state or a specific government as an ideological movement, shadowy in form but malevolent in intent.

As universal as this conflict was, and as much as International Communism was embodied in the Soviet Union, Eisenhower's rhetoric about the USSR itself was quite different. In both his inaugural addresses, he never mentions the Soviet state by name, focusing instead on the larger ideological movement of the communist threat. But in his landmark address before the United Nations General Assembly on December 8, 1953 – the "Atoms for Peace" speech – Eisenhower said nothing at all about International Communism but a great deal about the Soviet Union as a state. In so doing, he described a Soviet Union that, though clearly a competitor with the United States, was not at all an enemy in the classic sense. Rather than reverting to "paper tiger" imagery typical of enemy images, Eisenhower described Soviet capabilities in measured, factual tones: "the Soviet Union has exploded a series of atomic ... devices" and "it has devoted extensive resources to atomic weapons." Discussions of Soviet motivations in the context of ongoing negotiations were similarly measured. He noted that "we have received from the Soviet Union what is in effect an expression of willingness to hold a four-Power meeting.... we were pleased to see that his note did not contain the unacceptable preconditions previously put forward." He conceded that "[w]e never have, we never will, propose or suggest that the Soviet Union surrender what is rightfully theirs." And he vowed that the "United States ... is instantly prepared to meet privately with such other countries as may be 'principally involved,' to seek 'an acceptable solution' to the atomic armaments race," noting later in the speech that "[o]f those 'principally involved' the Soviet Union must, of course, be one."[20] When isolated from the larger discussion of ideological enmity, therefore, Eisenhower's publicly expressed view of the Soviet Union as a state was in fact much closer to the Complex end of the spectrum than the Enemy end.[21]

Even John Foster Dulles, one of the figures most associated with a hawkish view on the Soviets, made rhetorical distinctions between the Soviet Union as a state and International Communism as the primary enemy. In his 1957 speech to the AP, he was certainly harder on the USSR than Eisenhower was in the "Atoms for Peace" address, chiding the Soviets for vetoing UN resolutions. Here Dulles introduced a distinction very stereotypical of Enemy images: a separation between the Soviet government and Soviet citizens. He accused "Soviet rulers" of "prefer[ing] that the free nations should be weak and divided," of stealing "the independence of a dozen nations," of "pour[ing] out abuse against" US-led defensive alliances. When faced with a common defense, he argued, "the Soviet rulers emit threats." As for the Soviet people, Dulles pointed out that "[w]ithin the Soviet Union there is increasing demand for greater personal security, for greater intellectual freedom, and for greater enjoyment of the fruits of labor."[22] This divided image – a unified group of evil rulers lording over an oppressed population – is a standard component of the classic Enemy image.[23]

But Dulles directs his most damning critiques not at the Soviet state or its rulers, but at the broader forces of "international communism." It is communism writ large that represents "despotism," that is "cruel" and "aggressive" and "devious." In describing the response of the communists to the conditions of poverty in the Third World, Dulles argues that "Communism boasts that it could change all that and points to industrial developments wrought in Russia" – separating out communism as a larger force from the specific instance of Russia as a state. Like Eisenhower, and Truman in the late 1940s, Dulles argues that in the struggle with this ideological enemy, "[t]here is no safe middle ground."[24]

Why this bifurcated image, describing an ideological enemy with which no common ground is possible, yet a Soviet state that can be treated diplomatically like other states? The Eisenhower administration was faced with a dilemma: driven by the Soviet explosion of the atomic bomb in 1949 and the hydrogen bomb a few years later, war had become an unacceptable option. In his "Atoms for Peace" speech, Eisenhower pointed out that "[e]ven against the most powerful defense, an aggressor in possession of the effective minimum number of atomic bombs for a surprise attack could probably place a sufficient number of his bombs on the chosen targets to cause hideous damage" – a condition facing both sides, leading to a world in which "two atomic colossi are doomed malevolently to eye each other indefinitely across a trembling world."[25] On the other hand, as Dulles argued in 1957, "history suggests that a conflict as basic as that dividing the world of freedom and the world of international communism ultimately erupts in war."[26]

The challenge of US foreign policy was thus to deal rationally with the Soviet state – to engage it in negotiations to find ways of stabilizing the relationship so that global war would not occur – while simultaneously conducting a struggle against an implacably hostile ideological foe, communism. The rhetorical solution was thus to separate the two, treating the Soviet Union as a competitor state which *could* be negotiated with (something that Roosevelt, for example, never considered in dealing with Nazi Germany), while conducting an ongoing struggle against that part of the enemy, given amorphous form, that represents the real crux of the conflict, with which no accommodation is possible. Things that were associated with "international communism" could thus be dealt with by the standard means of fighting an enemy, namely warfare and violence – provided that doing so did not jeopardize the ongoing state-to-state relationship with the Soviet Union. This was of course a difficult balancing act, since the Soviet state was in fact behind or affiliated with many elements of International Communist activity. But the creation of a twofold enemy – one part rational state, one part malevolent force – enabled US foreign policy to simultaneously engage in "shadow wars" and low-level violence (in Iran, in Central America, and in Indochina) while maintaining an ongoing dialogue (however hostile it might be) with the Soviet government.

Cold War solidified: Kennedy, Johnson, and the institutionalization of the Cold War

Although the linked administrations of John F. Kennedy and Lyndon Johnson are remembered for their Cold War foreign policy events – the Bay of Pigs, the Cuban Missile Crisis, the Vietnam War – both presidents much preferred in their major addresses to discuss domestic politics. The rhetoric of both toward the Soviet Union, and communism in general echoed much of what was said during the Eisenhower administration, but there was movement in their portrayals of the enemy from 1961 to 1969, signaling an institutionalization of the Cold War in both words and deeds.

Unlike both Eisenhower and Truman before him, Kennedy's inaugural address of January 20, 1961, contained no references at all to communism, the Soviet Union, or indeed to foreign enemies of any kind. Remembered for its ringing calls to "pay any price, bear any burden, meet any hardship," even the vague references in the speech to foreign policy spoke entirely of cooperation, not of conflict – in keeping with the optimistic tenor of the speech as a whole.[27] In his 1961 State of the Union address to Congress, Kennedy continued in this general vein, spending most of his time on issues of the domestic economy. When he did turn to foreign policy, Kennedy identified three sources of threat: Chinese Communists, who "menace the security of the entire area [Asia]"; "Communist agents seeking to exploit [Latin America's] peaceful revolution of hope"; and the Soviet Union which, along with China, continued to harbor "ambitions of world domination."[28] To this point in the Cold War, this was fairly typical rhetoric, identifying the main motives of the enemy with a desire to take over the world and impose its system on others. In keeping with Eisenhower's portrayals, Kennedy separated out the Soviet Union from communism in general as a potential partner for state-to-state cooperation, particularly in scientific endeavors. In so doing, he continued the tradition of maintaining a somewhat complex view of the Soviet Union as a state, while identifying with communism the aggression and tyranny that characterize the motives of the classic enemy.

Kennedy maintained this pattern in both his 1962 and 1963 State of the Union addresses. In both, the first half of the speech dealt with domestic affairs. In his 1962 address, Kennedy characterized the realm of foreign affairs as "a global civil war," involving a "basic clash of ideas and wills" – in many ways typically Enemy-stereotyped language. But he was remarkably vague about who the enemy in this civil war was, mentioning communists only once and the Soviet Union not at all in that context. The only specific mention of the USSR in his 1962 speech was connected to the negotiations over Berlin, in which he said, "I believe ... a resolution can be found, and with it an improvement in our relations with the Soviet Union." All Enemy-stereotypic references – to "tactics of terror," "attempted subjugation," "occupation," and the enemy's "grand design" – were reserved for the more generalized enemy, the communists (wherever they may be found).[29] In a similar vein, Kennedy's 1963 State of the Union address contains only four references of any kind to the USSR, two of which were of the emerging Sino-Soviet split. In contrast there were a dozen references to communism in general, mostly negative regarding its motives ("aggression," "coercion," "social chaos"), or dismissive as to its capabilities, in keeping with the classic "paper tiger" image of the Enemy stereotype. Thus, Kennedy argued that "communism sought to convey the image of a unified, confident, and expanding empire.... But few people would hold to that picture today."[30] In his State of the Union addresses, Kennedy kept very much to the formula that the Soviet Union is an adversary that can be negotiated with, while the real enemy is communism writ large.

In Kennedy's two most famous foreign policy addresses, he continued this same pattern. On October 22, 1962, President Kennedy addressed the nation in the midst of the Cuban Missile Crisis, perhaps the defining moment of his presidency. In that address, as the United States was facing its most serious challenge from the Soviet state of the Cold War, Kennedy's rhetoric was remarkably measured. He did talk about "deliberate deception and offensive threats" and of the "Soviet threat to world peace." But he also described a Soviet Union that had, up to that point, "deployed strategic nuclear weapons with great care." And in calling for an end to the crisis, Kennedy wished to move forward, not to a world in which the Soviet Union would be eliminated, but one characterized by "a search for peaceful and permanent solutions."[31] Even at this most tense of moments, Kennedy did not resort to the sort of strident Enemy imagery that Roosevelt employed against Nazi Germany, the kind of rhetoric that leads inevitably to the conclusion that the enemy can never be bargained with and must be destroyed. Rather, Kennedy's portrayal of the USSR always left room for rationality, reasoned dialogue, and the potential for negotiated solutions – policy options not usually associated with extremely strong enemy imagery.

The other side of the coin was evident in Kennedy's famous "Ich bin ein Berliner" speech, delivered in West Berlin on June 26, 1963. In ringing tones, he decried the failures of communism in general – the "offense against humanity, separating families, dividing husbands and wives and brothers and sisters" – and pointed out that "we have never had to put a wall up to keep our people in." But never once in the speech did he mention the USSR, or any state in particular. The enemy – the "evil system," in his words – was not a state at all, but an ideology.[32] By this point in the Cold War, this argument had become essentially routine, having characterized US foreign policy rhetoric for a decade.

With the ascension to the presidency of Lyndon Johnson, this routine took on an increasingly institutionalized and detailed form. Johnson's inaugural speech on January 20, 1965 (after his election in 1964) contained not a single reference to foreign enemies, even vague ones. His 1965 State of the Union address, however, broke with Kennedy's tradition by focusing first on foreign affairs. In this, he continued the now well-established pattern of referring generally to "Communist aggression," while arguing that "[w]ith the Soviet Union we seek peaceful understandings."[33] In his 1967 State of the Union speech, he again referred to the Soviet Union itself in almost exclusively cooperative terms – lauding "a cultural agreement with the Soviet Union," "direct air flights," a "consular convention," and pledging that "[w]hen we have differed with the Soviet Union ... I have tried to differ quietly and with courtesy, and without venom." Johnson even went so far as to argue that "an important link between Russia and the United States is in our common interest, in arms control and disarmament."[34] Here Johnson reached the culmination of over a decade's rhetorical development, having managed to eliminate nearly all Enemy-stereotypical references to the Soviet state.

The more general threat of "Communism," for Johnson, became increasingly tied to the very concrete conflict in Vietnam. In his 1967 State of the Union address, he continued to describe communism in classic enemy terms: "threatens the peace," "aggression," "adversary who is committed to the use of force and terror to settle political questions." But all of these arguments, which for previous presidents had had a broad global quality, were made in the specific context of the Vietnam conflict. Here was an enemy bent, not on world domination, but on "taking over South Vietnam" and on "external Communist conquest in many Asian nations."[35] By his 1968 State of the Union speech, all enemy-style references were tied to very specific events in Vietnam: the "enemy continues to pour men and material across frontiers and into battle," "[a]ggression will never prevail."[36] Two months later, as Johnson gave his "renunciation speech" on March 31 announcing his withdrawal from the presidential race to focus on the Vietnam conflict, his description of the conflict had become entirely bogged down in details of expenditures and forces levels and "maximum combat effectiveness." Mired in what had become by that point the longest and costliest war in America's history, Johnson's description of the enemy contained no substantive references to communism or the ideological clash between East and West, no adversarial references to the USSR, and only a basic description of the enemy's (North Vietnam's) motives: "taking over the South by force."[37] The great ideological threat so stridently described by Truman and Eisenhower had become just another regional war between minor states on the periphery of the world, in which the United States had a reflexive interest from over a decade of identifying communism, whenever and wherever found, as the enemy.

Conclusions: rhetoric of the enemy and the experience of war

The journey from Truman to Johnson followed the path from the origins of the Cold War to its stabilization and institutionalization on the eve of Nixon and Kissinger's détente. From the beginning, the conflict was always an ideological one, and the enemy always characterized in ideological tones. In a sense, this is not at all surprising, for Americans believe that they are united precisely by their ideology (the ringing Enlightenment ideals of the Revolution) and nothing else. For American leaders to describe racial or religious enemies (typical of other corners of the world) would have been to violate the basic self-understandings of most Americans.

But this tendency to equate enemies *only* with ideologies, largely divorced from specific state actors, carried with it very real consequences for the American experience of war. It is one thing to have an ideological conflict with a specific state, as the United States did with Nazi Germany in World War II. There, the calculus of relations with the enemy is clear: so long as the opposing government holds to an ideology that is diametrically opposed to one's own, no peace is possible until that government changes. This basic logic – that state-to-state compromise, the stuff of diplomatic politics, was impossible – undergirded Roosevelt's call not just for victory, but for unconditional surrender on the part of the Axis powers.

Is it possible that, but for the development of nuclear weapons, the United States might have adopted a similar posture towards the Soviet Union in the wake of World War II? The rapid onset of mutually assured destruction, however, made "total victory" irrelevant and peaceful coexistence a necessary evil. Thus, even during the initial height of the Cold War in the 1950s, Eisenhower was careful to separate the Soviet Union as a state from the communist enemy in general, lest the "us or them" logic of extreme Enemy images lead to destruction.

But the separation of enemy image rhetoric, and its placement onto the more general and stateless form of "communism," meant that the United States had a new logic for getting involved in new sorts of wars. Because an ideological enemy, separate from any particular state, can be anywhere, you must be prepared to fight it everywhere. This broadened the nature of threats that must be addressed, and made the ideological scorecard – the tally of which states were in the "free world" or the "communist world" – the sole metric by which success or failure was measured.

A conflict with a particular state enemy – Nazi Germany or the USSR – has a particular form, particular boundaries, and a particular end. A conflict with a stateless ideology, on the other hand, has no boundaries, and is not confined to the well-worn pathways of state interest that had defined wars and diplomatic relations for centuries. Given the rhetoric employed by successive US presidents, it is little surprise that the United States found itself, from 1945 to 1969, involved in an increasingly wide set of conflicts, in places increasingly distant from any obvious strategic interests, and in increasingly more direct and costly ways. In this sense, the Vietnam War and the 1954 overthrow of the Guatemalan government, or the 1962 Bay of Pigs invasion, or even the 1953 toppling of the government of Iran, are not isolated incidents, but very much of a piece. These various adventures in far-flung wars, now widely regarded with distaste if not outright rejection, were justified by divorcing America's rhetoric regarding the enemy from the concrete sovereign state units of the international system.

Although the Cold War has ended and communism now largely forgotten in American foreign policy calculations, the rhetorical experience of the early Cold War period holds lessons for the United States in the twenty-first century. Since September 11, 2001, American rhetoric regarding its enemies abroad has again been substantially disconnected from specific states and toward broad, amorphous, ideological villains. With the exception of a couple of months toward the end of 2001, when the government of Afghanistan was squarely targeted for having supported the 9/11 attackers, the "War on Terror" has largely not identified any particular states as enemies, or even as adversaries. Instead, the rhetorical enemy – "the terrorists" – is spoken of much as "the communists" were in the 1950s and 1960s. American leaders argue that the United States faces a broad enemy united by an aggressive ideology inherently inimical to the Western values of freedom and democracy. With this enemy, it is said, there can be no compromise – just as democracy could not compromise with the tyranny of communism.

In this rhetorical environment, then, we should expect the American experience of war to again echo the Cold War. If the enemy is ideological and everywhere, it must be fought anywhere and everywhere it is found. We should expect, if this past pattern holds, that so long as America defines its enemies in these terms, it will involve itself in far-flung wars – not only in Iraq (where, it could be argued, the United States has more naked strategic interests than it did in Vietnam), but anywhere where "terrorism" (specifically, radicalized Islamic terrorism) occurs. By the present map, this potentially includes much of Africa, the Middle East, Central and Southeast Asia, plus areas like Europe with large immigrant Muslim populations. While we cannot predict the outcome of this struggle, any more than we could predict the end of the Cold War in the 1950s, it is clear that so long as American rhetoric stays its present course, the United States – a nation which believes firmly in its own inherent peacefulness –

will be involved in wars around the world. Given our historical understanding of the Cold War experience, in which many of those peripheral conflicts are now viewed with regret, this is not at all a pleasant prospect. It will continue to fuel the argument that, despite the insistence of many Americans, the United States is a country steeped in the experience of war. And it means that the constant American rhetorical longing, to be at peace in the world, will be put off for yet another generation or more.

Notes

1 Fritz Heider, *Psychology of Interpersonal Relations* (New York: Wiley & Sons, 1958). A similar dynamic can be seen in the Fundamental Attribution Error, in which we judge ourselves and our own motives differently from those of others; see Susan Fiske and Shelley Taylor, *Social Cognition*, 2nd edn (New York: McGraw-Hill, 1991), 67–72.
2 Brett Silverstein, "Enemy Images: The Psychology of U.S. Attitudes and Cognition Regarding the Soviet Union," *American Psychologist* 44 (1989): 903–913.
3 Richard W. Cottam, *Foreign Policy Motivation: a General Theory and a Case Study* (Pittsburgh: University of Pittsburgh Press, 1977); Richard Herrmann, *Perceptions and Behavior in Soviet Foreign Policy* (Pittsburgh: University of Pittsburgh Press, 1985); ibid., "The Empirical Challenge of the Cognitive Revolution," *International Studies Quarterly* 32 (1988): 175–203. See also Richard Herrmann and Michael Fischerkeller, "Beyond the Enemy Image and Spiral Model: Cognitive-Strategic Research After the Cold War," *International Organization* 39, 3 (1995): 415–450.
4 Herrmann and Michael Fischerkeller, "Beyond the Enemy Image."
5 Ibid., 428.
6 Kenneth Waltz, *Theory of International Politics* (Reading: Addison-Wesley, 1979); Hans Morgenthau, *Politics Among Nations*, 6th edn (New York: Alfred A. *Knopf,* 1985).
7 According to Cottam, *Foreign Policy Motivation,* and Herrmann and Fischerkeller, "Beyond the Enemy Image," the Ally image is a derivative of the Enemy image. Just as Enemies are seen in stark, stereotypical, universally negative terms, Allies are perceived in universally positive terms (providing affective balance by grouping positive attributes together and ignoring negative ones) only in the presence of an enemy. That is, when there are no extant threats, one can afford to be a bit critical even of one's friends and perceive their flaws; but under conditions of threat by an external enemy, decision-makers will tend to ignore the flaws of their allies and cast them in mostly or entirely positive terms, giving rise to Winston Churchill's famous declaration that "If Hitler invaded Hell I would make at least a favourable reference to the Devil in the House of Commons."
8 Franklin D. Roosevelt, "The Great Arsenal of Democracy" speech, December 29, 1940, American Rhetoric. Online, available at: www.americanrhetoric.com. See also Herrmann and Fischerkeller, "Beyond the Enemy Image," 428.
9 Roosevelt, "The Great Arsenal of Democracy" speech, December 29, 1940.
10 Franklin D. Roosevelt, State of the Union Address, January 6, 1945, From Revolution to Reconstruction. Online, available at: odur.let.rug.nl/~usa/P/fr32/speeches/su45fdr.htm. See also Herrmann and Fischerkeller, "Beyond the Enemy Image," 428.
11 Roosevelt, State of the Union Address, January 6, 1945. See also Herrmann and Fischerkeller, "Beyond the Enemy Image," 428.

12 Harry S. Truman, State of the Union Address, January 21, 1946, From Revolution to Reconstruction. Online, available at: odur.let.rug.nl/~usa/P/ht33/speeches/su46hst.htm.

13 George C. Marshall, "The Marshall Plan," Address at Harvard University, June 5, 1947, American Rhetoric. Online, available at: www.americanrhetoric.com.

14 Harry S. Truman, "Truman Doctrine," Address to Joint Session of Congress, March 12, 1947, American Rhetoric. Online, available at: www.americanrhetoric.com.

15 Harry S. Truman, Inaugural Address, January 20, 1949, American Rhetoric. Online, available at: www.americanrhetoric.com.

16 Dwight D. Eisenhower, Inaugural Address, January 20, 1953, American Rhetoric. Online, available at: www.americanrhetoric.com.

17 Dwight D. Eisenhower, Inaugural Address, January 21, 1957, Avalon Project, Yale Law School. Online, available at: www.yale.edu/lawweb/avalon/presiden/inaug/eisen2.htm.

18 John Foster Dulles, "Dynamic Peace," Address to the Associated Press, April 22, 1957, Modern History Sourcebook. Online, available at: www.fordham.edu/halsall/mod/1957Dulles-peace1.html.

19 Dwight D. Eisenhower, "Farewell Address," January 17, 1961, American Rhetoric. Online, available at: www.americanrhetoric.com. Interestingly, although Eisenhower's Farewell Address contains some of his typical rhetoric against communism, he spends most of the speech warning about *domestic* dangers to the United States – the military-industrial complex, the danger of a "scientific-technological elite" gaining too much policy influence, and the threat of mounting debt. He closes with a wish, not for the destruction of the Soviet Union or even an end to communism, but simply a peaceful and disarmed world. In the end, it appears that Eisenhower could see beyond even the universal moral struggle with communism to issues he considered higher and more important.

20 Dwight D. Eisenhower, "Atoms for Peace," Address to United Nations General Assembly, December 8, 1953, American Rhetoric. Online, available at: www.americanrhetoric.com.

21 Cottam, *Foreign Policy Motivation*; Herrmann and Fischerkeller, "Beyond the Enemy Image."

22 Dulles, "Dynamic Peace," Address, April 22, 1957.

23 Cottam, *Foreign Policy Motivation*; Herrmann and Fischerkeller, "Beyond the Enemy Image."

24 Dulles, "Dynamic Peace," Address, April 22, 1957.

25 Eisenhower, "Atoms for Peace," Address, December 8, 1953.

26 Dulles, "Dynamic Peace," Address, April 22, 1957.

27 John F. Kennedy, Inaugural Address, January 20, 1961, American Rhetoric. Online, available at: www.americanrhetoric.com.

28 John F. Kennedy, State of the Union Address, January 30, 1961, From Revolution to Reconstruction. Online, available at: odur.let.rug.nl/~usa/P/jk35/speeches/jfk61.htm.

29 John F. Kennedy, State of the Union Address, January 11, 1962, From Revolution to Reconstruction. Online, available at: odur.let.rug.nl/~usa/P/jk35/speeches/jfk62.htm.

30 John F. Kennedy, State of the Union Address, January 14, 1963, From Revolution to Reconstruction. Online, available at: odur.let.rug.nl/~usa/P/jk35/speeches/jfk63.htm.

31 John F. Kennedy, Cuban Missile Crisis Address to the Nation, October 22, 1962, American Rhetoric. Online, available at: www.americanrhetoric.com.

32 John F. Kennedy, "Ich bin ein Berliner," June 26, 1963, American Rhetoric. Online, available at: www.americanrhetoric.com.
33 See Lyndon B. Johnson, Inaugural Address, January 20, 1965, Avalon Project, Yale Law School. Online, available at: www.yale.edu/lawweb/avalon/presiden/inaug/johnson.htm, and ibid., State of the Union Address, January 4, 1965, From Revolution to Reconstruction. Online, available at: odur.let.rug.nl/~usa/P/lj36/speeches/su65lbj.htm.
34 Lyndon B. Johnson, State of the Union Address, January 10, 1967, From Revolution to Reconstruction. Online, available at: odur.let.rug.nl/~usa/P/lj36/speeches/su67lbj.htm.
35 Lyndon B. Johnson, State of the Union Address, January 10, 1967, From Revolution to Reconstruction. Online, available at: odur.let.rug.nl/~usa/P/lj36/speeches/su67lbj.htm.
36 Lyndon B. Johnson, State of the Union Address, January 17, 1968, From Revolution to Reconstruction. Online, available at: odur.let.rug.nl/~usa/P/lj36/speeches/su68lbj.htm.
37 Lyndon B. Johnson, "Renunciation Speech" On Vietnam and Not Seeking Reelection, March 31, 1968, American Rhetoric. Online, available at: www.americanrhetoric.com.

6 From Vietnam to Iraq

The first television war and its legacies

Chester Pach

Editor's introduction

> Both Lyndon B. Johnson and Richard M. Nixon concluded that TV news distorted Americans' views of the Vietnam War in ways that eroded popular support for the war. The author illustrates how Johnson and Nixon reached these conclusions and examines the ways that officials in the Reagan and Bush administrations drew on the experience of Vietnam as they devised new ways of managing news coverage of the operations in Panama (1989) and in the Persian Gulf War (1991). In his conclusion, the author draws comparisons between the coverage of the conflict in Vietnam and the current war in Iraq.

As he closed the *CBS Evening News* on March 28, 2003, a little more than a week after the beginning of the Iraq War, Dan Rather observed that "no people in history have ever seen a war the way we are seeing this one: real-time coverage, up close on the battlefield, live on television, twenty-four hours a day." This new kind of living-room war had affected US public attitudes almost immediately, Rather believed. Even though polls showed that a strong majority supported President George W. Bush's decision to begin military action, "gone are hopes it will be over in a matter or days or even weeks." Instead, most people expected that the war would last "many months." Rather concluded that "reality, much of it harsh, is setting in about this ultimate in reality television." Television news, he believed, had helped disabuse the American people of unrealistic expectations and enabled them realize that victory, even in a war that he thought was so far going well, would not be quick or easy.[1]

Secretary of Defense Donald Rumsfeld also thought that the television reporting was remarkable, but he reached a different conclusion about whether it helped the public understand the war. "We're probably watching something that is somewhat historic," the secretary declared at one of the briefings for reporters that soon made him into a (short-lived) media celebrity. "We have 24-hours a day coverage," from hundreds of journalists who were embedded in US military units. Yet the extensive and detailed reporting provided only a limited view of the war. "What we are seeing is not the war in Iraq," Rumsfeld maintained, but "slices" of it. Each TV story offered "a particularized perspective that that reporter, or that commentator or that television camera happens to be able to see at that moment." Round-the-clock coverage and hundreds of stories could not capture what the war was really like or explain how well it was going. Television, in Rumsfeld's view, provided many glimpses of the war without revealing the big picture.[2]

In the differing assessments of Rather and Rumsfeld were echoes of similar discussions that had occurred more than three decades earlier during the Vietnam War.

Although there was no real-time reporting or round-the-clock coverage from the battlefields of Southeast Asia on the three broadcast networks, Americans had not previously seen war on television the way they saw the fighting in Vietnam. There had been TV cameras and reporters in Korea during the early 1950s, but Vietnam was the first US war that got extensive daily coverage on network newscasts. It was also the first war during which a majority of Americans said that they relied on television as their principal source of news and the first – at least, in the twentieth century – in which US military authorities did not impose censorship.[3]

Rather, who was a CBS correspondent in Vietnam during 1965–1966, was one of many journalists who tried to understand the effects of the unprecedented TV coverage. He wrote in 1967 that television journalists had made extraordinary efforts "to inform the American people in a meaningful way of the complexities of the Vietnam Story." Rather conceded that errors occurred because of deadline pressure, and simplifications arose because of heavy reliance on film to explain complicated issues. But still he thought that television news had gotten stories from Vietnam "fast" and "right." Frank Reynolds, an ABC anchor and correspondent who also covered Vietnam, believed that TV reporting made Vietnam different than previous American conflicts. "Because this is the first war to be covered by television, it is really, in one sense, the first war to be brought home to the American people," Reynolds declared on the *ABC Evening News* in May 1967. Reynolds thought that TV's coverage – or, at least, ABC's reporting – had not sensationalized the war or shocked viewers but instead helped them to understand the experience of Americans in combat.[4]

Yet, like Rumsfeld more than three decades later, Lyndon Johnson and Richard Nixon reached very different conclusions than Rather or Reynolds about television's war. Johnson frequently complained that television journalists were out to "get" him and discredit his Vietnam policies. He also thought that the "vivid scenes" that TV news "brought into the American home" from Vietnam produced emotional reactions rather than measured understanding. He even suggested on the day after his stunning announcement that he would not run again for president that television news coverage was mainly responsible for the sharp drop in popular support for his Vietnam policies during the Tet Offensive of 1968.[5] Nixon made even more extreme allegations. He insisted that network reporters, editors, and executives deliberately slanted the news against him and his Vietnam policies. He tried to shift discontent over the war from the White House to the networks, as he mobilized a "silent majority" to help him overcome antiwar critics and hostile news media in his quest for "peace with honor" in Vietnam. During Johnson's and Nixon's presidencies, the first television war became, in part, a war about television and the ways that TV news coverage affected US involvement in Vietnam and public support for it.[6] The conflicts over television coverage of the Vietnam War had legacies that endured long after the last US helicopter left Saigon.

Progress or stalemate?

CBS reporter Bert Quint thought that he had spent a day in the Mekong Delta in South Vietnam with a US infantry unit taking "a walk in the sun," a term that correspondents used for a combat mission when "nothing happens." The troops made no contact with the enemy on that day in early August 1967, so Quint had no film of any action and no story. But he resolved that after "sweating my balls off here for ten hours, ... I'm not going to come up with nothing. Let's see, what kind of story can I tell over the pictures we are getting?" Quint had only been in Vietnam for a little more than a month, surely not very long, "but long enough," he recalled, "to give me this feeling" that US strategy was "leading to nothing."[7]

That idea produced an unusual – and important – story that aired on the *CBS Evening News* on August 8, 1967. Instead of a snapshot of a small part of the war, his report provided the "big picture," something that Quint rarely tried to do. His theme was that the war was a stalemate. The lack of any action or what TV journalists called "bang, bang" in the film – a deficiency that often doomed a combat report – became an asset, since it revealed the frustration of US troops and the ineffectiveness of their strategy. As the film showed soldiers slogging through swamps and jungles, Quint explained,

> It's a painful, foot-by-foot, paddy-by-paddy, stream-by-stream pursuit of an enemy that rarely stands and fights, that prefers to hit and then run, make for sanctuary in Cambodia when the going gets too tough, regroup, infiltrate back into Vietnam, and then hit again.

The "statements by American officials that there is no stalemate, that real progress is being made, ring hollow down here," he concluded.[8] Although US combat forces had been fighting in Vietnam for more than two years and there were more than 450,000 American troops stationed in Southeast Asia in August 1967, Quint insisted that the US strategy was not working.

Quint's report aired just a day after a junior White House aide had begun monitoring the network newscasts, something the Johnson administration had not previously done in any organized or sustained fashion. The aide was Peter Benchley, who seven years later became the best-selling author of *Jaws*. Benchley wrote a critical report about Quint's story as well as some other "anti-administration material" that he saw on the CBS evening newscast that Walter Cronkite then anchored. He described the stories as examples of "lazy" journalism. But the president had a different explanation after reading Benchley's report. He told his young aide, "If there's one man who is more against me on Viet Nam than Bill Fulbright, it's Walter Cronkite. . . . He's out to get me."[9]

Johnson had expressed similar reactions to stories that criticized the US war effort from the time that he committed large numbers of combat troops to Vietnam in 1965. He was angry, for example, over a sensational report by Morley Safer on the *CBS Evening News* in August 1965 that showed a US marine using a cigarette lighter to burn a thatched hut during a search and destroy mission in the village of Cam Ne. Johnson insisted that Safer's report showed that CBS was "out to get us." The president thought that Safer had "Communist ties," but investigations instead showed conclusively that he was a Canadian.[10] Four months later, the president complained that "on NBC today it was all about what we are doing wrong." He also declared that "Viet Cong atrocities never get publicized," even though that evening both ABC and CBS reported about an enemy terrorist who threw a hand grenade into a US troop truck in Saigon. By early 1967, Johnson accounted for critical stories by charging that the networks were "infiltrated" and announcing that he was "ready to move on them if they move on us." He even alleged that CBS and NBC were "controlled by the Vietcong" at a dinner in March 1967 that correspondents from both networks attended. Such outbursts showed that Johnson expected the news media to support the US war effort, perhaps even to the point of serving as the "handmaiden" of administration policy.[11]

Television coverage of the war during 1965–1967 was more balanced than the president believed. TV journalists at times expressed support for the US war effort. Some reported about "our" troops or planes engaged in combat against the "Reds." Others, like Walter Cronkite, the anchor of the *CBS Evening News*, visited Vietnam in July–August 1965, flew on a combat mission aboard a B-57 aircraft, and assured viewers that "we're using [these planes] very effectively . . . to dive bomb the Vietcong." In a prime-time special, ABC commentator Howard K. Smith analyzed the Johnson administration's policies in Vietnam and declared, "It is entirely good what we're doing." Only on rare occasions in 1965–1966 did network TV journalists question Johnson's decision to commit US combat forces or the basic reasons for US intervention. One of those unusual instances occurred when NBC correspondent Frank McGee closed a documentary in December 1965 by suggesting that if the president and his aides could not make "a compelling argument" that overcame the widespread public doubts "about the legality and morality of our actions," then they ought to consider withdrawal from South Vietnam.[12]

McGee was the exception. Most journalists did not question the Johnson administration's contention that the United States was fighting to stop the expansion of communism and to protect the right of the South Vietnamese to choose their own form of government. Most stories on the evening newscasts concentrated on US troops in combat. Many emphasized the advantages that General William C. Westmoreland, the commander of US forces, thought would eventually lead to success in Vietnam: sophisticated military technology, heavy firepower, and the courage, commitment, and skill of Americans in uniform.[13]

Yet television reports also showed the complications and hardships of subduing an elusive enemy and winning the hearts of minds of civilians. As early as October 1965, ABC's Lou Cioffi pointed to a major problem, when he stated that "the United States has brought in a fantastic amount of military power here in Vietnam. But so far we've not been able to figure just exactly how to use it effectively in order to destroy the Vietcong."[14] There were stories about the persistent problems with pacification programs and the many ways that heavy firepower was disrupting – and destroying – the lives of Vietnamese civilians. At least indirectly, some of these stories – especially those by CBS's John Laurence – raised questions about whether US military intervention actually benefited Vietnamese peasants. Some reporters, like Dan Rather, concluded after a few months in Vietnam that official assessments of the war effort failed to "match what [was] happening on the ground." His stories, like those of some other correspondents, showed that success in Vietnam would be difficult and costly.[15] ABC's Malcolm Browne even made the startling prediction in late 1965 that victory might require twenty-five years of waging war.[16]

Johnson worried about even occasional critical stories because of the power and influence of television. He thought that dramatic images in film reports and the inevitable simplification in thirty-minute newscasts could profoundly influence public support for the war. He also knew that a majority of Americans relied on TV as their principal source of news and considered it the most reliable of the mass media. Despite his concerns, Johnson and his aides rejected censorship of the news from Vietnam because they thought that it would be difficult to enforce and might even produce a hostile backlash. Instead, administration officials in Washington and Saigon tried "to build the necessary understanding" of US involvement in what they called this "new kind of 'twilight' war." They hoped that by meeting with editors and reporters to explain policy, providing confidential information to friendly journalists, and helping correspondents to secure transportation to battlefields and interviews with commanders, they would encourage sympathetic coverage.[17]

The results, however, were disappointing. US reporters in Saigon ridiculed the official daily briefings, calling them the "Five O'Clock Follies" because they consisted of a mix of spin and deception. CBS's Safer, for example, after checking geographic coordinates, found that an official briefer had located a major battle in the South China Sea. The information officer subsequently admitted that the engagement had never occurred and that he had made up the report on a "slow" day for news.[18] In Washington, Johnson's unique mixture of cajolery and intimidation in dealing with reporters often failed to produce the intended effects. Some journalists resented his boasts that he could make their reputations with exclusive interviews or privileged information if they covered his presidency and policies favorably. Others disliked his heavy-handed efforts to pressure them, as when he mentioned his friendship with CBS president Frank Stanton. Still others found odd, weird, or crude his clumsy efforts at intimacy, which included inviting reporters into his bedroom or even his bathroom.[19]

By mid-1967, declining public support for the administration's Vietnam policies intensified LBJ's concern about the reporting of the war. In August 1967, polls showed widespread discontent with the president's handling of the war, as critics outnumbered supporters by a margin of 54 to 32 per cent. High draft calls, mounting casualties, and rising inflation all contributed to public anxiety. Even more important was the failure of military action or diplomatic contacts to create hope for an early end to the war. Johnson knew that the poll numbers endangered his chances of winning a second term as well as the prospects of some congressional Democrats who faced re-election in 1968. He admitted to White House visitors that he was "in deep trouble," yet insisted that "there had never been a major war when there hasn't been major trouble at home."[20]

Johnson believed that frequent reports that the war was a stalemate, a theme of many stories during the summer of 1967, were a major reason for his difficulties. Top administration aides who visited Vietnam reinforced LBJ's suspicions. War correspondents, they said, were skeptical and antagonistic and were "out there to win Pulitzer prizes for sensational articles rather than objective reporting." Bert Quint's story about failed US strategy in a deadlocked war seemed to be the latest manifestation of such sensationalism. Johnson complained that TV journalists ignored the achievements of US forces, who not only fought courageously and effectively but also improved the quality of life in many villages by constructing schools or providing healthcare. Once more, Johnson charged that the networks were out to "get" him. "I can prove that Ho [Chi Minh] is a son-of-a-bitch, if you let me put it on the screen – but they want me to be the son-of-a-bitch," he insisted. Johnson agreed with ABC's Howard K. Smith that "the Administration's greatest weakness was its inability to get over the complete story" on Vietnam. Because of this failure, the American people were "skeptical, cynical, and – more often than not – uninformed."[21]

To deal with this problem, the administration began a new public relations effort to show that the United States was indeed making progress in achieving its war aims. This Progress Campaign reflected the president's conviction that the news reports about stalemate were fundamentally wrong. Yet Johnson and his national security advisors were also determined to accentuate the positive. The White House urged US officials in Saigon to "search urgently for occasions to present sound evidence of progress in Vietnam," and the president instructed his aides "to sell our product" and "to get a better story to the American people." Johnson followed his own advice in a news conference on November 17, during which he wore a lapel microphone that allowed him to move around freely and use his imposing physical attributes and persuasive skills to make what one reporter called a "passionate and articulate" argument that the US war effort was succeeding. Even more notable was a speech that General Westmoreland gave at the National Press Club in Washington, DC, four days later. "We have reached the point when the end begins to come into view," Westmoreland declared, as he predicted that a continuation of recent progress would allow American troops to begin coming home from Vietnam within the next two years. These optimistic statements produced improvement in the polls by the end of 1967.[22]

Those gains quickly evaporated once the Tet Offensive began in late January 1968. South Vietnam suddenly experienced "hard, desperate, Communist attack," in the words of NBC's Brinkley, with fighting in more than 100 places, from remote villages to major cities and even assaults on the US embassy in Saigon and the South Vietnamese presidential palace.[23] Many film reports on the evening newscasts were spectacular and frightening; both NBC and ABC showed the chief of the South Vietnamese police, General Nguyen Ngoc Loan, executing an enemy prisoner after a street battle in a Saigon suburb. On all three networks, there were scenes of journalists wounded while covering the fighting. "What the hell is going on?" asked CBS's Cronkite as he struggled to understand how the North Vietnamese and the National Liberation Front could launch their boldest and biggest offensive of the conflict. "I thought we were winning the war."[24]

Cronkite went to South Vietnam to find out for himself what had happened, and he provided a famous assessment of the Tet Offensive in a special, prime-time program on February 27. "The Vietcong did not win by a knockout," he told viewers in what he called a personal assessment of the war, "but neither did we." "We are mired in stalemate," he concluded, and the best way out was through negotiations "not as victors but as an honorable people who lived up to their pledge to defend democracy and did the best they could."[25]

"If I've lost Cronkite, I've lost the country," Johnson lamented.[26] Cronkite's call for disengagement did affect Johnson, since he thought that the "main front" on the war was "here in the United States" and network reporting about Vietnam had a major effect on public attitudes. But there were many other indications of divisions and dissatisfaction over the war, in Congress, the Democratic Party, and even among the president's advisors. With barely one-quarter of the public expressing confidence in his handling of the war, Johnson went on national television on the evening of March 31 to announce that he was seeking negotiations to end the war and that he would not run for another term as president.[27]

On the eve of his speech withdrawing from the presidential race, Johnson insisted that no president could govern effectively in the face of opposition from the major news media.[28] As his standing in the polls and his credibility plummeted during the Tet Offensive, Johnson thought that a major reason for his difficulties was that Vietnam was the first television war. His real problem, though, was with the war that television showed – how it diverged from the president's optimistic pronouncements, how it failed to produce reliable progress toward victory or a negotiated settlement, how the costs at home and abroad in the opinion of millions of Americans were simply too great.[29]

"Our worst enemy seems to be the press"

As they watched the evening news on April 1, 1971, officials in the Nixon White House could easily have wondered whether someone was playing an April Fools' joke on them. On ABC – the one television network that they considered reasonably balanced and fair in its news coverage – they were seeing something that they hardly could have expected. More than half of the newscast consisted of ABC's four principal Vietnam reporters criticizing the US military and the Nixon administration for obstructing their efforts to cover one of the biggest operations of the war – the South Vietnamese invasion of Laos – and attempting to discredit their stories about the poor performance and the disorderly retreat of some of the South Vietnamese troops. Correspondent Don Farmer bluntly summed up the problems that he and his colleagues encountered when he declared, "We've been lied to so many times that you begin to suspect that no one ever tells you the truth." Former ABC diplomatic correspondent John Scali, who had just joined the White House staff as an assistant on media relations, hardly provided his new colleagues with much comfort when he informed them that network editors had cut out "some of the most damning comments" in order "to keep the presentation balanced and ... to include only the charges that could be backed up."[30]

The ABC report came during one of the most tense periods in White House–news media relations during the Vietnam War. Nixon had long considered the television networks as antagonists. But during the Laos campaign, his thinking had reached the point that he declared, "our worst enemy seems to be the press."[31] Many journalists, on the other hand, thought that the Laos operation raised troubling questions not only about the effectiveness of the US and South Vietnamese war effort but also about the role of the news media in covering war.

Even more than Johnson, Nixon considered the news media hostile to him and his policies. Nixon declared that he had "entered the Presidency with less support from the major publications and TV networks than any President in history."[32] He directed White House aides to monitor the evening newscasts and prepare summaries that would alert him to unfair coverage. The official in charge of compiling the news summaries was Patrick J. Buchanan, someone who even Nixon described as an "advocate" rather than "objective" compiler of information.[33] Presidential assistants also maintained lists of journalists who they designated friendly or hostile. A listing of television reporters in November 1969, for example, designated only three correspondents as "Generally for Us," while categorizing twelve as "Generally Against" the administration.[34]

To counter this alleged media hostility, the Nixon White House made public attacks on the networks. Vice President Spiro T. Agnew stoked public discontent with the networks with inflammatory charges of liberal, anti-Nixon bias. Nixon thought that Agnew's flamboyant attacks along with those of other prominent Republicans had shrewdly shifted credibility problems from the White House to the networks. While administration officials criticized the networks, the president used television as a medium of direct communication with the American people on many issues, including Vietnam. Nixon considered himself a master of electronic communication. He explained to this staff that he used TV to talk "directly to the country" while bypassing as much as possible the reporters, editors, and commentators who "'filter[ed]' his ideas to the public." Increasingly believing that TV was the most important communications medium, Nixon relied heavily on televised speeches to appeal directly to what he called the "silent majority," patriotic citizens who supported his Vietnam policies but who got little, if any, attention from the news media.[35]

However ambitious, shrewd, or ruthless these political initiatives were, in Nixon's view, they had not achieved their most important goal: to create a strong, enduring image of Nixon as leader. At the end of 1970, Nixon wrote to his Chief-of-Staff, H.R. Haldeman, that "we simply are not getting across a strong image on any of the things that really matter – even in the handling of Foreign Policy." He complained, for example, that there was "little recognition of the courage and boldness" of his decision to send US troops into Cambodia in April 1970 and the success of his policy of Vietnamization or transferring combat responsibility for the war to the South Vietnamese armed forces. During his first two years in office, Nixon had admonished his staff to "build a mythology" about him as president, since he believed that it was this "mystique" of the president that most affected voters. At the same time, Nixon thought that in dealing with the news media, his staff had "to start playing much more aggressively and much harder in knocking down false stories and building up our positive points."[36]

Political considerations influenced the Nixon administration's planning of the South Vietnamese invasion of Laos. Code-named Lam Son 719, the operation began in late January 1971. US ground troops could not enter Laos because of a Congressional prohibition, but American air power and artillery played critical supporting roles. Administration officials told Nixon that there might be strong enemy resistance in Laos. The president approved the operation on 18 January, with the warning that whatever the outcome, it could not look like defeat. The official line would be that Lam Son 719 was an attack on North Vietnamese sanctuaries and supply routes in Laos and that all claims of success should be modest until the fighting was over. Nixon instructed Haldeman in early February to attend all critical meetings concerning Laos and to make sure that "PR factors" got considered. The president did not want decisions about war and international affairs to be made only "by the generals and Under Secretaries."[37]

As South Vietnamese and US forces prepared in their bases for operations against Laos, the US military command imposed an embargo on all information concerning Lam Son 719. Reporters could cover the preparations for the attack on Laos, but they could not publish or broadcast any of that information. Anchors on the evening newscasts could not at first even acknowledge that there was an information blackout, since US authorities placed an embargo on the embargo. The embargo lasted a week, but crumbled shortly after its imposition. Even while technically observing the restrictions on reporting, newscasters on all three networks began discussing speculation about a South Vietnamese operation into Laos.[38] To illustrate one of its stories, ABC showed an outline map of Laos with a big question mark next to it. Military authorities in Saigon and Washington said the reasons for official silence were to protect Allied troops and to prevent sensitive information from reaching the enemy. But CBS Pentagon correspondent Bob Schieffer wondered whether there was any good reason for continuing the news blackout when news agencies around the world, including those in the Soviet Union, were reporting details of the impending attack. Secretary of Defense Melvin Laird smiled and replied to Schieffer, "*Izvestia* does not speak the truth."[39]

Neither, perhaps, did US military authorities. General Creighton Abrams, the commander of US forces in South Vietnam, believed that there were legitimate military reasons for the embargo. But William Hammond, the author of the excellent official army history volumes on the military and the media during the Vietnam War, concluded that "Abrams was disposed to do as little as possible to assist newsmen." Recent reports about drug use, poor morale, combat refusals, and violations of rules of engagement, Hammond wrote, had upset Abrams.[40]

Such reports had become increasingly common on the network newscasts, and they illustrated what young officers such as Colin Powell, who finished his second tour of duty in Vietnam in July 1969, had learned from painful experience. As Fred Anderson and Andrew Cayton explain in *The Dominion of War*, Powell believed that "something had gone badly wrong in the war" and that the army was "in deep trouble."[41] Gary Shepard's sensational report on the *CBS Evening News* in late 1970 about drug use in a unit of the 1st Cavalry showed why Powell was so concerned. The soldiers in Shepard's story used drugs to escape a war that had little meaning for them. A squad leader allowed the camera operator to film him and the members of his unit smoking marijuana from the barrel of a shotgun. Other stories provided evidence of deteriorating morale and discipline. In Chu Lai, Steve Bell found several soldiers wearing t-shirts with peace symbols and one who declared, "I don't believe in this war, the way it's being run." A documentary in October 1969 showed troops from Minnesota who explained that unlike Americans during World War II, they "had nothing to fight for." A final scene with GIs sitting in a circle, shirtless and with floppy hats so they could not be identified, made clear that they did not care about what ultimately happened in Vietnam as long as they survived. As one member of the group explained, "I'm gonna go home ... [and] forget the whole dinger."[42] Such reports apparently antagonized Abrams and made him inclined not to cooperate with reporters covering US operations in Southeast Asia.

Once he lifted the embargo on the reporting of the Laos operation, Abrams insisted on new restrictions on journalists. Most notable was his requirement that reporters travel into Laos on helicopters reserved only for them and that were controlled by South Vietnamese military authorities. Citing the dangers of flying into heavy anti-aircraft fire, the South Vietnamese were reluctant to transport reporters across the border. The dangers were real; one helicopter crashed after taking hostile fire and carried four Western journalists to their deaths.[43] Yet the risks of covering Lam Son 719 were hardly unprecedented. What was different was the unwillingness of US military authorities to provide transportation and information as they had in the past.

These restrictions came at a time when skepticism and mistrust of many official sources of information were at a high point among US correspondents in Vietnam. NBC reporter George Lewis, who arrived in Vietnam in August 1970, quickly concluded that the Five O'Clock Follies were "b.s." ABC's Jim Giggans, who about the same time began a tour in Vietnam that lasted more than two years, thought the Follies were "a joke," since briefers were "cooking the books." Steve Bell, who started reporting from Vietnam in March 1970 for ABC, considered the overall lack of censorship and the access to information "remarkable" for a nation at war. Yet he also believed that the controversies over the war had produced a "siege mentality" in the US military that accounted for the obstacles that journalists faced in covering Lam Son 719. Official reminders about the dangers of flying into Laos seemed like thin rationalizations to correspondents who had had close brushes with death in other war zones, especially in Cambodia. Lewis thought that attributing the restrictions on travel to the South Vietnamese was part of an "access game" in which US officials tried "to shut us down." Giggans characterized the welter of excuses mixed with expressions of concern about reporters' safety as "Big Brother."[44]

The inability to get into Laos where most of the heavy fighting was occurring was especially debilitating for TV reporters, who knew that their producers in New York wanted "bang-bang." "Frankly, they wanted to see blood," Giggans asserted. But in the base areas of Khe Sanh or Lang Vei, there was little, save for scenes of casualties arriving on medevac helicopters. TV reporters thus tried to make their own arrangements to get to the action by relying on personal relationships with officers who controlled access to helicopters. Bell, for example, flew in the command helicopter of an officer who had long been a friend, and doing so allowed his camera operator to get the only film of areas along the Ho Chi Minh Trail where South Vietnamese troops swung into action on the first day of the main attack into Laos.[45] Yet these expedients by no means satisfied journalists. The result was that the arrangements for handling the news media produced a backlash and made the credibility of official explanations one of the main stories of the Laos operation.[46]

While many reports on the evening newscasts included caveats about the difficulty of knowing exactly what was happening because reporters could not get to the sites of battle, some pointedly suggested that US authorities were trying to mislead, misinform, or conceal the truth. For example, Harry Reasoner, the ABC co-anchor, used his commentary in early February to declare that the embargo had a "smell" about it, that it seemed designed to keep the public from knowing what was happening. George Lewis made a similar argument at the end of the month, when he reported from the forward base at Ham Nghi about stranded journalists who could not fly into Laos because General Hoang Xuan Lam, the commander of South Vietnamese troops in Laos, had cancelled their helicopter flight. Lewis stated that a majority of the reporters thought that "there has been a deliberate attempt by the military to cover up what's going on" in Laos. The risks of flying into North Vietnamese anti-aircraft fire, he concluded, could be "a convenient excuse" for keeping the correspondents "from seeing things that might embarrass the South Vietnamese army and the Nixon administration's Vietnamization program." Such criticisms became more frequent, as South Vietnamese troops encountered unexpectedly strong counterattacks and began to withdraw their troops from Laos earlier than planned. CBS's long-time Vietnam correspondent, Don Webster, back in New York after covering the first phases of Lam Son 719, stated that "rarely, if ever before, in the Vietnam War has there been such a discrepancy between what Washington and Saigon say is happening and reports we have been gathering from the field." The purposes of the operation – first cutting the Ho Chi Minh Trail, then severing a part of it, then capturing the important North Vietnamese supply bases around the Laotian town of Tchepone – seemed "to shift with almost every press release." On the same newscast, CBS reporter Ed Rabel interviewed a US helicopter pilot, who declared that the statistics about lost US helicopters "were not necessarily false, but they're not exactly true either." Only those downed helicopters that could not be retrieved from crash sites were counted as destroyed. Little wonder that CBS anchor Walter Cronkite introduced Webster's report by declaring that he was "confused."[47]

The main drama in the Laos operation was the collapse of the South Vietnamese military effort. During the last half of March, TV news concentrated on the South Vietnamese army's withdrawal from fire bases inside Laos in the face of heavy enemy attacks. Some reports juxtaposed the Pentagon description of "preplanned mobile maneuvering" with the assessments of US helicopter pilots, who said that the South Vietnamese troops were pulling out because of fierce North Vietnamese counterattacks. TV news crews at bases in the rear areas finally got the dramatic film footage they had long sought when helicopters landed with South Vietnamese soldiers clinging to their skids. Giggans described the evacuating troops as "frantic to leave." NBC's Tom Streithorst called them "panicked." CBS's Bert Quint said "they came out any way they could."[48]

As North Vietnamese attacks turned rear areas into front lines, TV news showed problems in some US units near the Laotian border. NBC's Lewis remembered having dinner with a young West Point graduate, who confided that he kept "having this nightmare. I say to my troops 'follow me, men,' and they all say, 'fuck you, sir.' "[49] The nightmare seemed to be turning into reality, as combat refusals occurred occasionally in units that faced exceptional danger and fatigue. Lewis himself did a story about one member of the 2d squad, 17th Cavalry who would not fly into Laos. The squad commander made clear that this was an isolated occurrence, and Lewis pointed out that the missions into Laos were the "most dangerous flying" that the pilots had ever done because of the concentration of antiaircraft fire. A much larger incident occurred when fifty-three soldiers in two platoons of the Americal Division refused an order to travel down a dangerous stretch of Highway 9 near the Laos border to retrieve a disabled armored personnel carrier. One soldier explained that they were willing to fight and had done so under trying circumstances, but there was "no sense in risking more lives" to save damaged equipment. The men did not face disciplinary action; instead the captain who gave the order was reassigned. Jed Duvall's report of this incident on CBS portrayed the soldiers as neither cowards nor rebels. But on ABC, Howard K. Smith described the replacement of the captain, rather than the disciplining of the soldiers, as "a non sequitur rapidly becoming typical in Vietnam."[50]

Convinced that they were "getting clobbered on Laos," White House officials made determined and elaborate efforts to counteract the gloomy reports on TV and in other news media. They had no illusions, however, that it would be easy to get out "a positive, let alone neutral, evaluation" of Lam Son 719. Indeed, Nixon insisted in discussions with his advisors that the news media wanted the operation "to fail" and were eager to use the problems against the Nixon administration. "The bastards," he exclaimed, were "trying to stick the knife right in our groin."[51] Still, administration officials and Republican members of Congress pressed their interpretations by arguing that a few panicked soldiers were no measure of the achievements of Lam Son 719. They insisted that the disruption of North Vietnamese logistics – something the cameras did not show – would only become apparent in succeeding months.[52]

Yet such hopeful assessments put the best face on an operation that the president and some of his top advisors privately criticized for failing to meet their expectations. At an Oval Office meeting with Nixon and Haldeman, National Security Advisor Henry Kissinger judged Lam Son 719 "as clearly not a success, but still a worthwhile operation." Both Kissinger and Nixon blamed General Abrams for misleading them and persisting in a plan "even though it was clear that it wasn't working." Nixon thought that Abrams was a World War II general that time had passed by. He even talked about relieving Abrams. But since US military operations in South Vietnam were coming to an end, there was no point in doing so.[53]

Despite these private reservations, the Nixon administration renewed its efforts to blame the networks for the bad news from Indochina. Irate over reports on the newscasts that raised doubts about official claims of South Vietnamese progress, Nixon called on his aides "to start a campaign against TV coverage of Laos." Nixon asked Charles Colson and Jeb Stuart Magruder, both noted for their hardball tactics in dealing with the networks, to lead this effort. Magruder compiled regular reports about White House efforts to correct "little lies" – the Nixon administration's term for inaccuracies, omissions, distortions, errors, and unacceptably critical remarks or conclusions that appeared in news stories. Special attention went to dealing with NBC, whose reporting about Laos was repeatedly described as overwhelmingly negative in the news summaries. Alvin Snyder, who worked in the White House Office of Communications, took charge of "counterattacking NBC" by talking to network officials and pointing out their alleged biases or failings. Snyder's protests may well have had some effect, as George Lewis got a telex from editors in New York after his report about journalists' frustrations over getting into Laos that cautioned him not to be "too argumentative." CBS and ABC executives also learned about White House discontent over coverage of the Laos operation in meetings with Nixon and Colson.[54]

More prominent was the administration's public campaign to discredit network news. At the end of February, the president suggested that Agnew "might consider blasting TV for its distorted coverage of Laos." In a speech in Boston on 18 March, he did just that. He insisted "that a widening credibility gap ... exists between the national news media and the

American people." The vice president focused his criticism on CBS, particularly its recent documentary, "The Selling of the Pentagon," and charged that the reliability of the network's news programs was deeply in doubt. While Agnew did not mention the coverage of Laos, Senator Robert Dole of Kansas, the chair of the Republican National Committee, held a news conference the next day and asserted that the vast majority of stories about Laos on CBS and NBC either stated or implied criticism of the South Vietnamese operation. Nixon himself questioned the veracity of network reporting. As he told Haldeman, it was time to "pick an enemy . . . and the networks should be it." In a press conference in early March, Nixon decried a nightly "drum beat" of criticism of Lam Son 719 on the evening newscasts. He returned to this theme in a prime-time interview with Howard K. Smith, noting that all the dire predictions in the news media about the effects of the Cambodian invasion a year earlier simply had not come true. The clear implication was that viewers should dismiss the criticisms about Laos.[55]

In a memo that circulated through the White House in spring 1971, Mort Allin, Buchanan's colleague in preparing the news summaries, explained what he found especially unsettling about TV news. The harnessing of television's "artistic assets" – sophisticated camera work and emotional narration – to news reporting was Allin's principal concern. Instead, he wanted TV news to play it "basically straight: . . . give the facts, let the viewer draw his own conclusions." If the networks would not do so, he recommended a variety of pressure tactics, including more speeches from administration officials "blasting networks," fomenting "insurrection among the affiliates," an ultimatum from Colson to network executives with the reminder that the "FCC and Justice are in our control," and an approach to "the corporate honchos who are our people" who managed the companies that bought advertising time on the evening newscasts. The coverage of the war in early 1971 thus only solidified Nixon's conclusions that the networks were "out to get us," that it was imperative to be "tough" and "ruthless" in dealing with them, and that the most important goal of public relations was to create an image of strong presidential leadership, especially on Vietnam.[56]

The conflicts over reporting about Vietnam issues in early 1971 made some TV journalists suspicious and even fearful. Jim Giggans recollected that the unprecedented and incomprehensible restrictions on journalists led to the long wrap-up report that he and his three ABC colleagues did at the conclusion of Lam Son 719. "Because we couldn't cover Laos, because we couldn't get the story out, that became the story." Journalists, he said, began to wonder, "why wouldn't they let you do your job?" Steve Bell reached less troubling conclusions. Even though "terrible" things happened in military–media relations, these conflicts had "complex" causes, he concluded, when viewed "in total perspective." George Lewis saw a continuing effort, even after Lam Son 719, to restrict access in covering the war. Walter Cronkite worried about far greater dangers. "Many of us see clear indication on the part of this administration," he declared in a speech in May, "of a grand conspiracy to destroy the credibility of the press." Colson ridiculed Cronkite as "paranoid." But John Scali informed Nixon that several "responsible and fair-minded" journalists, such as John Chancellor of NBC and even Howard K. Smith, had reached similar conclusions. For them, "the war on television" had taken on an ominous, double meaning.[57]

Legacies

In *The Dominion of War*, Fred Anderson and Andrew Cayton make the important observation that the "experience of defeat in Vietnam ... profoundly influenced the nation's approach to the rest of the world for more than a generation."[58] The painful lessons of Vietnam, for example, shaped Colin Powell's thinking about strategy and warfare for the remainder of his public career, both as chair of the Joint Chiefs of Staff and as Secretary of State. As Anderson and Cayton emphasize, Powell was determined that there would be no more Vietnams. For Powell, Clausewitz provided the necessary guidance about how to avoid repeating the past. From *On War*, he learned that it was essential that any future war have a clear objective and that strategists devise precise and specific plans for achieving that goal. In addition, "the people must support a war." As the Vietnam War dragged on, Powell wrote, "that essential pillar had crumbled."[59]

The belief that TV coverage undermined popular support of the Vietnam War led to new restrictions on war reporting during the 1980s. So, too, did concern that new technology could compromise military security or jeopardize the lives of US forces in action. Even as early as 1967, Dan Rather imagined that communication satellites had made live coverage of war technically feasible.[60] By the 1980s, what had been conceivable twenty years earlier had become a reality. New Pentagon regulations called for journalists in war zones to refrain from reporting sensitive military information as a condition of their accreditation. Commanders also had the discretion to allow only small groups of journalists into battle zones and to have them share their reporting with their colleagues. This pool system got its first test when US troops invaded Panama in December 1989, and it prevailed during the Persian Gulf War of 1991. Colin Powell played a central role in devising a strategy of overwhelming US force, which he rightly believed would quickly force Iraqi troops to relinquish control of Kuwait. Powell thought that a quick, decisive war had the best chance of retaining the support of the American people. He also worried that televised images of casualties or frightful views of combat could jeopardize public backing of the war effort. Such concerns, a product of his Vietnam experience, made Powell a strong advocate of terminating the ground war quickly. Overall, the administration of George H.W. Bush was pleased with its management of the television coverage of the Gulf War. Secretary of State James A. Baker described "that poor demoralized rabble – outwitted, outflanked, outmaneuvered by the US military. But I think, given time, the press will bounce back."[61]

The first President Bush proclaimed the death of the Vietnam Syndrome in 1991. His declaration might have been premature. Comparisons between Vietnam and the current Iraq War are common. Usually they are misleading or even simplistic.[62] Yet in one way the two wars have a similarity. The system of embedding journalists – attaching more than 600 correspondents to specific military units at the beginning of major combat in March 2003 – seemed like a return to the arrangements that prevailed during the Vietnam War. Actually, very few correspondents who covered Vietnam spent extended periods with a single unit. But embedding did provide reporters with greater freedom to cover combat than in any US conflict since Vietnam. The embedding system, however, produced mixed reviews. Some observers praised the "intimate, immediate, almost addictive coverage." Others complained that they saw only rare glimpses of firefights.[63]

The more important debate, however, is the one that Rather and Rumsfeld joined about the accuracy and the effects of such reporting. It is hard to argue with Rumsfeld's contention that TV reporters – especially those embedded with military units – provided only narrow glimpses of the war. But behind this sound observation was the implication that TV coverage could be misleading and unreliable, that it suffered from "mood swings" and included "breathless" updates that could be "somewhat disorienting." Rumsfeld added "sensationalism" to this catalog of media deficiencies when the Abu Ghraib scandal dominated the news from Iraq.[64] For Rather, the current war reporting, whatever its limitations, provided viewers with information that enabled them to assess official policies and to understand, even in the first days of fighting, that the war would not be as easy as they had expected. This debate is not the same as those that took place during the Progress Campaign or Lam Son 719. But in some ways the discussions about television and warfare during US involvement in Vietnam seemed quite timely and relevant a generation later during the Iraq War.

Notes

1 CBS Evening News, March 28, 2003.
2 Transcript, DoD News Briefing, Secretary Rumsfeld and Gen. Myers, March 21, 2003. Online, available at: www.defenselink.mil/transcripts/2003/t03212003_t0321sd1.html.
3 Report, "Emerging Profiles of Television and Other Mass Media: Public Attitudes, 1959–1967," Roper Research associates, Television folder, Office Files of Fred Panzer, Box 421, Lyndon B. Johnson Library, Austin, Texas [hereafter LBJL].
4 Memo by Rather, n.d. [approx. August 1967]; and questionnaire, Defense Information School, August 1, 1967, both in folder 3, Papers of Dan Rather, Box 11, Howard Gotlieb Archival Research Center, Boston University;

comments by Reynolds, ABC, May 31, 1967, A97 pt. 2, Weekly News Summary, Assistant Secretary of Defense for Public Affairs, Record Group 330, National Archives, College Park, Maryland [hereafter DODNS].

5 *Public Papers of the Presidents of the United States: Lyndon B. Johnson, 1968–69*, 2 vols (Washington, DC: Government Printing Office, 1970), 1: 482–486.

6 Chester J. Pach, Jr., "The War on Television: TV News, the Johnson Administration, and Vietnam," in *A Companion to the Vietnam War*, Marilyn B. Young and Robert Buzzanco (eds) (Malden: Blackwell Publishing, 2002), 463.

7 Author interview with Quint, July 6, 2001, Langley, VA.

8 Ibid.; report by Quint, CBS, August 8, 1967, A107, DODNS.

9 Memorandum, Christian to President, August 14, 1967, folder Chronological August 1967, Aides – George Christian, Box 6, White House Central Files, LBJL; Benchley oral history transcript [hereafter OH], 44, LBJL.

10 Report by Safer, CBS, TV-6412.2, Museum of Broadcast Communications, Chicago, Illinois (hereafter MBC), Barry Zorthian Oral History Interview, II: 8, LBJL; memo, Rather to Reedy, n.d.; and memo, Moyers to president, n.d., both in Folder August 1–15, 1965, Box 9, Handwriting File, LBJL; William M. Hammond, *Public Affairs: The Military and the Media, 1962–1968*. (Washington, DC: Center of Military History, United States Army, 1988), 188–191; Morley Safer, *Flashbacks: On Returning to Vietnam* (New York: Random House, 1990), 88–97; Chester J. Pach, Jr., "And That's the Way It Was: The Vietnam War on the Network Nightly News," in *The Sixties: From Memory to History*, David Farber (ed.) (Chapel Hill: University of North Carolina Press, 1994): 90–118; Pach, "The War on Television," 451–452.

11 Notes of meeting, December 17, 1965, *Foreign Relations of the United States, 1964–1968*, vol. 3: *Vietnam, June–December 1965* (Washington, DC: US Government Printing Office, 1996, 644–645; Robert Dallek, *Flawed Giant: Lyndon Johnson and His Times, 1961–1973* (New York: Oxford University Press, 1998), 286–288, 452–453; comments by Jennings (ABC) and Cronkite (CBS), both December 17, 1965, A20, DODNS, memo, "Dinner at Home of Sen. Henry Jackson," March 10, 1967, Folder 1, Box 4, Rather Papers; Safer, "Television Covers the War," 91; Pach, "The War on Television," 456.

12 Alfred E. Kroeger, "Vietnam: Television's Cruelest Test," *Television* 23 (May 1966): 26; CBS News, *Vietnam*, 5 vols (Beverly Hills: Fox Video, 1994), vol. 3: *Fire From the Sky*; Walter Cronkite, *A Reporter's Life* (New York: Alfred A. Knopf, 1997), 249–252; Howard K. Smith, *Events Leading Up to My Death: The Life of a Twentieth-Century Reporter* (New York: St. Martin's, 1996), 325–329; memo, Cater to president, May 14, 1965, Folder Douglas Cater Memos [1 of 2], Reference File – Vietnam, Box 1, LBJL; "ABC Scope: The Vietnam War," Part 34, "Howard K. Smith, One Man's Opinion," July 16, 1966, TV-1505.1, MBC; and "Vietnam: December 1965," NBC, December 20, 1965.

13 See Pach, "The War on Television," 452–454; Pach, "And That's the Way It Was," 94–100.

14 Report by Cioffi, ABC, October 14, 1965, A10, DODNS.

15 Author interview with Rather, New York City, November 15, 2000.

16 Pach, "The War on Television," 454.

17 Ibid., 452; Chester Pach, "Television," in Alexander DeConde, Richard Dean Burns, and Frederik Logevall (eds), *Encyclopedia of American Foreign Policy*, 3 vols, 2nd edn (New York: Charles Scriber's Sons, 2002), 3: 551.

18 Author interview with Morley Safer, July 23, 2001, Chester, CT.

19 Author interviews with David Brinkley, February 22, 2000, Bal Harbor, FL; John Rich, 23 February 2000, Ft. Pierce, FL; Jack Perkins, February 24, 2000, Sarasota, FL; and Murray Fromson, May 23, 2000, Los Angeles, CA; Pach, "The War on Television," 455.

20 Table, "Public Approval of LBJ's Handling of the War ...," October 5, 1967, Folder October 1967, Office Files of Fred Panzer, Box 398, LBJL; Burns W. Roper, "What Public Opinion Polls Said," in Peter Braestrup, *Big Story: How the American Press and Television Reported and Interpreted the Crisis of Tet 1968 in Vietnam and Washington*, 2 vols. (Boulder: Westview Press, 1977), 1: 700; *The Gallup Poll: Public Opinion, 1935–97* (Wilmington: Scholarly Resources, 2000), CD-ROM edn, 1967: 2074–2075; and notes, president's meeting with educators from Cambridge, MA, September 26, 1967, Tom Johnson's Notes of Meetings [hereafter TJ notes], Box 1, LBJL; Pach, "The War on Television," 457.

21 Dallek, *Flawed Giant*, 452–453; notes, meeting with Australian broadcast group, September 20, 1967, folder "September 1967 – Meetings with Correspondents," Box 3, Meeting Notes File, LBJL; notes of meetings, July 12 and 13, *Foreign Relations of the United States, 1964–1968*, vol. 5: *Vietnam, 1967* (Washington, DC: US Government Printing Office, 2002), 600–609, 611–614; notes, meeting between president and Smith, March 31, 1967, Folder Notes on Meetings – President, 1967, Box 1, Papers of George Christian, LBJL; Pach, "The War on Television," 456–458; memo, Tom Johnson to Christian, August 15, 1967, PR 18, Confidential File, White House Central Files, LBJL.

22 Larry Berman, *Lyndon Johnson's War: the Road to Stalemate in Vietnam* (New York: Oxford University Press, 1989); *Public Papers of the Presidents of the United States: Lyndon B. Johnson, 1967*, 2 vols (Washington, DC: Government Printing Office, 1969), 2: 1058–1059; Kathleen J. Turner, *Lyndon Johnson's Dual War: Vietnam and the Press* (Chicago: University of Chicago Press, 1985), 204–205; remarks by Brinkley, NBC, and by Cronkite, CBS, both November 21, 1967, A122, DODNS; Braestrup, *Big Story*, 1: 695, 700; *The Gallup Poll*, 3: 2074, 2075, 2078, 2089, 2091; Dallek, *Flawed Giant*, 499.

23 Comment by Brinkley, NBC, February 1, 1968, A132, DODNS.

24 Chester J. Pach, Jr., "Tet on TV: US Nightly News Reporting and Presidential Policy Making," in *1968: The World Transformed*, Carole Fink, Philipp Gassert, and Detlef Junker (eds) (New York: Cambridge University Press, 1998): 55–81; Pach, "Television," 3: 551–552.

25 "Who, What, When, Where, Why: Report from Vietnam by Walter Cronkite," CBS, February 27, 1968, A596, Museum of Television and Radio, New York, NY.

26 Author interview with George Christian, August 25, 1999, Austin, Texas.

27 Pach, "Television," 3: 552.

28 David Culbert, "Johnson and the Media," in *Explaining the History of the Johnson Years*, Robert A. Divine (ed.) (Austin: University of Texas Press, 1981), 214–248; Randall Bennett Woods, "LBJ, Politics, and 1968," *South Central Review* 16–17 (1999–2000): 21–22.

29 Pach, "The War on Television," 464.

30 Report by Giggans, Howard Tuckner, Farmer, and Bell, ABC, April 1, 1971, 4256, White House Communications Agency Video Tape Collection (1968–1974) [hereafter RN Tapes], Nixon Presidential Materials, National Archives, College Park, Maryland [hereafter Nixon Papers]; memo, Scali to Colson, April 14, 1971, folder Colson Action Memos [5 of 7], Box 1, John Scali Files, Nixon Papers.

31 William M. Hammond, *Public Affairs: the Military and the Media, 1968–1973* (Washington, DC: Center of Military History, United States Army, 1996), 460.

32 Memo, Nixon to Haldeman, January 6, 1970, folder Memos January 1970, Box 2, White House Special Files [hereafter WHSF]: Staff Member and Office Files [hereafter SMOF], President's Personal File; Nixon Papers; memo, Nixon to Haldeman, March 8, 1971, folder Haldeman Memos from the President, 1971, Box 140, WHSF: SMOF, H. R. Haldeman Files, Nixon Papers.

33 Memo, Nixon to Ehrlichman, February 4, 1969, folder Memos – February 1969,

Box 1, WHSF: SMOF, President's Personal File, Memos from the President (Contested Documents), Nixon Papers. For more information on Buchanan and the news summaries, see memo and attachments, Haldeman to Klein and Ziegler, July 23, 1970, folder H.R. Haldeman II [1 of 5], Box 1, WHSF: SMOF, Hebert G. Klein Files, Nixon Papers; and transcript, "Thirty Minutes With ..." (guest: Patrick J. Buchanan), May 4, 1972, folder Network Coverage Bias [3 of 4], Box 5, WHSF: SMOF, W. Richard Howard Files, Nixon Papers.

34 Memo, Ziegler to Haldeman, November 25, 1969, folder Press and Media #2 [Part 2], Box 141, WHSF: SMOF, H.R. Haldeman Files, Nixon Papers; memo, Klein to Haldeman, March 21, 1970, Folder 1, Box 1, WHSF: SMOF, Patrick J. Buchanan Files (Contested Documents), Nixon Papers; Pach, "Television," 552. See also, memo, Klein to Haldeman, June 3, 1969, folder H.R. Haldeman [1 of 3], Box 1; Klein Files; memo, Allin to Haldeman, n.d., folder Press and Media #2 [Part 1], Box 1, Haldeman Files; and memo, Nixon to Haldeman, November 30, 1970, folder HRH Presidential Memos Project 1970, Box 138, Haldeman Files; memo, Nixon to Haldeman, January 31, 1971, folder Memos from the President – January 1970, Box 2, President's Personal Files.

35 Memo, Nixon to Haldeman, January 6, 1970, folder Memos – January 1970, Box 2, President's Personal Files; memo, Nixon to Haldeman, November 30, 1970, folder HRH Presidential Memos Project 1970, Box 138, Haldeman Files; Melvin Small, *The Presidency of Richard Nixon* (Lawrence: University Press of Kansas, 1999), 59–95; Jeffrey Kimball, *Nixon's Vietnam War* (Lawrence: University Press of Kansas, 1998), 1–15; Pach, "Television," 552.

36 Memo, Nixon to Haldeman, December 18, 1970, folder Memos from the President 1970 [1 of 2], Box 138, Haldeman Files; memo by Haldeman, "General PR Objectives," January 18, 1971; and memo by Haldeman, January 19, 1971, both in folder P.R. [1], Box 141, Haldeman Files; memo, Nixon to Haldeman, folder Haldeman Memos from the President, 1971, Box 141, Haldeman Files; memo, Nixon to Ehrlichman, January 25, 1969, folder 1 of 6, Box 1, President's Personal Files (Contested Documents); H.R. Haldeman, *The Haldeman Diaries: Inside the Nixon White House* (CD-ROM version) (New York: Sony Electronic Publishing, 1994), July 21, 1969 [hereafter *Haldeman Diaries*]; Small, *The Presidency of Richard Nixon*, 230.

37 Hammond, *The Military and the Media, 1968–1973*, 401–407; Kimball, *Nixon's Vietnam War*, 241–245; *Haldeman Diaries*, February 3, 1971.

38 Typical were NBC anchor David Brinkley's comments:

It is apparent tonight there is some major new development in Southeast Asia in the war. But there are no official details at this hour. The speculation is that it's an invasion of Laos by South Vietnam's army with heavy American support, mainly in the air.

(Brinkley, NBC, January 30, 1971, 4153, RN Tapes)

39 ABC graphic, February 2, 1971, ibid.; report by Schieffer, CBS, February 2, 1971, ibid.

40 Hammond, *The Military and the Media, 1968–1973*, 408.

41 Fred Anderson and Andrew Cayton, *The Dominion of War: Empire and Liberty in North America, 1500–2000* (New York: Viking, 2005), 416.

42 Report by Shepard, CBS, November 13, 1979, CBS News, *Vietnam*, 5 vols (Fox Video, 1994), vol. 5: *America Pulls Back*; report by Bell, ABC, July 4, 1971, A311, DODNS; "Grunt's Little War," Minneapolis, MN, 1969, MBC.

43 Hammond, *The Military and the Media, 1968–1973*, 420–422, 430–432.

44 Author interview with Lewis, May 23, 2000, Los Angeles, CA; author interview with Giggans, May 17, 2001, Los Angeles, CA; author interview with Bell, February 9, 2001, Muncie, IN.

45 Interview with Bell; report by Bell, ABC, February 8, 1971, 4174, RN Tapes.
46 Interview with Giggans; interview with Lewis.
47 Commentary by Reasoner, ABC, February 2, 1971, 4153, RN Tapes; report by Lewis, NBC, February 28, 1971, 4209, ibid.; reports by Webster and Rabel and comments by Cronkite, CBS, March 17, 1971, 4226 pt. 2, ibid.
48 Comments by Reasoner, ABC, March 17, 1971, 4226, RN Tapes; comments by Cronkite, CBS, March 17, 1971, 4226 pt. 2, ibid.; report by Quint, CBS, March 20, 1971, 4241, RN Tapes; report by Giggans, ABC, March 22, 1971, ibid.; and report by Streithorst, NBC, March 22, 1971, ibid.
49 Author interview with Lewis.
50 Report by Lewis, NBC, February 17, 1971, 4184 pt. 2, RN Tapes; comment by Smith, ABC, March 22, 1971, 4241, RN Tapes; report by Streithorst, NBC, March 22, 1971, ibid.; report by Duvall, March 23, 1971, A296, DODNS.
51 Conversation 459–452, February 27, 1971, audio tapes, Nixon Papers.
52 Memo, Colson to Haldeman, March 25, 1971, folder Colson 1971 [2 of 2], Box 3, Buchanan Files; memo, Allin to Haldeman, March 22, 1971, folder Magruder 1971, Box 4, Buchanan Files; Hammond, *The Military and the Media, 1968–1973*, 479–486.
53 *Haldeman Diaries*, March 23, 1971.
54 Nixon marginal comments, news summary, February 25, 1971, folder February 1971, Box 32, Annotated News Summaries; memo, Magruder to Haldeman, February 22, 1971; and memo, Magruder to Haldeman, March 22, 1971, both in folder Magruder 1971, Box 4, Buchanan Files; John Anthony Maltese, *Spin Control: the White House Office of Communications and the Management of Presidential News*, 2nd edn (Chapel Hill: University of North Carolina Press, 1994), 82–89; author interview with Lewis.
55 Nixon marginal comments, news summary, February 25, 1971, folder February 1971, Box 32, Annotated News Summaries; transcript, address by the Vice President, March 18, 1971, folder CBS 146, Box 18, WHSF: SMOF, Ronald L. Ziegler Files, Nixon Papers; *Washington Daily News*, March 11, 1971, folder Press File #1 [2 of 6] 104, Box 20, ibid.; report by Schoumacher, CBS, March 19, 1971, 4227 RN Tapes; "The Selling of the Pentagon," CBS, February 23, 1971, 4191, RN Tapes; *Haldeman Diaries*, March 5, 1971; Hammond, *The Military and the Media, 1968–1973* 481.
56 Allin to Colson, April 28, 1971, folder Press and Media #2 [Part 2], Box 141, Haldeman Files; memos (2), Nixon to Haldeman, May 9, 1971, folder Mr. Haldeman, ibid.
57 Author interviews with Giggans, Bell, and Lewis; memo and attachment, Colson to Scali, May 19, 1971, folder Colson Action memos [4 of 7], Box 1, Scali Files; memo, Scali to President, May 11, 1971, folder Media Policy [2 of 2], Box 1, Scali Files (Contested Documents).
58 Anderson and Cayton, *The Dominion of War*, 410.
59 Ibid., 417.
60 Memo by Rather, n.d. [approx. August 1967], folder 3, Papers of Dan Rather, Box 11.
61 Warren P. Strobel, *Late-Breaking Foreign Policy: the News Media's Influence on Peace Operations* (Washington, DC: United States Institute of Peace Press, 1997), 19.
62 Chester Pach, "'The Past Has Another Pattern': Vietnam and Iraq," *Passport: the Newsletter of the Society for Historians of American Foreign Relations* 35 (December 2004): 15–17.
63 Terence Smith, "Defining News in the Middle East," and Paul Friedman, "TV: a Missed Opportunity," both in *Columbia Journalism Review*, May–June 2003. Online, available at: www.cjr.org/issues/2003/3.
64 Smith, "Defining News in the Middle East."

7 Global war and the foundations of US systemic leadership

William R. Thompson

Editor's introduction

> The author analyzes the American ascent to global power and argues that war's effects on development, especially the 1914–1945 era of global war, are absolutely crucial to US history, but not as a monovariate shock or series of shocks alone. Wars, rather, are nested prominently within a complex of other drivers, including technological and organizational change. He concludes that the US ascent story is not as distinct as previous scholars have supposed, but can be explained by systemic perspective and leadership long cycle theory.

The customary approach to accounting for the rise of the United States to global primacy is descriptive, American-centric, and heavily reliant on the distinctiveness of the ascent.[1] Once strictly a producer of raw materials in the world economy, the United States emerged as an increasingly competitive economy in the late nineteenth century and had even managed to overtake the world economy's previous leader, Britain, well before 1945. As such, it is one of history's more remarkable illustrations of the possibilities of dependency reversal. Size, location, and resource endowment are often noted as causal factors in this move upward in status. After 1945, though, there was little doubt that the economy of the United States was the world's most advanced center of high technology and manufacturing production. It also emerged in 1945 as the leading political–military actor and the head of a coalition of the most economically advanced states in the world system. Interwoven in the customary story are World Wars I and II, major wars in the late 1910s and early 1940s (from a US perspective). The US entered World War I late and had less impact than might otherwise have been the case. At war's end, the US is often thought to have retreated from the world stage. It entered the second one late as well, but definitely had more impact and, thanks in large part to the exhaustion of everyone else, emerged in 1945 as king of the planetary hill. In contrast to what happened after World War I, the United States, after World War II, assumed its pre-eminent role in world politics.

This ascent story is well known. Presumably, there are no great mysteries concerning what took place that await revealing. Thus, what follows is not a wholly new story but a familiar one told in a different way, causal rather than descriptive, seeking to explain the ascent in terms of the interaction among specific processes rather than the decade-by-decade course of events. One of the more important processes is global warfare, in the present analysis, for the period 1914–1945. The two world wars that most people designate as occurring in 1914–1918 (or 1917–1918) and 1939–1945 (or 1941–45) were not really separate wars but early and late phases of a period of systemic crisis. War's effects on development are absolutely crucial to US history, but not as a monovariate shock or series of shocks alone. Wars, rather, are nested prominently within a complex of other drivers of change.

This version of the story is avowedly systemic-centric. No abstract and external deus ex machina caused the US ascent to global primacy to occur, nor were some Olympian gods rolling dice to see on whom good fortune might fall. Rather, the ascent happened because certain things fell into place that made global primacy highly probable. "Highly probable" is not a synonym for inevitable. Nothing is inevitable. But given what did transpire, the United States evading global primacy by 1945 would have been a very interesting trick. Human agency was certainly involved. People have to make choices and execute them for things to happen. Moreover, some of the choices that were made proved to be more important than others. But these choices are not the main story. It is the systemic context in which they are made that is most critical. Finally, the "certain things" that came together had done so before. What happened to the United States in the late nineteenth and early twentieth century certainly had distinctive and unique elements, but it was not the first time global primacy had been achieved in this manner. It may not be the last time somebody follows this path to the apex of the system either.

Understanding this particular story requires, as a prerequisite, understanding two main clusters of ideas: the Twin Peaks model and a co-evolutionary argument. The Twin Peaks model refers to an argument developed within leadership long-cycle theory to explain the causal processes most important to systemic leadership and long-term economic growth. The Twin Peaks refer to spurts of economic growth separated by a period of intensive conflict. In the US account, World Wars I and II were preceded by accelerated economic growth in the late nineteenth century and followed by another spurt of growth in the mid-twentieth century. This part of the application should not be considered particularly controversial. More interesting and controversial is the extent to which these developments were dependent on one another. In other words, the first growth spurt did not simply precede two world wars. The first growth spurt led to the outbreak of two world wars, which, in turn, led to a second economic growth spike, along with a host of other phenomena.

Elaborating the Twin Peaks model is one preliminary objective. But, while the Twin Peaks model helps to isolate the factors that are most important in the ascent of the United States, it does not provide a full explanation of the phenomena at hand. A fuller theoretical explanation requires a co-evolutionary model that highlights interdependent changes in political-economy, political organization, military organization, weaponry, and threat environment. The basic dynamic is that major changes in one or more of these areas tend to lead to changes in the other areas. That is, the six spheres tend to co-evolve over time. While it is conceivable that change in any sphere could drive change in any of the other spheres, it appears from other analyses that it is major changes in political-economy that are most likely to stimulate co-evolutionary processes. The story of US ascent gives every appearance of adhering to this principle as well.

The Twin Peaks model

The argument underlying the Twin Peaks model subsumes theories of long-term economic growth and the evolution of world politics. Long-term economic growth is viewed as depending greatly on intermittent spurts of radical technological innovation that fundamentally alter the technological frontier and the way the most advanced economies function. The innovations tend to be monopolized by one pioneering economy at a time. This pioneering lead economy undergoes the transformations associated with a particular package of innovations and related implications for energy sources. It then reaps the material profits of leading the way to new commercial and industrial best practices.

Possession of the world's lead economy implies several collateral developments. The lead economy becomes the system's primary source of investment capital geared to the surpluses generated by the highly profitable innovations. As a matter of self interest, the lead economy also becomes the principal protector of a global economic system geared initially to long-distance trade and increasingly technologically sophisticated industrial output. In turn, this role generates a need for the development of global reach superior to that possessed by all other actors.[2] Given the distribution of land and water on Earth and the lower transaction costs associated with contemporary maritime exchange, global reach capabilities have tended to concentrate on naval power over much of the last millennium. The system's lead economy, therefore, must develop a relative monopoly in blue water naval capabilities to provide the military armature for its system protection activities.

Economic and technological sophistication does not guarantee predominant influence in the global layer of long-distance exchange and industrial production. World politics remains fairly primitive in the sense that political and policy leadership continues to be a prize that must be won by force.[3] Typically, the global political economy experiences periodic crises that take the following form. The prevailing techno-economic paradigm of one era gives way to a new set of innovations and economic procedures.[4] The lead economy associated with the older paradigm is in relative decline. So, too, is its ability to protect the networks of exchange and production developed in the preceding era. Other economies may be generating economic challenges in the form of new innovations and new techno-economic paradigms. The pecking order of the global layer is destabilized. The ability to make policy and rules for the global layer is up for grabs. The crisis, therefore, is whether, when, and in which direction a new political–economic status quo will emerge.

In the past 500 years, these crises have led to global wars – bouts of intensive warfare fought increasingly throughout the planet in which most or all of the most powerful states participate. An added quirk to this process is that, between 1494 and 1945, one region developed political–military centrality thanks in part to its escalatory, intra-regional competition for predominance and the byproduct of advantages in military organization and lethality. On repeated occasions, one state in the region sought (or was perceived to be seeking) regional hegemony. This European state (Spain, France, Germany), for its time, tended to have the largest regional population, a strong agrarian economy, and the largest army. The principal strategic approach to regional hegemony consisted of military conquest and control of adjacent territories.

Intermittent attempts at regional hegemony presented survival problems for weaker states located within the European region. Such efforts also constituted a threat to the global political order. If one state controlled Western Europe, it would also control European ports, maritime resources, and considerable commercial–industrial potential. Territorial expansion in Western Europe also meant absorbing the old lead economy (Venice, Portugal, the Netherlands, Britain) and its resources. A European regional hegemon, as a consequence, would be a potent contender for power at the global, inter-continental layer. Not only was an aspiring regional hegemon a direct threat to the old system leader, it usually constituted a proximate threat to new centers of technological prowess as well. By at least the end of the nineteenth century, the aspiring regional hegemon was also a leading candidate to usurp the central technological innovation position as well. Thus, when they overlap in time, global crises have tended to fuse with European regional crises (for example, by the 1930s, the struggle for Asian regional hegemony also fused with European and global crises). The outcome has been global warfare in 1494–1517, 1580–1609, 1688–1713, 1792–1815, and 1914–1945.

Global wars have seen a fairly simple yet consistent line-up of opposing actors. On one side, there is an aspiring regional hegemon and its allies that choose to, or are forced to, bandwagon. Typically, these allies are not among the strongest actors in their home region. They also may turn out to be more liability than asset. On the other side, are the maritime/global actors that include the old leader and, if applicable, the most likely successor. They are joined by at least one powerful land power that is a principal rival with the aspiring regional hegemon. The maritime/global actors provide naval capability, maritime blockades of resources entering the main war theaters, commercial–industrial supplies to their allies, and coordination of a planetary-wide struggle. Their land allies typically provide the bulk of the armies to oppose the aspiring regional hegemon.

The typical outcome of these intensive global blood-lettings is that most of the actors who participate are exhausted, at least temporarily. In particular, the aspiring regional hegemon is defeated and limitations may be placed on its subsequent involvement in international affairs. Whether or not that happens, considerable time is necessary to rebuild its shattered economic and military capabilities. Many of the winners of global wars have become exhausted by the effort as well. The land powers on the winning side carry the brunt of the land campaigns. The old system leader is apt to be financially exhausted if it has not developed a strategy for retaining pioneering technological innovation.

One state, however, tends to profit immensely from the global war. One state emerges with a relative monopoly of global reach capabilities built up as part of the global war effort. This state was also a leading contender for the lead economy status prior to the outbreak of war. With its rivals exhausted by global war and its own political–military–economic capabilities expanded by participation in global war, one state emerges as the new system leader. As the lead economy in the world economy, the new system leader is in an optimal position to usher in, and pioneer in as well, a new round of technological innovation, the development of which was in turn accelerated by the global war effort.

The twin peaks of this process, therefore, are the spurts of radical technological innovation that precede and follow periods of global war. The first spurt helps to stimulate global war. The consequent global war helps to stimulate a second spurt of technological innovation. A new period of systemic leadership is facilitated by the first peak and the global war. The subsequent peak in systemic leadership is more or less co-terminous with the second peak of technological innovation. Throughout this process, systemic leadership is not to be equated with global hegemony. One state has a decisive edge in commercial–industrial productivity and in naval capabilities. It has considerable global reach but it also has significant limitations in what it can do with its global reach, depending in part on the number, nature, location, and timing of its opponents.[5] In some centuries, systemic leadership has enjoyed something of an extended honeymoon without much competition (for instance, Britain's nineteenth-century Pax Britannica). In others, the opposition emerges or re-emerges quickly (as in the Dutch–Spanish rivalry of the first half of the seventeenth century or the US–Soviet rivalry of the second half of the twentieth century). The system leader never rules the world. It only has a position of pre-eminence in global political economy for a finite period of time that is geared to the superiority of the techno-economic paradigm and global reach capabilities that provide a platform for a preponderance in affluence and influence.

The Twin Peaks model is not simply an abstract set of generalizations. It has been tested empirically over the past 500 years.[6] In the past half-millennium, each successive system leader (Portugal, the Netherlands, Britain, and the United States) pioneered new commercial routes and industrial technology generating a wave of leading sector growth. Global war followed and in each global war, an incumbent system leader emerged with 50 percent or more of the global system's pool of global reach capabilities, such as naval power. Subsequently, the incumbent system leader has pioneered and presided over a second round of leading sector growth. Thus, the intention here is not to test the Twin Peaks model in the American iteration. The fundamental sequence of growth peak–global war–growth peak has already been established.[7] Instead, the Twin Peaks model will be used to help to structure and elaborate the twentieth-century ascent of the United States to world pre-eminence.

The co-evolutionary argument

The Twin Peaks model stipulates that accelerated economic growth in the world system leads to global war and more accelerated economic growth. Why should this be the case? One historical answer is that this seems to be the way things have worked in the last millennium.[8] A more general explanation is associated with co-evolutionary processes of change, in the realms of politics, economics, and emergence of a new source of threat. Take, for instance, the following scenario: the threat is centered on attacks from nomads coming from the south. Light cavalry can be met with either light or heavy cavalry, but light cavalry is greatly facilitated by a non-sedentary political economy focused on protecting migrating herds by armed horsemen. Absent a considerable nomadic sector, traditional agrarian economies tended to rely more on heavy cavalry to deal with light cavalry raiders. But heavy cavalry requires that numbers of large horses and well-armored warriors be developed, trained, and available for responding to attacks. This is a very expensive undertaking that can be paid for in one of two main ways. Either one develops a strong imperial central government capable of extracting sufficient resources, as in China, or one develops a decentralized political system in which a central ruler with limited financial capability can diffuse military costs by exchanging provincial political power for military services on demand, as in the European feudal system.

The point of this non-hypothetical illustration is that it encompasses a number of changes of differing extent. There is a change in the threat environment. A new type of threat emerged that required or encouraged a particular type of response, in this case, either a new or a reinforced development of heavy cavalry to cope with the light cavalry threat (though, since the Romans had already introduced heavy cavalry throughout Western Europe, this was not entirely a novel development either). Whether an entirely new political economy and political organization are involved is a matter of timing. When Western Europe was confronted with Muslim raiders from the south, it was already decentralized in the aftermath of the disintegration of the western Roman Empire. A new light cavalry threat probably only reinforced feudal tendencies that were already present.

The point is that there tends to be continual interaction among threat environment, political economy, political and military organization, weaponry, and war. Regardless of where change emerges first, there is some probability that the other spheres of activity will demonstrate change that corresponds to the magnitude of the initial stimuli.[9] That is not to say that all six spheres of activity are equally likely to usher in system-wide change. In general, changes in political economy and perhaps political organization are probably more significant sources of fundamental change than are changes in weaponry and military organization. War and threat environment appear to fall somewhere in-between. Still, there are obvious exceptions to these generalizations. Chariots, gunpowder, and nuclear weapons, for instance, are hardly minor sources of weaponry change. The most simple and safest theoretical premise is to proceed on the presumption that all six spheres tend to co-evolve. Change in one of the six arenas, assuming some threshold of significance is attained in terms of the nature of the change, is likely to be followed by changes in the other five arenas. Figure 7.1 depicts one version of this argument even though it omits, for the sake of simplicity, many arrows that could be drawn among the six spheres of activity.

This co-evolutionary theory has not been applied before to the problem of ascent in world politics. It may not prove to fit very well. Many of the appropriate ingredients, however – changes in threat environment, political organization, military organization, weaponry, political economy, and war – are definitely present. Therefore, it seems a good bet to provide some further explanatory grist for the Twin Peaks mill. In this respect, though, the utility of the co-evolutionary perspective is being tested in this chapter.

The ascent of the United States to systemic leadership

Where should we begin? The crux of the Twin Peaks interpretation is that ascension to systemic leadership takes place in a very specific context. It does not happen randomly. Nor does it take place in a totally unique manner. The probability of systemic leadership ascension is most probable after a fundamental change in techno-economic paradigms and related acceleration in economic growth have destabilized the world economic,

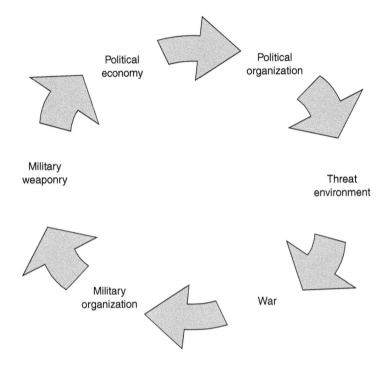

Figure 7.1 Co-evolutionary processes.

and therefore the world political, pecking order. Global war is likely to ensue as challengers compete for pre-eminence in world politics. The state most likely to ascend to systemic leadership at the end of the global war interval is the state most closely linked to the fundamental and radical innovations in political economy paradigms that are ultimately responsible for destabilizing change.

In the twentieth-century case, radical changes in political economy initially helped to create a threat environment that emphasized the potential for systemic leadership transition and replacement. Once this threat/opportunity was in progress and not resolved immediately, we can draw on Bruce Porter's excellent argument that defeat in World War I essentially encouraged or facilitated the emergence of fascism and communism in states attempting to catch up quickly to the more economically developed winners.[10] The takeovers of Russia, Italy, Germany, and, to a lesser extent, Japan by adherents to these formulas for rapid and militarized economic development made the systemic crisis all the more acute. World War II, along with other combat in the inter-war years, was the outcome and amounted to a showdown between diametrically opposed approaches to organizing regional and global orders.

Table 7.1 Changes in techno-economic paradigms

Timing (Leader)	Label	Main carrier branches	Key factors	Infrastructural focus	International regime
1770s–1840s [Britain]	Industrial Revolution	Textiles Iron working	Cotton Pig iron	Canals Roads	British supremacy
1830s–1890s [Britain]	Steam	Steam engines Railroads	Coal	Railways World shipping	Pax Britannica
1880s–1940s [Germany/ USA]	Steel	Steel construction Electrical engineering Chemicals	Steel	Electricity supply and distribution	Imperialism/ world wars
1930s–1990s [USA]	Fordist mass production	Motor vehicles Petrochemicals Aircraft	Oil	Highways Airlines; airports	Pax Americana
1980s– [USA]	Information technology	Computers Software Electronic goods	Micro- chips	Telecommunications Satellites	Military unipolarity/ economic multipolarity

Source: based selectively, and with some modifications, on Christopher Freeman and Car-lotta Perez "Structural Crises of Adjustment, Business Cycles and Investment Behavior," in *Technological Change and Economic Theory*, Giovanni Dosi, Christopher Freeman, Richard Nelson, Gerald Silverberg, and Luc Soete (eds) (London: Pinter, 1988: 50–57).

Table 7.1 provides an overview of fundamental changes in the world economy over the past two centuries or more. The British Industrial Revolution of the late eighteenth century initiated a sequence of industrial changes that proceeded in five waves. The late eighteenth-century revolution focused on changes in the mass production of textiles and iron. The next wave, also British led, was built around the many implications related to introducing steam engines as a principal source of propulsion. Steel, chemicals, and electricity, beginning in the second half of the nineteenth century, led to the introduction of a new cluster of revolutionary "carrier branches" in which the United States and Germany were the leading pioneers.[11]

Techno-economic paradigms refer to the fundamental principles characterizing how economies are organized to produce. Major or radical innovations create paradigmatic shifts. Examples include making textiles by machine, propelling trains by steam, or creating automobiles on assembly lines. These innovations are initially applied to specific leading sectors that attract new investment and generate high profits. They tend to be dependent on some "key factor" such as cotton or oil that is both readily available and inexpensive. In time, the new innovations diffuse throughout the economy (e.g., steel replaces iron, assembly lines are adapted to

Table 7.2 Shares of world manufacturing output

	Britain	USA	Germany	France	Russia	Italy	Austria-Hungary
1880	22.9	14.7	8.5	7.8	7.6	2.5	4.4
1900	18.5	23.6	13.2	6.8	8.8	2.4	4.7
1913	13.6	32.0	14.0	6.1	8.2	2.4	4.4
1928	9.9	39.3	11.6	6.0	5.3	2.7	
1938	10.7	31.4	12.7	4.4	9.0	2.8	

Source: Paul Bairoch, "International Industrialization Levels from 1750 to 1980," *Journal of European Economic History* 11 (1982: 296).

the assembly of other products, computers revolutionize mathematical calculation and writing alike). They also require entirely new economic infrastructures in order to maximize the effectiveness of the new products. Finally, they also tend to lead to new international regimes organized around the pioneering lead economy which has a major stake in maintaining the order of the global economy.

Table 7.2 captures the destabilization implicit to the late nineteenth-century changes in the political–economic sphere. Britain's manufacturing lead was surpassed by the United States in the last two decades of the nineteenth century. Germany, well behind the United States in many respects, had also caught up to the British position by 1913. A long era of Pax Britannica had to give way to some new organizing principle. World Wars I and II were waged to determine who would supply the new organizing rules, the United States or Germany.

The US's edge in this competition, clearly demonstrated in Table 7.2 is also suggested strongly in the preceding Table 7.1. The fourth industrial wave was predicated on interchangeable parts and automobile assembly lines as a production mode that revolutionized manufacturing, gas engines that became the new principle source of propulsion, and petroleum as the new central and increasingly primary energy source, as illustrated in Figure 7.2. These developments are sometimes labeled "Fordist" in honor of the entrepreneur who began assembling Model Ts in Detroit, Michigan prior to World War I.[12] Unlike the late nineteenth-century innovations in steel and chemistry, the Fordist mass production changes in manufacturing were very much an American development. The automobile itself initially had been a European innovation but one characterized by more traditional craftsmanship.[13] The mass assembly changes in Detroit changed all of that and much more. For instance, it gave the United States a pioneering monopoly in the early twentieth century's best-practice manufacturing technology, as suggested by the American lead in motor vehicle production reproduced in Table 7.3. Equally impressive is the increase in production volume. Automobile output increased by more than a factor of ten between 1910 and 1920. Between 1940 and 1950, it almost

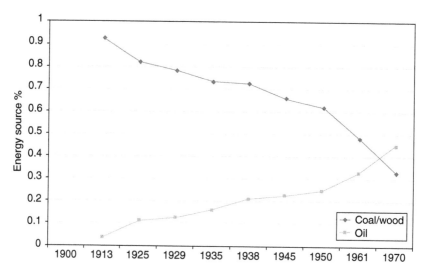

Figure 7.2 The transition to oil.

Table 7.3 Automobile production in the big five economies (thousands)

	United States	Japan	France	Germany	United Kingdom	Total
1900	4.1					
1910	181			9.4		
1920	1,906 (94.4%)		41		71	2,018
1930	2,787 (86.3%)		194	77	170	3,228
1940	3,717 (83.0%)	1.6	182	275	305	4,481
1950	6,666 (86.9%)	1.6	257	219	523	7,667
1960	6,675 (87.1%)	165	1,136	1,817	1,353	11,146
1970	6,547 (37.7%)	3,179	2,458	3,529	1,641	17,354
1980	6,400 (29.9%)	7,038	3,488	3,530	924	21,380
1990	6,078 (24.1%)	9,948	3,293	4,634	1,302	25,255
2000	5,542 (23.5%)	8,359	2,880	5,132	1,642	23,555

Source: R. Mitchell, *International Historical Statistics: Africa, Asia & Oceania, 1750–2000*, 4th edn (New York: Palgrave Macmillan, 2003); ibid., *International Historical Statistics: the Americas, 1750–2000*, 5th edn (New York: Palgrave Macmillan, 2003); and ibid., *International Historical Statistics: Europe, 1750–2000*, 5th edn (New York: Palgrave Macmillan, 2003). 2000 information online, available from: www.autoindustry.co.uk/statistics/production/world.

doubled.[14] The success of the Model T also virtually ended the experimentation going on in different modes of automobile propulsion. Steam and electricity-based alternatives lost to the gasoline engines placed in Ford automobiles, thereby further reinforcing the twentieth century's gradually growing dependency on petroleum.

The control of appropriate energy sources is critical to this story. New technology does not always require new energy sources but there is some probability of shifts in the need for more potent fuels. Global commercial expansion in the fifteenth through eighteenth centuries relied on sail power (along with gunpowder) to create Portuguese, Dutch, and English monopolies. Coal, abundantly available in Britain, fueled the steam-power age. Not coincidentally, the United States began its ascent as one of the principal suppliers of petroleum, a status that persisted through 1945, as is demonstrated in Figure 7.3.

War was extremely influential in this process. American discoveries in Pennsylvania immediately prior to the outbreak of the Civil War proved timely when Confederate maritime raiders were able to damage the Northern whaling fleets and reduce an important source of oil for lighting purposes. Electricity might have made oil much less significant if it had not been for the fortuitous emergence of gasoline engines in the late nineteenth century. Navies had begun converting to petroleum as their principal propulsion fuel for battleships prior to 1914, but World War I accelerated the demand for petroleum in a number of ways. Navies had discovered that they could build bigger ships that were capable of staying at sea longer, more capable of being refueled, and able to travel longer distances if they switched from steam engines to gasoline/diesel engines and to petroleum over coal. Trucks (and even French taxi cabs) became critical for supplying and ferrying troops during wartime. Gasoline-powered tanks were introduced as mechanized ways to break through stalemated front lines. Planes, initially used for scouting purposes, became fighters and bombers. All of these new military fighting platforms depended on various types of gasoline engines. As they developed into the central weapon platforms of the twentieth century, access to the fuel that drove them added compelling national-security incentives to the increasing industrial reliance on petroleum and petrochemicals.

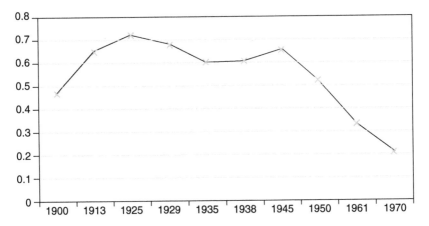

Figure 7.3 U.S. share of world oil production.

But the predominant US role in oil production/distribution in the American Century was not simply a function of fortunate geological circumstances. It was an outcome that was strongly influenced by deliberate corporate and governmental strategies.[15] Part of the US ascent to systemic leadership consisted of wrestling away control over non-American oil from the preceding system leader, Britain, especially in the Middle East.[16] Table 7.4 suggests that predominant US corporate control in non-American areas had not been achieved completely by the beginning of World War II. British and Dutch firms (note that the Netherlands was Britain's predecessor as system leader) still controlled most of the oil in the Middle East and southeast Asia. Yet within a few years of the close of World War II, US firms, as summarized in Table 7.5, were in control of a majority share of non-US/Soviet oil production.

This outcome is similar in significance to the estimate that the Mongols controlled over 50 percent of the world's horses in the early thirteenth century.[17] Both the Mongols and the United States, for a time and in their respective eras, dominated the key to military propulsion. The United States went one better by also controlling the production and/or distribution of what was to become the main industrial energy source of the twentieth century. The importance of this factor in the rise of the US economy

Table 7.4 Control of key producing areas outside the United States (%)

		Western Hemisphere	Middle East	Far East
1929	United States	58		5
	Britain/Netherlands	39	100	90
	Others	3		5
1939	United States	48	16	19
	Britain/Netherlands	36	78	73
	Others	16	6	8

Source: based on Ed Shaffer, *The United States and the Control of World Oil* (New York: St. Martin's Press) (1983: 68).

Table 7.5 Acquisition of control of key producing areas outside the US and USSR (percentages)

	1938	*1945*	*1953*
United States	33	41	53
Britain/Netherlands	53	41	33
Others	14	18	14

Source: Steven A. Schneider, *The Oil Price Revolution* (Baltimore: Johns Hopkins University Press) (1983: 36).

Table 7.6 Percent changes in US direct foreign investment by industry

1897–1914		1919–35		1946–70	
Other[1]	796	Utilities	688	**Petroleum**	1,450
Utilities	504	Manufacturing	135	Manufacturing	1,246
Mining/smelting	437	**Petroleum**	129	Other[3]	1,114
Manufacturing	408	Other[1]	44	Trade	1,000
Agriculture/timber	362	Mining/smelting	39	Mining/smelting	675
Petroleum	304	Sales	34	Public utilities	123
Sales[2]	198				
Railroads	77				

Sources: Ed Shaffer, *The United States and the Control of World Oil* (New York: St. Martin's Press) (1983: 36, 70, 83); C. Lewis, *America's Stake in International Investment* (Washington, DC: Brookings Institution) (1938: 579, 588, 605); Mira Wilkins, *The Emergence of Multinational Enterprise: American Business Abroad from the Colonial Era to 1914* (Cambridge, MA: Harvard University Press) and ibid., *The Maturing of Multinational Enterprise: American Business Abroad from 1914 to 1972* (Cambridge, MA: Harvard University Press) (1970: 110; 1974: 329).

Notes
1 Mainly banks and insurance.
2 Excludes petroleum.
3 Includes sales organization and agriculture.

as the system's lead economy is strongly hinted at in Table 7.6 which records the ascent of US direct foreign investment (DFI) in petroleum-related assets. Table 7.6 cannot be read as a summary of petroleum's share of DFI, but it does underline the weight of petroleum investments abroad in establishing economic leadership in a techno-economic era heavily reliant on oil.

Another way of underscoring the importance of Fordist assembly lines, gasoline engines, and petroleum as the core package for economic ascent is provided by Table 7.7's list of World War II war-material production. One interpretation is that the United States-led coalition won World War II because it was in a position to out-produce the opposing coalition. We do not need to adopt this interpretation exclusive of other factors to recognize that the Allied victory was certainly facilitated mightily by the very strong Allied material advantage. If World War I fighting introduced petroleum-powered fighting platforms (tanks, battleships, and planes), World War II fighting was heavily dependent on these vehicles. The Allied side consumed twenty times the crude oil available to the Axis powers. One of the reasons for this is that the Allied side produced six times the number of military trucks, four times the number of tanks/self-propelled guns, and three times the number of combat planes.

The fourth column in Table 7.7 calculates the US production share of this war material advantage. The US economy clearly did not generate all of the war materials for its side and in some categories (tanks/self-propelled guns and artillery) was not even the leading producer. But the

Table 7.7 The Selective production of war materials, 1939–45

	Axis	Allied	USA %
Coal	2,624.9	4,283.6	50.2
Iron ore	266.1	591.1	67.1
Crude steel	191.8	497.1	67.3
Aluminum	2,503.3	4,642.7	88.8
Crude oil	50.45	1,043.0	79.9
Tanks/self-propelled Guns	51,845	227,235	38.9
Artillery	179,694	914,682	28.1
Military trucks	594,859	3,060,354	77.8
Military aircraft			
Combat	145,584	417,219	47.4
Trainers	28,516	103,578	55.6
Transport	4,897	43,045	55.6

Source: based on John Ellis, *Brute Force: Allied Strategy and Tactics in the Second World War* (New York: Viking) (1990: statistical appendix, 157).

United States did contribute nearly 80 percent of the petroleum and military trucks, as well as about half of the aircraft. The rapid production of shipping was another US specialty. Since a respectable proportion of the non-petroleum US material contribution was generated via converted automobile factories using assembly line techniques, it follows that much of the "arsenal of democracy" was predicated on the same Fordist-petroleum foundation that rocketed the US economy to its position of world pre-eminence.

Winning the 1939–1945 combat is definitely a part of the US ascent story. One does not have to denigrate the Soviet contribution on land to the outcome of World War II to acknowledge US leadership in the planning, coordination, and supplying of the Allied side.[18] At best, US pre-eminence might have been restricted to the Americas. With the Allied victory over what may have been the last coercive attempt to unify Western Europe, US pre-eminence was guaranteed throughout what became known as the "free world." That systemic leadership after 1945 failed to encompass the entire planet is hardly surprising given the evolutionary trajectory of this form of global predominance.

In the early 1500s, Portugal, the first global system leader, managed to control parts of South America, some African coastline, parts of the Indian Ocean, with other scattered bases in southeast and east Asia. The Dutch and British system leaders managed to build on this foundation and extend it in subsequent centuries, but there have always been areas beyond the reach (and often the interest) of global leaders concerned with intercontinental and oceanic trade. US systemic leadership has been more focused on industrial production than in the Portuguese, Dutch, and first British eras, but its geopolitical concerns with the defense of Western Europe, the "rimland" of Eurasia, and problem areas in Africa and Latin America would not have seemed all that remarkable to decision-makers in earlier system leaders. They fretted about the same areas as sources of global policy problems.

So, what do these changes add up to? We have radical political–economic changes being wrought by major economic innovations. Their political–military implications alter the major power-threat environment by creating an opportunity for systemic leadership transition that is traditionally fused with efforts to establish regional hegemony in Europe. Two of the most intensive wars ever fought, thanks in part to the new technology, were waged to decide the leadership succession issue. In the process, major power military organizations and weaponry were organized around weapon platforms that reflected the technological changes (battle-ships, aircraft carriers, submarines, tanks, fighters, and bombers).[19] That is another way of saying that political–economic changes encouraged co-evolution in the threat environment, war, military organization, and weaponry. Only political organization seems omitted.

This is an oversight that is easily remedied. Prior to the twentieth century, US government was typically characterized as a federal system with a weak center. There were occasional lapses, as in the American Civil War, but, in general, the federal government reigned but did not rule the American political system. The co-evolutionary changes of the twentieth century changed all that. The US central government expanded in size and political clout primarily as a function of its wartime participation. The basic pattern was the well-known ratchet effect. Political systems engaged in war must mobilize resources and personnel. The more intensive the war participation, the greater is the demand for resources and personnel. Governmental intervention and coordination of the war effort, as a consequence, is all the greater and more essential. Moreover, technological changes expanded the scope and range of warfare, and made more civilian participation in the war effort (both in factories and as military targets) more necessary and probable.

Once the fighting had ended, some movement back to pre-war conditions was feasible but it was unlikely that the pre-war status quo would be regained. In the US case, federal revenues more than quadrupled between 1910 and 1920, before declining to a level roughly triple the 1910 level by 1930 (see Table 7.8). Between 1940 and 1950, federal revenues increased by a factor of six and never returned to anything resembling pre-World War II levels. Lest these numbers be dismissed as ignoring infla-tion, which also tends to ratchet upwards in wartime situations, Table 7.8 also reports data on public debt per capita and number of military person-nel. Public debt, a device innovated by earlier system leaders to pay for global wars, expanded on a per capita basis by a factor of nineteen during World War I. World War II brought about another five-fold increase.

Table 7.8 The expansion of the US central government

	Federal revenues	Public debt per capita	Military personnel (000s)
1900	$653	$16.60	125.9
1910	962	12.41	139.3
1920	4,261	228.23	343.3
1930	2,634	131.51	255.6
1940	7,000	325.23	458.4
1945			12,123.5
1950	43,527	1,696.67	1,460.3
1960	99,800	1,584.70	2,476.4
1970	205,562	1,811.12	3,066.3

Standing military personnel almost tripled as a function of World War I. The increase between 1940 and 1950 was closer to a quadrupling. In the case of this indicator of governmental size, the Cold War ensured that the numbers began to rise again after initially retrenching from the heights of 1945.

Another dimension of this governmental expansion is captured in Figure 7.4. The series plotted in the figure measures the federal proportion of total governmental revenues in the United States. It gives us some sense of the extent to which the US federal political system became more centralized in the twentieth century. Prior to World War I, local and state governmental revenues claimed the majority of governmental financial extractions. World War I almost created a 50:50 situation, but only temporarily. The Great Depression, World War II, and the ensuing Cold War permanently changed the federal role in the US political system.[20] The greatly increased centralization of the federal government was of course highly convenient for a state in a position to assume systemic leadership.

But it was not just the federal government that became more centralized. Within the federal layer, the division of power among the three nominally equal main branches had also been altered. War and crisis had brought about what Arthur M. Schlesinger, Jr. has termed the Imperial Presidency,[21] or a centralization of political power within the executive branch vis-à-vis Congress and the Supreme Court.[22] Schlesinger's argument has an attractive evolutionary flavor. If the original constitutional system created a web of checks and balances on the three branches of the federal center, the likely outcome was governmental stalemate unless one branch seized the initiative. Crises and external threat favored the presidency becoming the supreme branch because the executive branch could claim to be the best informed and was most prepared to act coercively in response to perceived attacks or opportunities. Thus, the more acute the sense of external threat, the greater is the power of the presidency.

Although Schlesinger does not use the ratchet metaphor, it seems as

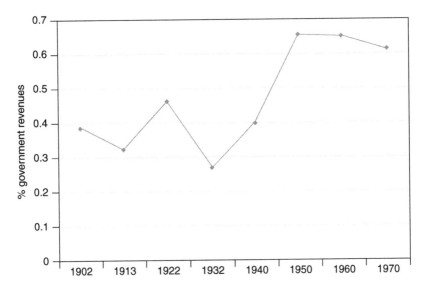

Figure 7.4 The centralization of the federal government.

appropriate here as it did in reference to revenues, debt, and military size. Between the American Civil War and immediately prior to World War I, the US federal government is usually characterized as Congressionally-centered. Foreign (and domestic) policy problems in the twentieth century have swung the central governmental role towards the office of the President. This movement has not been inexorable. Crises come and go creating opportunities for greater Congressional influence in "the troughs" of relative tranquility. But each successive twentieth-century crisis has further expanded the powers of the Presidency to the extent that it has become difficult to expect much in the way of genuine checks and balances in the US federal government, especially when it comes to dealing with crises and threats.

Conclusion

The argument that has been advanced here is that the ascent of the United States to world pre-eminence is not as exceptional as is often imagined. That the ascent of the United States marked a major sea change in world politics is without question. How it came about is a more controversial issue that, no doubt, will continue to be debated from different perspectives. The perspective adopted here is that the Twin Peaks model, based on a leadership long-cycle reading of the past millennium's developments, and with the assistance of an auxiliary, co-evolutionary process interpretation, is quite capable of constructing a strong explanation of what transpired and why things worked the way they did.

Fundamental change in the political economy sphere led to long-term economic growth and destabilization of the world's political hierarchy. A new threat environment emerged that was focused on the dangers associated with systemic leadership transition, and subsequently compounded by fascist and communist strategies and political takeovers in some major powers. Global war ensued. Military organizations and weaponry were transformed to correspond to the assembly line/gasoline engine/petroleum-related technological changes that were radically modifying the way things worked in the twentieth century. Political organizations were also transformed to better correspond to the new times. Winning World War II set the stage for a new round of techno-economic change, one in which much of Western Europe was allowed to catch up to the US lead in a number of respects. The stage was also set for the next paradigmatic shift tied to information technology that became most evident toward the end of the twentieth century, even though its main carrier, the computer, first emerged in World War II. Figure 7.5 attempts to depict the complexity of the interactions among the co-evolving processes.

Amid these changes, the state that was most responsible for introducing the radical innovations underlying the technological changes benefited most. Its economy expanded greatly and became more advanced than any other economy for a time. For better or worse, its political system became more centralized and more capable of acting on the world stage. It not only made money in waging global wars, it used its material advantages to finance, supply, and increasingly coordinate victorious coalition warfare. Winning the global war made it likely that its own preferences (as opposed to the preferences of the losing side) would be pre-eminent in the post-war era. Finally, it was the superiority of its economic technology and global reach that conferred systemic leadership on the United States and not the context of general exhaustion on the part of friends and foes alike, although this certainly did not hurt. Generational change is one of

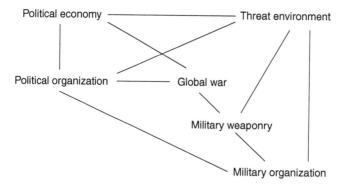

Figure 7.5 An abstract summary of the argument.

several processes that we have not yet integrated very well with other factors such as war and technological change, yet clearly it also helped that US elites were more prepared to accept the role of system leader in the 1940s than they had been in the 1920s. All things considered, the Twin Peaks story appears to work well as a guide to these structural changes.

Throughout American history, war figures prominently as a shaper and driver of change.[23] This generalization holds equally well in the first half of the twentieth century as it does for earlier periods. Yet war does not take place in a vacuum. Wars are embedded in fields of political, economic, and military processes. Wars are made more (or less) probable by other political, economic, and military factors that may be in flux. In turn, wars may also reinforce the direction taken by the larger complex of interrelated changes that are underway. There is no reason to take away from the significance of war-induced changes – a generally under-recognized process in its own right – in suggesting that wars are part of a larger explanatory package. At the same time, wars are hardly minor factors in the bigger picture.

Notes

1 Examples of quite useful treatments of American ascent and/or the impact of wars of the twentieth century include Alan S. Milward, *Economy and Society, 1939–1945* (Berkeley: University of California Press, 1977); Arthur A. Stein, *The Nation At War* (Baltimore: Johns Hopkins University Press, 1978); David M. Kennedy, *Over Here: the First World War and American Society* (New York: Oxford University Press, 1980); ibid., *Freedom from Fear: the American People in Depression and War* (New York: Oxford University Press, 1999); Peter Fearon, *War, Prosperity and Depression: the US Economy, 1917–45* (Lawrence: University Press of Kansas, 1987); Stephen Ambrose, *America's Rise to Globalism: American Foreign Policy since 1938* (New York: Penguin, 1988); Ronald Shaffer, *America in the Great War: the Rise of the War Welfare State* (New York: Oxford University Press, 1991); Robert J. Maddox, *The United States and World War II* (Boulder: Westview, 1992); David Reynolds, "Power and Superpower: the Impact of Two World Wars on America's International Role," in *American Unbound: World War II and the Making of a Superpower*, Warren F. Kimball (ed.) (New York: St. Martin's Press, 1992); Donald C. Watt, "US Globalism: the End of the Concert of Europe," in ibid.; Russell F. Weigley, "The Legacy of World War II for American Conventional Military Strategy: Should We Escape It?," in ibid.; Paul A.C. Koistenen, *Mobilizing for Modern War: the Political Economy of American Warfare, 1865–1919* (Lawrence: University Press of Kansas, 1997); ibid., *Planning War, Pursuing Peace: the Political Economy of American Warfare, 1920–1939* (Lawrence: University Press of Kansas. 1998); ibid., *Arsenal of World War II: the Political Economy of American Warfare, 1940–1945* (Lawrence: University Press of Kansas, 2004); Michael Sherry, *In the Shadow of War: the United States Since the 1930s* (New Haven: Yale University Press, 1997); Hugh Rockoff, "The United States: From Ploughshares to Swords," in *The Economic of World War II: Six Great Powers in International Comparison*, Mark Harrison (ed.) (Cambridge: Cambridge University Press, 1998); Kevin Phillips, *The Cousins' Wars: Religion, Politics and the Triumph of Anglo-*

America (New York: Basic Books, 1999); Fareed Zakaria, *From Wealth to Power: the Unusual Origins of America's World Role* (Princeton: Princeton University Press, 1999); and, most recently, Fred Anderson and Andrew Cayton, *The Dominion of War: Empire and Liberty in North America, 1500–2000* (New York: Viking, 2005) and David R. Mayhew, "War and American Politics," *Perspectives on Politics* 3 (September 2005): 473–493. Most of these studies, perhaps with the exception of Stein (1978), stress or seem to assume the uniqueness of the American path. Ira Katznelson, "Rewriting the Epic of America," in *Shaped by War and Trade: International Influences on American Political Development*, Ira Katznelson and Martin Shefter (eds) (Princeton: Princeton University Press, 2002) rightly notes that American political development analyses tend to overlook the arguments of Peter Gourevitch, "The Second Image Reversed: the International Sources of Domestic Politics," *International Organization* 32 (Autumn 1978): 881–912, or the external environment's impact on domestic processes. This propensity further reinforces the exceptional interpretations of the American rise.

2 Rafael Reuveny and William R. Thompson, *Growth, Trade, and Systemic Leadership* (Ann Arbor: University of Michigan Press, 2004).

3 This statement is not necessarily one that will hold for all time. The costs of military conquest and the attractions of economic development and trade appear to be chipping away at this propensity. See, for instance, the argument and evidence in Karen Rasler and William R. Thompson, *Puzzles of the Democratic Peace: Theory, Geopolitics and the Transformation of World Politics* (New York: Palgrave Macmillan, 2005).

4 The emphasis on the techno-economic paradigm is borrowed from the highly compatible "Sussex school's" approach to long waves of economic growth. See, among others, Christopher Freeman and Carlotta Perez, "Structural Crises of Adjustment, Business Cycles and Investment Behavior," in *Technological Change and Economic Theory*, Giovanni Dosi, Christopher Freeman, Richard Nelson, Gerald Silverberg, and Luc Soete (eds) (London: Pinter, 1988).

5 Barry Posen, "Command of the Commons: the Military Foundation of US Hegemony," *International Security* 28 (2003): 22, advances the concept of "contested zones" or "arenas of conventional combat where weak adversaries have a good chance of doing damage" to intrusive system leaders.

6 See George Modelski and William R. Thompson, *Leading Sectors and World Powers: the Coevolution of Global Economics and Politics* (Columbia: University of South Carolina Press, 1996).

7 A 50 percent share of global reach capabilities is used as a benchmark to denote a minimal concentration of resources required for systemic leadership. The usual pattern is that a new system leader's naval concentration peaks in global war or shortly thereafter (due to war-induced construction) and then experiences a gradual decline in relative capabilities. It is not something that has been studied closely, but it is assumed that leadership activities, other things being equal, are more feasible when a system leader's capabilities are greater than when they are lesser. See George Modelski and William R. Thompson, *Sea Power in Global Politics, 1494–1993* (London: Macmillan, 1988).

8 The leadership long-cycle interpretation traces the origins of the Twin Peak phenomenon to Sung China around 1000 CE. Intensive conflicts were present early on but global war only emerged in the late 1400s. George Modelski and William R. Thompson, "Long Cycles and Global Wars," in *Handbook of War Studies*, Manus Midlarsky (ed.) (Ann Arbor: University of Michigan Press, 1989). See also William R. Thompson, *On Global War: Historical–Structural Approaches to World Politics* (Columbia: University of South Carolina Press, 1988); Karen Rasler and William R. Thompson, "Global War and the Political

Economy of Structural Change," in *Handbook of War Studies II*, Manus Midlarsky (ed.) (Ann Arbor: University of Michigan Press, 2000).

9 This argument has been made elsewhere. See William R. Thompson, "A Test of a Theory of Co-evolution in War: Lengthening the Western Eurasian Military Trajectory," *International History Review* 28 (September 2006): 473–503; and Jack S. Levy and William R. Thompson, *The Arc of War* (Englewood Cliffs: Prentice Hall, 2007).

10 Bruce D. Porter, *War and the Rise of the State: the Military Foundations of Modern Politics* (New York: Free Press, 1994), chapter 6. Minimally, Porter's argument can be read as suggesting that World War I setbacks made it less likely that wartime regimes would survive. More maximally, participation in World War I dramatically demonstrated the need for new strategies in competing with other major powers. "Defeat" in World War I is used elastically. Russia would have been on the winning side if it had avoided or survived its revolution. Russian defeats early in World War I, however, made German-assisted revolution more likely. Italy was also on the winning side but Italian opinion that none of its war aims had been achieved was widespread. Porter's focus is on the European powers, but the rise of more aggressive regimes in Japan can also be traced to the World War I-intensified perception that Japan required access to Manchurian resources. See also Karen Rasler and William R. Thompson, *War and State Making: the Shaping of the Global Powers* (Boston: Unwin and Hyman, 1989).

11 Sources used for statistical data in this chapter include US Department of Commerce, *Historical Statistics of the United States: Colonial Times to 1970* (Washington, DC: US Department of Commerce, 1975); Paul Bairoch, "International Industrialization Levels from 1750 to 1980," *Journal of European Economic History* 11 (1982): 290–296; Brian R. Mitchell, *International Historical Statistics: Africa, Asia & Oceania, 1750–2000*, 4th edn (New York: Palgrave Macmillan, 2003); ibid., *International Historical Statistics: the Americas, 1750–2000*, 5th edn (New York: Palgrave Macmillan, 2003); and ibid., *International Historical Statistics: Europe, 1750–2000*, 5th edn (New York: Palgrave Macmillan, 2003).

12 Naturally, the radical technological changes that were introduced in the early twentieth century were not the work of a single individual. Nor was Ford necessarily directly responsible for the idea of the assembly line. But the Ford Motor Company did produce Model Ts and they were the initial products of the new age of manufacture.

13 James P. Womack, Daniel T. Jones, and Daniel Roos, *The Machine That Changed the World* (New York: Macmillan, 1990), 21–24, describe the classical craft production system approach to automobile construction which involved highly skilled specialists fitting non-standardized parts together one vehicle at a time relatively slowly and at high expense. Mass assembly of standardized parts simplified construction tasks which, in turn, accelerated the process, facilitated the use of less-skilled labor, permitted much greater production volume, and lowered costs as volume increased. These payoffs, of course, were not restricted to automobile production alone.

14 Equally difficult to avoid is the diffusion of the Detroit assembly line to other advanced economies. Between 1960 and 1970, US automobile firms continued to produce about the same number of vehicles annually but their share of world production had dropped dramatically. Table 7.3 understates the extent of contemporary diffusion by ignoring South Korean and Chinese auto production.

15 See C. Lewis, *America's Stake in International Investment* (Washington, DC: Brookings Institution, 1938); Mira Wilkins, *The Emergence of Multinational Enterprise: American Business Abroad from the Colonial Era to 1914* (Cambridge, MA: Harvard

University Press, 1970); and ibid., *The Maturing of Multinational Enterprise: American Business Abroad from 1914 to 1972* (Cambridge, MA: Harvard University Press, 1974).

16 Ed Shaffer, *The United States and the Control of World Oil* (New York: St. Martin's Press, 1983); Hans J. Bull-Berg, *American International Oil Policy: Causal Factors and Effect* (New York: St. Martin's Press, 1987). See also Steven A. Schneider, *The Oil Price Revolution* (Baltimore: Johns Hopkins University Press, 1983), and John G. Clark, *The Political Economy of World Energy: a Twentieth Century Perspective* (Chapel Hill: University of North Carolina Press, 1990).

17 Samuel A.M. Adshead, *Central Asia in World History* (New York: St. Martin's Press, 1993).

18 See John Ellis, *Brute Force: Allied Strategy and Tactics in the Second World War* (New York: Viking, 1990).

19 Military organization agents first choose which weapons platforms they feel will be most efficacious for their mission. Once chosen, however, the weapons platforms will influence the organization of the military services. This effect is seen in the ascendancy and decline of groups within each military organization (e.g., tank versus infantry commanders in the Army, bomber versus fighter pilots in the Air Force, and battleship versus aircraft carrier versus submarine commanders in the Navy. Much the same can be said about doctrine and strategy.

20 In this perspective, the world depression of the 1930s was a function of the intermittent introduction of new technology. Each new wave of technological change requires greater or lesser adaptations. The more difficult the transition from one wave to the next, the deeper is the downturn in economic growth (i.e., depression).

21 Arthur M. Schlesinger, Jr., *The Imperial Presidency* (Boston: Houghton Mifflin, 1989); ibid., *War and the American Presidency* (New York: W.W. Norton, 2004).

22 The argument and outcome were predicted in 1832 by Alexis de Tocqueville, *Democracy in America*, J.P. Mayer (ed.) (Garden City: Anchor, 1969), 126, when he wrote:

> If the Union's existence were constantly menaced, and if its great interests were continually interwoven with those of other powerful nations, one would see the prestige of the executive growing, because of what was expected from it and what it did.

23 Argued most recently by Martin Shefter, "International Influences on American Political Development," in *Shaped By War and Trade: International Influences on American Political Development*, Ira Katznelson and Martin Shefter (eds) (Princeton: Princeton University Press, 2002), and Anderson and Cayton, *Dominion of War*.

8 Domestic challenges to American hegemony

Steven W. Hook

Editor's introduction

> Convinced that history does indeed repeat itself, the author brings together the work of historians and political scientists to challenge the tradition of American exceptionalism, arguing that it is a cultural delusion that hurts the nation's efforts in foreign policy. Accepting the neoliberal view that soft power is of greater importance today than the traditional hard power of military superiority, he extends upon themes explored in other, historical chapters of this book and projects these themes into an uncertain future for the maintenance of America's present position as global hegemon.

As other chapters in this volume demonstrate, the rigorous study of American diplomatic history is essential to reveal the patterns of behavior that shaped the nation's origins and subsequent development. The recurring pattern in North America of morally sanctified political violence, a central theme of Fred Anderson and Andrew Cayton's *The Dominion of War* (2005), both precedes the founding of the United States and transcends its physical boundaries. Such continuity is particularly striking at a time that the nation is engaged in an open-ended "war on terrorism" that is routinely framed by government officials around universal moral themes. History, we learn again, does repeat itself.

Within the fields of political science and international relations, scholars have benefited from major works of diplomatic history. The studies of Thomas Bailey, William Appleman Williams, John Lewis Gaddis, Walter McDougall, and others continue to inform rival claims among scholars from the realist, liberal, and neo-Marxist traditions in international relations theory. Historical detail is equally vital to constructivist theory, particularly as it pertains to the role of public discourse in defining the identity of states, manipulating public opinion, and conducting routine diplomacy.[1]

In testing and building theories of international relations, political scientists seek to understand foreign policy at differing levels of analysis. The defining of these levels of analysis is that of the international system, in which sovereign states pursue their interests in an anarchic, threatening environment, and seek to maximize relative as well as absolute gains by adapting favorably to shifting regional and global balances of power.[2] Whereas the pessimism of traditional realism is rooted in a dubious view of human nature, structural or neo-realists believe that the absence of world government, which inherently forces states into competitive and antagonistic relations with one another, is sufficient to understand war. Neo-realists further argue that power balances, however essential to geopolitical stability, are by nature fragile and temporary, and their break-down leads to interstate conflict.

This pessimism applies to the longevity of unipolar world orders such as that which exists today in a power balance characterized by US preponderance. In particular, hegemonic stability theory identifies recurring cycles in which the costs to dominant states of providing global public goods gradually rise and ultimately become prohibitive, leading to systemic warfare and the changing of the hegemonic guard. To Robert Gilpin (1981), world history reveals the "increasing costs of dominance" that burdened past empires as they faced rising challengers.[3] This pattern is not dissimilar to that identified by historian Paul Kennedy (1987), although the causes of "strategic overstretch" in his analysis were not rooted in theories of public goods.[4]

System-level theories help us to appreciate the context in which state action takes place, and hegemonic stability theory provides insight into the sources of order in a unipolar world. But to more fully understand the behavior of the United States during its ascension as a dominant power, and to better grasp the limitations facing policy-makers at this pivotal moment in history, it is necessary to examine behavioral dynamics inside the "black box" of foreign-policy-making. For this reason, this chapter focuses on domestic sources of foreign policy. It is here that distinct substantive features of the American experience can be discerned that are neglected by system-level studies.[5] And it is through examining these features that a paradox of America's world power appears that reinforces the doubts of systemic theorists about the capacity of the United States to sustain its predominance long into the future.

As this chapter will argue, in seeking to consolidate its primacy, the United States is increasingly constrained by the very forces that propelled its rise as a world power. These forces, which create growing vulnerabilities for the US government, are expressed in enduring, but contrary, societal impulses to detach the United States from world politics and to transform the system of states in the US image.[6] Derived from an eighteenth-century model, the cultural traits and governing structures of the United States are remarkably persistent in the twenty-first century. Yet the world order the nation played a leading role in creating has changed in critical ways, along with the nation's role in that order.

In *The Dominion of War*, Anderson and Cayton note the irony that the "power-abhorring ideology of resistance, republicanism, formed the basis of political culture in what soon proved one of the most dynamically expanding territorial empires in world history."[7] This chapter projects this historical trend line into the present and future and asks whether this irony, visible in current foreign-policy behavior, may soon imperil the United States as it confronts the "radically unpredictable, often destabilizing effects" of its military interventions and designs for global hegemony. Indeed, it is worth considering whether the tensions that have long defined America's world power, including those between empire and liberty, are already eroding the predominance strenuously pursued by national leaders for more than two centuries.

Of interest in this chapter are institutional arrangements that represent structural manifestations of the nation's cultural values and aspirations. These institutional arrangements, including transnational organizations as well as domestic governing structures, restrict the range of choice available to policy-makers.[8] Transnational institutions include intergovernmental organizations (IGOs) such as the United Nations and non-governmental organizations (NGOs), ranging from multinational corporations to human-rights and environmental groups and terrorist organizations. Pressure from IGOs has intensified to the point that many are seeing as threatening US sovereignty. Well-organized NGOs, an outgrowth of US-backed democratic reforms and technological innovations, have mobilized in many areas against US actions and preferences. The equation of US and global interests, a presumption of the "constitutional" world order created after World War II,[9] is inconceivable today with the United States increasingly alienated from this transnational civil society.

Domestic institutions, including constitutional arrangements and federal agencies engaged in foreign policy, bring their own pressures and organizational interests to bear on the policy process.[10] While the ambiguities of the US constitution and electoral politics endow the president with dominant power, the diffusion of policy-making authority across the executive branch, combined with the relative weakness of the state vis-à-vis civil society, hinder the White House's ability to manage foreign policy. The tangle of domestic institutional arrangements has led to a steady stream of legislative stalemates, intelligence breakdowns, and bureaucratic rivalries that hinder the nation's ability to protect itself against emerging threats. To the 9/11 Commission, the "missed opportunities" to prevent the attacks were "symptoms of a broader inability to adapt the way the government manages problems to the new challenges of the twenty-first century."[11]

The paradox of America's world power is intimately connected to the democratic nature of its political system. A "weak state" relative to civil society, such as that in the US case, is likely to be captured by powerful interest groups whose interests may overshadow those of the state. A fragmented state, further, is likely to lose coherence and cohesion as semi-autonomous bureaucracies grow and undertake more specialized functions. Drawing upon these impressions of the US government nearly two centuries ago, Alexis de Tocqueville advanced the claim that democracies are "decidedly inferior" to other governments. George Kennan eloquently revisited this notion in the early days of the Cold War:

> I sometimes wonder whether in this respect a democracy is not uncomfortably similar to one of those prehistoric monsters with a body as long as this room and a brain the size of a pin. He lies there in his comfortable primeval mud and pays little attention to his environment; he is slow to wrath – in fact, you practically have to whack his tail off to make him aware that his interests are being disturbed. But, once he grasps this, he lays about with such blind determination that he not only destroys his adversary but largely wrecks his native habitat.[12]

Opening the "black box" of US foreign policy reveals societal and state-level pressures that are historically resilient and unlikely to change appreciably even under acute duress. A central question remains how well the United States can provide the international leadership it espouses given the domestic and global constraints that are essential features of its political and system. Of particular concern is whether a political culture that is alternately indifferent toward foreign affairs and enmeshed with events overseas is suitable for this type of dominant world role on a long-term basis. How the US government manages the paradox of its own foreign policy will determine how long its "unipolar moment" will last in the turbulent new millennium.[13]

This study is divided into four parts. The first section highlights the military activism of the United States throughout its history and the degree of US primacy in world politics today. The second section describes salient cultural attributes of US political culture and identifies ways in which they contribute to the nation's paradoxical world power. Our attention then turns to dynamics within the US government that impede a coherent response to global problems, including the threat posed by Islamic terrorists. Finally, the chapter considers the implications of the study for the future use of US military force in the globalized "dominion of war."

Military activism and American foreign policy

The US government has freely and frequently employed its military forces throughout its "rise to globalism."[14] A 2002 study by the Congressional Research Service identified 299 instances of overt military force between 1798 and 2002, or about 1.5 military actions per year.[15] Of this total, 168 occurred through 1945, an average of 1.14 per year. After slowing during the Cold War, the pace of US military involvement accelerated in the 1990s. Seventy-eight such instances were recorded between 1992 and 2001, nearly eight per year. The terrorist attacks of September 2001 prompted a new burst of military action, including wars against Afghanistan and Iraq and US military support for dozens of foreign governments linked to the war on terrorism.

The nation's frequent resort to military force contributed to a degree of global predominance that is unprecedented in world history. The United States is the only country whose military forces literally patrol the entire world, through the deployment of troops across five regional commands.[16] In 2003, American troops operated out of 6,702 military installations around the world, including bases in Canada, much of Western Europe, Japan, Indonesia, and Australia.[17] More than 500,000 US troops are stationed at these bases, including about 200,000 troops deployed to Afghanistan and Iraq in 2005. The United States also provides military assistance and training to more than 150 countries in the world today.[18]

Other figures demonstrate the extent of US military superiority. The United States spends more than $400 billion on national defense, more than 40 percent of the global total.[19] Having grown considerably since the war on terrorism began, the US defense budget is larger than the combined budgets of the next twenty military spenders. American military predominance is even greater on qualitative terms, as US weapons have undergone rapid technological advances in such areas as ballistic missile systems and unmanned aerial surveillance. The United States also leads the world in global arms exports, cornering nearly half the global arms trade since the Cold War.[20] All this military strength is financed by the world's largest economy, which produced more than $12 trillion worth of goods and services in 2004, more than one-quarter of the global total.[21] The United States is also the world's foremost trading state, exporting more than any other nation while displaying a voracious appetite for overseas goods and services. Firms in the United States record about $1 trillion in annual exports, nearly 15 percent of the world total. The nation's imports are even larger in absolute terms ($1.4 trillion in 2001) and as a share of world imports (about 20 percent). More foreign direct investment (FDI) travels to the United States than any other country, and the amount of money invested in US stock markets matches that invested in all other stock markets combined. The concentration of economic and military power is particularly notable given that the United States contains about 300 million citizens, less than 5 percent of the world's population. The nation's primacy followed rapid territorial expansion that affirmed the government's hegemonic ambitions.[22]

Early American leaders sought an "empire of liberty" that would extend across the Western Hemisphere.[23] The closing of the western frontier simply opened the Pacific Ocean to US expansion. After the United States established itself as a great power in the two world wars, a central objective of US foreign policy was the preservation of a "predominance of power."[24] The Cold War strategy of containing communism was a means to this end of sustained US primacy. The Pentagon articulated this view most clearly by stating that the United States should "establish and protect a new order that holds the promise of convincing potential competitors that they need not aspire to a greater role."[25]

The coming to power of George W. Bush in January 2001, followed by the terrorist attacks in September, elevated the doctrine of US primacy to a new level. "America has, and intends to keep, military strengths beyond challenge, thereby making the destabilizing arms races of other eras pointless, and limiting rivalries to trade and other pursuits of peace," Bush told US Army cadets at West Point. Three months later, the president's *National Security Strategy of the United States of America* explicitly established US primacy as a pillar of US foreign policy. As the document stated, US military forces "will be strong enough to dissuade potential adversaries from pursuing a military build-up in hopes of surpassing, or equaling, the power of the United States."[26]

The doctrine of sustained US primacy cannot be properly implemented without continued, pervasive military interventionism and immersion of the United States in the global economy. "We are in the world with both feet now," Michael Hirsch observed. "We have achieved our Founding Fathers' fondest dream and, at the same time, their worst nightmare. We are a shining success, the supreme power on earth. And we are entangled everywhere."[27]

Cultural detachment and the paradox

Despite its position of global predominance, the United States faces a variety of challenges today. Military superiority has not allowed the US government to impose its will, and political system, on highly resistant Afghan and Iraqi societies. Nor has military superiority led to the capture of Osama bin Laden, the capitulation of al Qaeda, or the renouncing by Islamic religious leaders of continued anti-American terrorist attacks. The war on terrorism, combined with sweeping tax cuts approved by Congress and more recent domestic costs associated with Hurricane Katrina, has produced massive US budget deficits and borrowing from foreign governments. Other economic problems confront the United States, including a chronic trade deficit and the loss of manufacturing jobs to developing countries. Spiraling petroleum and natural gas prices have eroded the spending power of American consumers while demonstrating the extent and perils of continued US dependence on foreign energy sources. Taken together, these heightening strains illustrate the paradox of American world power.

The roots of this paradox may be found in the political culture of the United States. Political culture, a "historically transmitted pattern of meanings" by which citizens "communicate, perpetuate, and develop their knowledge about and attitudes toward life,"[28] is commonly expressed through popular conceptions of human nature and the relationship of individuals to public institutions. Public policies, both foreign and domestic, are natural outgrowths of these collective attitudes and beliefs. The United States, for example, is unique among industrialized nations in the intensity of public passions associated with abortion policies, in the limited scope of government-sponsored healthcare, and in the availability of citizenship to immigrants.[29]

Although cultural influences are difficult to identify with precision, the conduct of any country's foreign policy reflects its people's distinctive sense of place in the world, which itself is shaped by tangible factors such as geographical location, natural resources, the size and characteristics of the population, and historical experience.[30] Studies of US political culture tend to emphasize the nation's "exceptional" self-image, or being superior to other polities by virtue of its societal values, system of free enterprise, and governing institutions.[31] The "grand narrative" of exceptionalism is not unique to the United States, as students of the Roman, Spanish, French, Ottoman, and other empires can attest. Indeed, US exceptionalism is so genetically bound to that of the British Empire that the two cannot be easily separated. To Bernard Bailyn, early US leaders inherited essential elements of British political culture, including "a conviction of national superiority manifested particularly in the achievement of a degree of civil and political freedom unique in the world."[32]

Yet the Americans departed from their British ancestry in the peculiar time and place of the nation's founding. The first European settlers to North America proclaimed the founding of a "city upon a hill" that would inspire other societies far from its shores.[33] This observation set the evangelical tone in public discourse that persists today. To Thomas Jefferson, Americans had proven themselves to be "the chosen people of God, if ever he had a chosen people, whose breasts he has made his peculiar deposit for substantial and genuine virtue."[34] In the midst of the Spanish–American War, William McKinley claimed he sought, and received, divine guidance to "uplift and civilize and Christianize" the Philippines as an American colony.[35] And President George W. Bush, a born-again Christian, described the war on terrorism in starkly Biblical terms nine days after the September 11 attacks: "Freedom and fear, justice and cruelty, have always been at war, and we know that God is not neutral between them."

Religious zeal is linked to the moralistic nature of US foreign policy that is one of its defining characteristics. American leaders have consistently refused to justify their actions on the narrow basis of national interests, preferring instead normative rationales that draw upon universal moral principles. To Abraham Lincoln, the Declaration of Independence promised democracy "not alone to the people of this country, but hope to the world for all future time."[36] Woodrow Wilson captured this sentiment in arguing that the United States should enter World War I "for the ultimate peace of the world and for the liberation of its peoples."[37]

The nation's record of military interventionism has been sustained by moral rationales that have appealed to public sentiments regarding the appropriate use of force. Commonly cited examples include references to "manifest destiny" in justifying US westward expansion and war against Mexico, colonizing the Philippines as the "white man's burden," and entering World War I in order to make the world "safe for democracy." Similar rationales were used during the Cold War in the Korean and Vietnam wars, although these conflicts had less to do with territorial expansion than spheres of influence controlled by rival ideological blocs.

A sense of moral purpose has consistently guided the foreign-policy preferences of US citizens, a majority of whom reported in 2004 that "following moral principles" should be a top priority.[38] This acute sense of moralism and devoutness sets Americans apart from citizens of other countries. Americans ranked first among citizens of all countries in believing in a "personal God" in a survey of forty-three societies conducted in the early 1990s.[39] Americans ranked first among citizens of industrialized countries in believing that there are "absolute guidelines about what is good and evil" and that religion plays a "very important" role in their lives. A recent survey of US public attitudes about foreign policy finds religious beliefs to be directly linked to the opinions Americans hold on recent government actions in Iraq and elsewhere, with those reporting greater church attendance more likely to support the Bush administration's policies.[40]

Oddly, the US government's record of rapid territorial expansion unfolded amid a societal impulse for the United States to detach itself diplomatically and culturally from the outside world. American foreign policy conducted during the nineteenth century occurred without a sizeable diplomatic corps, a standing military force, or a network of alliances. Woodrow Wilson's failed attempt to include the United States in the collective-security mechanisms of the League of Nations was followed in the interwar years by US retreat and neutralism. While the United States became enmeshed in civil wars and regional conflicts during the Cold War, foreign-policy-makers viewed these interventions through the myopic ideological lens of anti-communist containment, and US involvement with IGOs was based almost entirely on this basis.[41] After the Cold War, Bill Clinton's proclaimed grand strategy of global "engagement" was stymied by an inward-looking Congress. And the "Bush Doctrine," which followed the 2001 terrorist attacks, combined a declaration of sustained US primacy with a pledge to dislodge the United States from multilateral institutions and commitments.

Detachment in this context is not synonymous with isolation, a term frequently and erroneously used to define US foreign policy prior to the twentieth century. Instead, detachment refers to a pervasive public and elite sentiment that the United States should keep its distance from foreign countries and their citizens. The basis of this detached posture rested in the location of the United States, combined with ample territory and natural resources, which together provided the US with the self-sufficiency it required to have "as little political connection as possible" with other states, as George Washington recommended in his farewell address. Secretary of State John Quincy Adams restated this position in 1821 by declaring that the United States "goes not abroad, in search of monsters to destroy." Two years later, the notion that the United States was "essentially different" from the European powers formed the basis of James Monroe's doctrine of US hegemony across Latin America.

American cultural detachment takes several forms, including a national educational system that pays little attention to foreign affairs, public mis-perceptions of foreign-policy issues, and a commercial news media that provided less coverage of world news as the United States became more predominant on the world stage. These elements either encourage disen-gagement from foreign affairs or encourage government interventions that ignore the complexities of regional or domestic conditions in the contested areas. The nation's detached posture has also led to a practice of acting alone, or unilateralism, that compounds the strains on the United States in the interdependent world of the twenty-first century.

Public opinion and news media coverage

The lack of broad public knowledge of the world beyond the United States has long been emphasized by students of the nation's political culture.[42] Despite their residence in the world's predominant state, Amer-ican citizens tend to focus on problems close to home and have little contact or familiarity with foreign nations. This cultural detachment, which mirrors the diplomatic detachment of the US government as described above, leads government leaders to neglect the nation's own historical experience and lessons in foreign affairs. As Walter Russell Mead has observed, political leaders and prominent private citizens

> do not know very much about the history of American foreign policy before World War II, do not particularly want to know more than they already know, and cannot think what practical purpose a deeper knowledge of American foreign policy history might serve.[43]

A few results from public-opinion surveys over the past several decades demonstrate the limitations of the knowledge Americans have had of the world around them. Nearly half of Americans in 1942 were unaware that India was a British colony, and in 1953 only 10 percent could identify the UN Secretary General. More than half of Americans in a 1964 survey thought the Soviet Union was a member of NATO, and in 1979 only 30 percent of survey respondents could identify the United States and Soviet Union as the two signatories of the SALT arms-control treaty. In 1988, with the Cold War winding down, only 40 percent could identify the purpose of NATO, and in 1994 less than half of Americans could identify the president of Russia.[44]

These indicators of limited knowledge can be traced to the primary-school system in the United States. In nationwide tests conducted in 2001, less than one-quarter of high-school students demonstrated proficiency in world history and geography, two areas consistently neglected in public schools.[45] Most school districts do not require courses in world politics at the high-school level, leaving courses in Western civilization or American politics as the closest most students come to foreign affairs.

This intellectual detachment can also be attributed to the traditional insulation of the United States from direct foreign threats. In this secure environment, "foreign policy, save in moments of grave crisis, has to labor under a handicap; it has to shout loudly to be heard even a little."[46] Such a pattern is especially evident when the United States is at peace. In 1999, when participants in a national survey were asked to identify the biggest foreign-policy problem facing the United States, they most often replied, "Don't know."[47] Only when foreign problems reach crisis proportions do they spark the public's interest. The result is a hasty demand for action by the US government, which responds impulsively, often with little knowledge of the underlying problems that provoked the crisis.

Public-opinion surveys consistently find that Americans favor an active role for the United States in world politics.[48] Americans also generally support US engagement in multilateral organizations, including the United Nations,[49] with 74 percent of Americans reporting in 2004 that the United States should play a "shared leadership role" rather than going it alone.[50] By large majorities, however, Americans oppose the nation playing the role of "world policeman," and they believe the government has played that role more than it should in recent years.[51] While the public generally supports high levels of military spending, Americans are strongly opposed to spending on military and economic aid.

Studies of US public opinion also suggest that the views of citizens and political leaders are often based upon faulty information. Among noteworthy recent examples: public opposition to foreign aid, one of the least popular federal spending programs, is fueled by exaggerated beliefs about the size of current aid programs.[52] Whereas the majority of survey respondents believe the US government spends between 10 and to 20 percent of the federal budget on foreign aid, the actual level of aid spending has been less than 1 percent in recent years.

Widespread misperceptions regarding conditions in Iraq prior to the US-led invasion in March 2003 sustained public support for the preventive war.[53] Specifically, most Americans either believed that clear evidence had earlier linked Saddam to al Qaeda, weapons of mass destruction had been found recently in Iraq, and global public opinion favored US military action. The strength of these misperceptions, which persisted long into the US occupation of Iraq despite frequent revelations to the contrary, was vital to the continued public support of the war effort.

While most Americans support multilateral cooperation in US foreign policy, they wrongly believe that most of their fellow citizens favor unilateral action. At the same time, a "false consensus" exists in the minds of unilateralists that their view is prevalent. These misperceptions had important consequences for public support of US foreign policy, as survey respondents who "incorrectly perceived the unilateral view as the majority view were more likely to support the invasion of Iraq and the shift in the defense strategy of the United States from deterrence to preemptive action."[54]

Members of Congress tend to share this perception of a unilateral public, and their false assumptions have led legislators to vote against majority preferences on key foreign-policy issues. These issues include the Comprehensive Test Ban Treaty, the International Criminal Court, the Kyoto Protocol, and the Ottawa Convention to ban land mines, all of which had broad public support but were rejected by Congress.[55] This pattern suggests either that US detachment from international institutions is based on a misreading of public opinion or that elected officials ignore public preferences in conducting US foreign policy.

Just as domestic public opinion plays a key role in American politics, global public opinion is important in an integrated world in which problems routinely cross national borders and require cooperative solutions. In this respect, it is noteworthy that global public opinion has turned against the United States in recent years. Most foreign respondents in a recent survey found the United States to be an "untrustworthy" world leader. Outside of Great Britain, the majority of those surveyed disagreed with the assertion that the United States was engaged in a "sincere effort" to stop terrorism but wanted instead to control Middle East oil, protect Israel, or "dominate the world."[56]

Critical overseas judgments of the United States are not new to the current period, nor should they be unexpected toward any dominant state in a unipolar world. The degree of anti-American sentiment, however, is greater than at any time since the Vietnam War, and it reflects a particular unease with the apparent self-righteousness with which the Bush administration approached the world. As James Kitfield observed, the "Bush revolution" in US foreign policy was based upon a "fundamental misjudgment" about the nation's world power:

> In their ideological fervor, the revolutionaries had convinced themselves and a goodly portion of their countrymen that good intentions and US military might make right in world affairs. They failed to see

how the perception of a superpower run amok would diminish the greater source of American power: the principles and ideals that others freely embraced and by which our good intentions and leadership are judged.[57]

Trends in public opinion are closely related to news media coverage of international affairs, which is the primary means by which American citizens learn about the world beyond their shores. Such coverage decreased dramatically after the Cold War as news outlets closed overseas bureaus and reduced the share of foreign news to about 10 percent of total coverage.[58] National surveys consistently reveal that foreign news is of least concern to US newspaper readers. According to one survey, foreign news coverage by the major networks dropped from more than 40 percent in the 1970s to less than 15 percent by 1995.[59] Among the top fifty magazines sold in the United States in 2001, only three – *Time* (ranked 10th), *Newsweek* (15th), and *US News and World Report* (33rd) provide detailed coverage of international news.[60]

The limited foreign reporting that remains, and the superficial bases upon which it normally rests in peacetime, has implications for US foreign policy. In 1992, President George H.W. Bush acknowledged that his deployment of troops to Somalia on a relief mission was based in part on his exposure to CNN images of starving Somali children. The impact of the "CNN effect" also relates to the failure of the US mission in Somalia, which followed broadcast images of Somalis dragging a slain American solider through the streets of Mogadishu. The public uproar over those images prompted Bill Clinton to withdraw from the mission and later, under congressional pressure, to issue a presidential directive severely restricting future deployments of multilateral peacekeepers. The popular and political backlash, in turn, ensured that the United States would not respond to the 1994 genocide in Rwanda and Burundi that claimed nearly one million lives.

Foreign news predictably regained its hold on media attention after the terrorist attacks of September 2001. In accordance with the "rally-around-the-flag effect," President Bush enjoyed favorable coverage as he executed his war plan against Afghanistan. A year later, the White House demonstrated its skill in "manufacturing consent" in preparing for the invasion of Iraq.[61] Despite their expressed reservations of the invasion, the editorial boards of major US newspapers "conditioned themselves to treat Bush's national-security argument with deference."[62] Reporters were "embedded" with US forces during the twenty-one-day blitzkrieg, providing first-hand accounts of the overthrow of Saddam's military forces and government. In approving this innovation in military journalism, the White House correctly anticipated that the embeds would identify with the troops and provide favorable reports of their missions.[63]

News organizations in the United States generally reinforce the government's tendency to depict foreign-policy problems as moral struggles between good and evil.[64] Government policies, most of which are of remote interest to news consumers, are rarely questioned in media reports. Only when internal divisions are exposed among US officials, a relatively rare occurrence in foreign policy, do the news media depart from the government's "frame" and create their own image of the foreign-policy problem.[65] Otherwise, news organizations freely grant government leaders access to their audience and adopt the government's ideology and viewpoints.[66]

Unilateralism

As noted elsewhere, the United States did not require substantial external assistance during its rise as a world power. The vigorous pace of Western expansion was facilitated by a power vacuum in North America. The major European stakeholders on the continent – Great Britain, France, Spain, and Russia in the far west – were increasingly unable to manage their continental holdings. The Monroe Doctrine merely codified this geopolitical reality.

Early US leaders demonstrated their faith in unilateralism by renouncing their alliance with France; their successors did not establish another peacetime alliance until 1949. The failure of Woodrow Wilson's effort to gain Senate support for the Treaty of Versailles, and the subsequent neutrality of the United States in the face of mounting tensions in Europe, reflected the firm hold of unilateralism even as the United States entered the ranks of the great powers. To Gaddis, while US leaders immersed themselves in foreign affairs during the nineteenth century, they were determined to "avoid commitments to act in concert with other great powers against future contingencies which no one could foresee."[67]

The lessons of US withdrawal after World War I, combined with the threat posed by the Soviet Union after World War II, prompted US leaders to diverge from this unilateral course and to erect a "constitutional" world order.[68] The primary agents of this order would be IGOs such as the UN, international financial institutions, and multilateral alliances – along with the array of international agreements signed by participating states. Under the institutional bargain struck between US leaders and their counterparts, the United States would cover the costs of public goods, including economic stability and military security, while other governments would defer to most US foreign-policy preferences. Such deference would not only bring material gains to other countries; they would be assured that the United States would not abandon them in the uncertain first years after World War II.[69]

The glue holding this bargain together included not only anticipated benefits regarding public goods and confidence in US self-restraint. The presence of the Soviet Union, its deepening hold over Eastern Europe, and the creation of the People's Republic of China in 1949 provided incentives for non-communist states to establish formal mechanisms of cooperation. The preponderance of the United States in these organizations, and its disproportionate financial contributions to them, resulted in institutional arrangements – e.g., weighted voting, command and control of NATO operations, veto power in the UN Security Council – that ensured US interests would not be neglected. The US government also reserved the right to operate outside the bounds of these institutions, as in the Vietnam War and a multitude of covert operations. In this respect, even in the presumed heyday of US multilateralism, a strong element of unilateral control remained in the hands of foreign-policy-makers.

Given the artificially high level of US predominance in the early days of this institution building – the United States produced half of global economic output just after World War II – it should not be surprising that other countries became more assertive as they recovered socially, economically, and politically. The rapid growth of the interstate system during the period of African decolonization in the 1950s and 1960s, itself a stated priority of the US government, directly affected the politics of the UN as a growing proportion of its members were from the developing world. The abrupt end of the Cold War, while affirming the founding values of US-led constitutional order, "weakened crucial supports" that kept the bargain intact.[70] Although George Bush identified US multilateral engagement as a key element of the "new world order," the failed US military intervention in Somalia prompted a unilateral backlash in the mid-1990s.

Criticism of US multilateral activism contributed to the electoral victories by the Republican Party in November 1994 that allowed it to reclaim control of both houses of Congress for the first time in four decades. While domestic policy dominated the new majority's "Contract with America," Republican leaders rejected the Clinton administration's embrace of multilateral engagement as a central pillar of US foreign policy. In their view, the United States was becoming paralyzed by the global missions and obligations accepted by foreign-policy-makers after the Cold War.[71] The United Nations emerged as a primary target of the unilateral turn in US foreign policy, and by Clinton's departure from office the United States owed the world body more than $1 billion in past dues.

All this occurred before George W. Bush came to power in 2001.[72] Bush's refusal to consider the Kyoto Protocol reflected his administration's stated intention to focus on US national interests rather than transnational concerns.[73] Bush's rejection of the International Criminal Court, once championed by the United States, was based upon his fears that the court would challenge US sovereignty. His skepticism of the UN found full expression in his decision to invade Iraq in 2003 without the Security

Council's blessing, marking the nadir of US–UN relations in the world body's history. Bush's recess appointment in 2005 of John Bolton, a controversial figure in the State Department long opposed to US multilateralism, further isolated the United States in the international community.

The revival of unilateralism in the 1990s and its persistence today is not in accord with the preferences of most Americans, as noted above. Nonetheless, the shift reflects a strong desire among many leaders to detach the United States from institutional commitments and instead either go it alone or cooperate temporarily through "coalitions of the willing." This view is particularly strong in the conservative wing of the Republican Party that has dominated Congress since 1994 and has served as the ideological base of the Bush administration since January 2001. In a 2004 survey, conservative Republicans were most likely to believe that the US government should act as the world's "single leader" and least likely to believe that declining respect for the United States overseas was a "major problem." Conservative Republicans were least likely to believe that the Bush administration had been too quick to use military force, and least likely to believe that past US wrongdoing may have motivated the September 2001 terrorist attacks on the United States.[74]

Although the consequences of this shift remain to be seen, strains have already appeared that suggest the US government's pursuit of sustained primacy, as outlined in the 2002 National Security Strategy, will face mounting obstacles in the absence of greater solidarity between the United States and other major powers. Anti-American coalitions in the UN General Assembly, the reluctance of European Union members to follow US policy directives, and institutional cooperation between Russia and China indicate that the pattern of Cold War "bandwagoning" may be giving way to balancing behavior.[75] If so, the United States will indeed be foiled by the very "networks of interdependence" it took a lead role in creating half-a-century ago.[76]

The state and the paradox

The institutional manifestations of US political culture are also present in domestic political structures. The dynamics of organizational behavior, distinctive in the United States given the constitutional arrangements for managing foreign policy as well as the diffusion of bureaucratic structures erected since World War II, support the importance of "bringing the state back in" the work of policy analysis.[77] "The central feature of American politics is the fragmentation and dispersion of power and authority. It is not clear in the United States where sovereignty rests, if indeed it rests anywhere at all."[78] A related question is whether the nation's democratic institutions, while vital to its success, also threaten to "undermine and weaken the power and authority of government and detract, at times seriously, from its ability compete internationally."[79]

The link between political culture and governing institutions is the subject of debate among political scientists. While some scholars argue that institutions cannot be said to derive from cultural influences,[80] this study adopts the view of John W. Kingdon, Steven R. Smith, and others that institutional behavior cannot be understood outside the context of cultural and societal forces.[81] This does not mean that governing institutions do not exhibit structural and behavioral dynamics that are intrinsic to them, only that understanding these dynamics requires that attention also be paid to the ideological milieu in which the institutions were established.

The model suggested in this chapter further presumes that institutional behavior follows a course of "path dependency" by which "initial conditions and early choices heavily affect the future course of events."[82] In this case, prominent cultural features of the United States at its founding, including an emphasis on constraining government by diffusing powers while reserving substantial prerogatives to the president, continue to affect government actions, often in dysfunctional ways. Federal officials operate both within a transnational civil society that invites interest-group pressure at home and overseas, and within domestic governing agencies that, although formally overseen by the president, maintain a high level of autonomy and capacity to pursue institutional self-interests at the expense of stated national interests. "American national security agencies are not created by international relations theorists who think in terms of organizational optimality," Amy Zegart observed. "They are created by political actors who must operate in a reality suffused with conflict, contention, and compromise at the domestic level."[83]

The foreign-policy malfunctions of the US government are literally written into its constitution. In disbursing foreign-policy powers across the legislative and executive branches, the architects of the US government extended an "invitation to struggle for the privilege of directing American foreign policy."[84] While the constitution is specific in some cases – the means of appointing ambassadors and ratifying treaties, for example – most of the general conduct of foreign policy occurs, in the words of former Supreme Court Justice Robert Jackson, in a "zone of twilight in which (the president) and Congress may have concurrent authority, or in which its distribution is uncertain."

Within this twilight zone rests a structural contradiction that contributes to the paradox of America's world power. The relative silence of the US Constitution on foreign policy permits formidable prerogative powers of the president and the executive branch in general. Presidential powers in foreign policy, traditionally stronger in wartime, were permanently strengthened with the coming of the Cold War. Yet this centralized power has been hindered by a fragmented bureaucratic structure that inhibits coherent policy-making. As Huntington observed:

In the United States any centralization of power produced by the expansion of government bureaucracy is mitigated by pluralistic forces that disperse power among bureaucratic agencies, congressional committees, and interest groups and that undermine efforts to subordinate lower-ranking executive officials to higher-ranking ones. Yet an increasingly sophisticated economy and active involvement in world affairs seem likely to create stronger needs for hierarchy, bureaucracy, centralization of power, expertise, big government specifically, and big organization generally.[85]

For all its virtues in allowing for bureaucratic specialization and autonomy, this fragmentation creates problems in the conduct of US foreign policy, which requires a unified statement of national purpose, clear chains of command, consistency, and timely action taken by the head of state. This section reviews how domestic institutions contribute to the paradox of America's world power. The role and limitations of Congress vis-à-vis the Executive Branch are first considered. Each of the primary foreign-policy institutions – the National Security Council (NSC), the State Department, the intelligence community, and the Department of Defense (DoD) – is then reviewed.

Of particular concern in this section is the impact of these institutional arrangements on recent US foreign-policy behavior, particularly the war on terrorism. Bureaucratic failures contributed to the US government's failure to prevent the terrorist attacks of September 2001, as demonstrated by numerous government investigations. Seven months before the attacks, the US Commission on National Security/21st Century (2001) found the US government to be "very poorly organized to design and implement any comprehensive strategy to protect the homeland."[86] The 9/11 Commission of 2004, the most authoritative examination to date, found the US government to be unprepared for the attacks.

Congress

The role of Congress in US foreign policy must be viewed in the context of the legislative branch's inherent limitations. The sheer size of Congress hinders its efforts to compete with the president, who sits alone atop the executive branch. Unity within Congress is a rare exception to the rule of partisan division, as Democrats and Republicans chronically disagree over the primary goals of US foreign policy and the means to achieve them. The legislative process is by nature laborious and time-consuming, a major constraint given the rapid pace of developments overseas. Further, presidents have greater and more immediate access to information regarding these developments, and their command of the "bully pulpit" gives them an additional advantage in shaping public opinion. As a result, "the calculation of where the public interest lies is often passed to the Executive in matters of foreign policy."[87]

Congress has received little help from the judicial branch in foreign-policy disputes. Court rulings have consistently acknowledged the president as the "sole organ" of foreign policy or dismissed as "political" the turf battles between the White House and Congress. The Supreme Court's refusal to rule on the constitutionality of the War Powers Resolution, despite repeated appeals by Congress that it do so, has encouraged presidents to dismiss the legislation.

Finally, electoral concerns inhibit the foreign-policy role of Congress. In order to stay in office, legislators must serve the specific needs of their constituents, and these needs most often have more to do with local or state interests than national or global concerns. Constituent self-interests are especially vital to House members, whose two-year terms in office force them into a nearly perpetual re-election campaign. In this pressurized environment, most members of Congress focus on domestic rather than foreign policy unless the United States faces an imminent crisis overseas. Legislators know that presidents will receive credit for any breakthroughs that may occur in foreign policy. And they protect themselves from blame if foreign-policy initiatives undertaken by the president fail. As congressional scholar Barbara Hinckley observed:

> This is a legislative body where time and influence must be carefully expended, where conflict must be kept within tolerable levels, and where many other policies can fulfill the goals of members better than foreign policy programs do. Seen in this light, foreign policy making by Congress should be the exception and not the rule.[88]

Among the committees with primary concern over foreign policy are the Senate Foreign Relations Committee (FRC) and the House International Relations Committee (IRC). The FRC is especially important because its members consider treaties and presidential appointments before the full Senate votes on them. With their focus on global affairs, both committees provide a large measure of visibility to their members, along with exposure to foreign leaders, intergovernmental organizations, and transnational interest groups. But the lack of material ties to constituent needs has made membership on these committees less attractive to legislators in recent years. Ratifying a treaty, in short, is not likely to enhance a legislator's prospects of re-election. "Foreign Relations has been kind of a wasteland," Senator Chuck Hagel (R-Nebraska) said in 1998. "It is not a particularly strong committee to fundraise from."

National Security Council

The creation of the National Security Council (NSC) moved sensitive functions of foreign policy, including crisis management, from the State Department to the White House itself. Yet the NSC has also amassed a sizeable staff of regional and functional specialists that effectively make for "two foreign ministries" in the US government.[89] Three issues are of primary concern regarding the NSC's role. The first of these is that Congress is left out of the NSC system. Significantly, the national security adviser and other high-level NSC staff members do not require Senate confirmation. Congressional leaders have sought, thus far without success, to gain this oversight power over NSC appointments, a power that seems consistent with constitutional intent. The second concern relates to the NSC's emergence as an independent power center and a rival rather than partner of other federal agencies. Critics allege that NSC staff members have overstepped their bounds by "taking formal policy positions and conducting ongoing relations with the Congress, media, American public, and foreign governments."[90] The council today remains closely identified with Henry Kissinger, Richard Nixon's national-security adviser who overshadowed Secretary of State William Rogers. Conflicts between Jimmy Carter's security adviser, Zbigniew Brzezinski, and Secretary of State Cyrus Vance ultimately led to the latter's resignation.

Finally, the secretive nature of the NSC system raises concerns about potential abuses that come from the concentration of power within the White House. This fear was realized in the 1980s when NSC staffers conducted secret, "off-the-shelf" military operations in the Middle East and Central America that led to the Iran–Contra scandal. A more recent controversy involved National Security Adviser Condoleeza Rice's initial refusal to testify before the 9/11 commission regarding her actions and conversations with President Bush prior to the attacks. Rice claimed such testimony would violate the separation of powers and would discourage future advisers from providing candid advice to the president that would later become public. The White House finally allowed Rice to testify, but only after insisting that her appearance not be considered a precedent.

The State Department

The State Department, originally designated the primary locus of foreign-policy decision-making, has long struggled to gain a high level of credibility within the US government. Early US leaders frowned upon the routine practice of diplomacy. Thomas Jefferson, the first secretary of state, described eighteenth-century diplomacy as "the workshop in which nearly all the wars of Europe are manufactured."[91] Republican Benjamin Stanton of Ohio declared in 1858 that he knew of "no area of public service that is more emphatically useless than the diplomatic service – none in the world."[92] In the popular imagination, the nation's early success, particularly the rapid pace of continental expansion, resulted from the government's rejection rather than embrace of diplomacy.

Largely for this reason, the US government did not create a full-scale foreign service until after World War I. Government leaders then agreed, however reluctantly, that the nation's arrival as a global power required that it "dirty its hands" in diplomatic activity. Even then, State Department budgets and salaries were kept at minimal levels, the travel and schedules of diplomats were closely scrutinized, and once the United States achieved the status of a great power, other government agencies – particularly the NSC – became enmeshed in the foreign-policy process. Although the State Department has retained its traditional role as the institutional base of the foreign service, the cacophony of voices speaking for US foreign policy creates confusion within foreign governments regarding the goals and intentions of the United States.

The experience of Secretary of State Colin Powell illustrates this point. Just before the terrorist attacks of September 2001, Powell had such a low profile in the Bush administration that Time magazine asked on its cover, "Where Have you Gone, Colin Powell?" Vice President Dick Cheney and National Security Adviser Condoleezza Rice carried more weight than Powell in policy deliberations. In addition, Bush frequently turned to Secretary of Defense Donald Rumsfeld and his deputy, Paul Wolfowitz, whose world views more closely matched his own.[93] Although Powell was formally part of Bush's inner circle, he did not play a decisive role in Bush's strategic choices in the war on terrorism. His public statements on behalf of the president's decision to invade Iraq in 2003 belied deep reservations within the State Department.[94]

The Intelligence Community

The Central Intelligence Agency, another product of the National Security Act of 1947, failed to "centralize" intelligence but merely added another component to the densely populated intelligence "community."[95] The intelligence complex includes fifteen federal agencies, of which the CIA is the only independent agency. Of the other fourteen, eight operate within the DoD, including a centralized Defense Intelligence Agency (DIA) and separate intelligence units in each of the four armed services. Six other intelligence agencies support the departments of energy, state, treasury, homeland security, the FBI, and the US Coast Guard, respectively. The chronic tensions between centralized authority and bureaucratic fragmentation that afflict other foreign-policy agencies are particularly troubling to the intelligence complex. The member agencies have long resisted a truly "central" intelligence agency, competing instead for their own niche in the process of gathering and disseminating intelligence.

Such fragmentation has contributed to a lack of coordination among the various agencies within the intelligence complex. As noted earlier, the failure of intelligence agencies to "connect the dots" prior to 9/11 eliminated any chance of averting the tragedy. To Condoleezza Rice, President Bush's national security adviser, "legal and structural impediments" made it impossible for the CIA and Federal Bureau of Intelligence (FBI) to compare their notes effectively regarding the growing threat of an al Qaeda attack on the United States.[96] While the CIA limited its scope to the gathering of foreign intelligence, the FBI's counter-terrorism units focused within the United States. Such a division of labor was entirely in keeping with the roles assigned to each agency, but ill-suited to the task of countering a transnational threat that defied political boundaries.

The reports of a gathering terrorist threat in 2001 came from several sources in the US government and foreign intelligence services. Considered separately, the warnings lacked sufficient detail to provoke strong action by President Bush, who spent the month of August vacationing at his Texas ranch. Instead, the departments of state and defense issued a series of urgent warnings to US forces, government offices, and private citizens overseas. The FBI, meanwhile, issued three nationwide warnings to federal, state, and local law-enforcement agencies, and the Federal Aviation Agency issued "security information circulars" to airports regarding possible hijackings. This gap in jurisdiction was compounded by a shared reluctance of the counter-terrorism units to communicate with each other. As former Senator Bob Kerrey, a member of the 9/11 commission, observed, "Everybody who does national security in this town knows the FBI and the CIA don't talk."

Intelligence analysts have repeatedly failed to provide adequate warning of important developments overseas. These included the strength of anti-American resistance in the 1961 Bay of Pigs crisis, the imminent overthrow of the Shah of Iran and the Soviet invasion of Afghanistan in 1979, and the entry of India and Pakistan into the nuclear club in 1998.[97] Beginning in 2001, George Tenet's CIA suffered four failures: the 9/11 attacks, the inability to capture Osama bin Laden, the lack of Iraqi weapons of mass destruction, and the strong resistance to the US occupation of Iraq.[98] The US government's response to this most recent failure was to create a new layer of bureaucratic control over intelligence and the creation of a new federal position – the national intelligence director – to oversee the process. While this structural reform is consistent with theories of organizational behavior, it remains to be seen whether even greater diffusion of authority will rectify these chronic problems.

The Department of Defense

The institutional dynamics of the Department of Defense (DoD) further complicate the task of managing US foreign policy in a manner that enhances the prospects for sustained US primacy in world politics. The DoD, also created in the aftermath of World War II, is by far the largest federal program in terms of personnel and annual discretionary spending by the US government. Like the CIA, the DoD was created in part to centralize functions that had previously been diffused across multiple agencies. In this case the DoD assumed control over the previously independent armed services – the Army and Navy – along with the newly created Air Force. The centralizing agent in the DoD's design was the Joint Chiefs of Staff, representing each armed service whose individual preferences would be reconciled by an appointed chairman and a civilian Secretary of Defense.

This design, however, failed to prevent ongoing inter-service competition over personnel, the development and deployment of weapons systems, and combat roles and missions. While the Goldwater–Nichols Reorganization Act of 1986 sought to remedy these problems, the independence of the armed services remains a stubborn fact of military life today. Ongoing resistance to more fully unifying the armed forces "can only be understood as proof of the institutionalized clout that the separate services had acquired over the previous five decades."[99] Institutional tensions also exist between the DoD and the State Department. Strong defense secretaries, including Donald Rumsfeld in the Bush administration, have prevailed over secretaries of state in critical matters of national security. The disparity in budgetary authority controlled by each agency – the DoD's budget of approximately $400 billion is nearly twenty times that of State – provides additional leverage for the Pentagon, particularly when the spillover effects of defense spending on the civilian economy are taken into account.

In this regard, the "military–industrial complex" about which President Eisenhower expressed concern in 1961 poses additional institutional challenges for the US government. Potentially excessive levels of military spending may result from this enmeshment of DoD operations within the US political economy. The nation's defense industry is often regarded as a prototypical "iron triangle" that includes Pentagon officials, arms contractors, and congressional committees that make decisions regarding the type, scale, and location of weapons programs.[100] Each actor in this institutional hybrid stands to gain from the approval of large programs, quite apart from the merits of the programs in serving US foreign-policy goals. Defense contractors such as General Dynamics and Lockheed maintain among the strongest lobbying presence of any domestic interest group in Washington, DC. Legislators have strong incentives to satisfy the contractors, which represent many jobs (and possible votes) in their districts and contribute generously to their semi-permanent election campaigns.[101]

Homeland Security

Efforts to merge federal agencies and functions are often plagued by clashing organizational cultures, disputes over budgets and missions, and other forms of bureaucratic rivalry. These problems have been clearly evident in the creation in 2003 of the Department of Homeland Security (DHS), the product of the largest reorganization of the federal government since the National Security Act of 1947. More than 20 federal agencies with nearly 200,000 employees became part of the DHS, whose mission was to prepare US territory for potential attacks or natural disasters.

Many agency leaders resisted their move to DHS, however, fearing the loss of autonomy and control. Amid these internal problems, public support for the department was diminished by high-profile missteps. A color-coded national alert system only seemed to confuse Americans, as did remarks by DHS officials that citizens should stock up on cellophane and duct tape to survive bio-chemical attacks on their neighborhoods. Long delays prevented the timely release of a terrorist "watch list" and national risk assessment. "Far from being greater than the sum of its parts," said journalist Michael Crowley, "DHS is a bureaucratic Frankenstein, with clumsily stitched together limbs and an inadequate, misfiring brain.... Even allowing for inevitable transition problems, DHS has been a disaster: underfunded, undermanned, disorganized, and unforgivably slow moving."[102]

Progress reports regarding Homeland Security from other sources have also been critical. The private Markle Foundation, for example, found the department's information-sharing role to be in disarray.[103] And the Gilmore Commission reported to Congress and the White House that, "with the lack of a clear articulated vision from the federal level," each of the fifty-five US states and territories "has been moving to combat terrorism in its own way."[104] Criticism of DHS escalated in 2005 after the federal government failed to act quickly and effectively after Hurricane Katrina devastated the Gulf Coast and New Orleans in August 2005. A common complaint was that the Federal Emergency Management Agency (FEMA), whose traditional role was oversee responses to natural disasters, had become too preoccupied with counter-terrorism programs. Funding for strengthening the New Orleans levee system, for example, had been cut in previous years as spending on fighting terrorism, including the war in Iraq, rapidly increased.

The paradox and the dominion of war

As noted by Anderson and Cayton, the long historical record of US militarism seems alien to the common association of peace as the normal state of foreign relations, with war as the exception. The "grand narrative" of American exceptionalism sets the United States apart from the warlike peoples of other nations, while justifying US military interventions in the name of liberty and universal moral values. This exceptional self-image aside, the conduct of US foreign policy throughout its history, including an unending pattern of coercive diplomacy and military interventions, is consistent with the imperial policies of Old World states founded on realpolitik. Still, American exceptionalism endures in the public imagination, and the costs of this cultural delusion are steadily increasing.

The widely perceived gap between America's exceptionalist self-image and its behavior creates growing problems for current and future foreign-policy-makers. By committing itself to lofty moral standards and often failing to live up to them, the United States exposes itself to charges of hypocrisy. The genocide of American Indians, the persistence of slavery for nearly a century after the nation's founding, the denial of women's voting rights, and imperial adventures in Mexico and across the Pacific Ocean at the turn of the nineteenth century violated key moral principles stated in the Declaration of Independence. The US role in toppling elected leaders during the Cold War – as in Iran in 1953, Guatemala in 1954, and Chile in 1973 – also departed from the country's stated principles. In the war on terrorism, the US government has created informal alliances with "front-line states" such as Pakistan, Tajikistan, and Indonesia that are known violators of human rights. Abuses by American soldiers at the Abu Ghraib prison, Guantanamo Bay, Cuba, and other detention centers further legitimate charges of hypocrisy.

Excessive US moralism and the attending double standards fuel skepticism of the United States, even when it acts on behalf of benevolent or humanitarian concerns. Critics charged that US intervention in the former Yugoslavia during the 1990s reflected imperial intentions in the post-Cold War era, not a desire to halt an escalating pattern of religious conflict and "ethnic cleansing" of Muslims. Similar arguments were made about the Somalia intervention, a country whose geopolitical significance to the United States had vanished with the Soviet Union.

Despite the shortcomings and duplicity of US-style democracy, a central goal of the nation's foreign policy has been to export this model to other countries. This effort has taken many forms, from the provision of development aid to the imposition of "democracy by force."[105] Iraq is only the latest in a long series of state-building operations designed to create civil societies and political institutions that make the orderly and democratic conduct of governance possible.[106] For the United States, democratization overseas not only satisfies the nation's normative goal to "uplift" foreign citizens; political reforms make the United States more secure by "the construction of a stable world order congenial to America's way of life."[107]

In many cases, particularly in Latin American during the 1970s, the combination of US economic support and political persuasion was sufficient to open the doors to US state builders. When foreign leaders objected, as in the case of Panama in 1989 and Haiti in 1994, the United States applied economic coercion, and later military force, when the non-violent measures failed. The end of the Cold War produced additional opportunities for state building, whose success varied as widely as the means undertaken by the US government. The 1992 US intervention in Somalia, while successful in providing emergency relief to thousands of starving victims of a war-induced famine, fell apart after US and UN peace-keeping forces tried in vain to create a viable government that would prevent more humanitarian nightmares after they left.

Three lessons emerge from the attempts by the US governments to export democracy.[108] First, state-building is unlikely to succeed without public support. Second, competitive elections do not ensure the coming to power of democratic leaders or the conduct of government policy that respects domestic freedoms or international norms. Elections may instead produce an "illiberal democracy,"[109] in which elected leaders such as Russia's Vladimir Putin suppress political rights and civil liberties. Finally, external support is most helpful to governments that have already initiated their democratic transitions. In countries where attempted transitions "are stagnating or slipping backward, democracy aid has few chances of reversing this trend."[110]

The war in Iraq represents a cautionary tale in this regard. The rationale for the invasion turned to building democracy only after the stated rationales linked to the war on terrorism proved unfounded. Public support for the invasion was based largely upon the stated rationales and was conditioned on the United States first gaining support from the United Nations. Early elections in Iraq brought a wide range of officials to power, many of whom claimed primary allegiance to their ethnic groups or religious sects rather than a unified Iraq. Perhaps most gravely, American efforts to create democratic institutions and constitutionalism in the country are further hampered by the nation's lack of a democratic tradition, by its lack of a consensual civil society, and by widespread hostility among Iraqi citizens toward the United States.

The diplomatic detachment of the US government from Iraq and the Persian Gulf region prior to the war further weaken its achieve its goals in the conflict. The lack of area expertise beyond the State Department, which was largely excluded from White House deliberations prior to the invasion, prevented policy-makers from receiving adequate information regarding Iraq's long history of autocratic rule, its splintered population, and the deep-seated cultural enmities between Islam and the West. The same knowledge gap doomed the US intervention in Vietnam, which was founded falsely on ideology rather than nationalism as the primary motivating factor of the Vietminh. Such misperceptions no doubt stem from the cultural equation of US foreign-policy interests with universal values, particularly the advance of human liberty. By applying this view to a wide variety of foreign conflicts, American leaders have "freed themselves from any obligation to understand other peoples and places on their own terms and in their own contexts."[111]

The frustrations of US democratic state-builders notwithstanding, the United States has contributed greatly to the trend toward global democratization that has resulted in a record number of democratic governments in place, as defined by a leading human-rights NGO, and a record number of world citizens living under democratic rule.[112] It is likely, however, that this trend owes as much to indirect US pressure as well as transnational forces outside US control than to direct US policy initiatives. More to the point of this chapter, the more democratic world of today not only supports US foreign-policy goals, normative as well as geopolitical, but also mobilizes social forces with goals that are incompatible with those of the US government. This is clearly evident within the IGO and NGO communities that have formed a central element of transnational civil society. Many reasons account for this outcome, including the gap between the traditional US conception of democracy, based largely upon the notion of individual liberty and legal equality, and the more widespread conception by other governments of democracy as also including state-supported efforts to enhance material equality.

In sum, the historic patterns of behavior outlined in *The Dominion of War* remain clearly visible in the formulation and conduct of US foreign policy today. The United States continues to pursue a greater scope of world power, it does so by relying heavily on military force, and it justifies such actions on the moral grounds of democratic liberation. This consistent pattern of behavior makes the lessons of *The Dominion of War* particularly vital as the US government struggles to extend its primacy in the turbulent new millennium. Overcoming these challenges will be very difficult, however, as cultural habits and bureaucratic inertia are notoriously resilient and the external environment becomes ever more complex and resistant to US manipulation.

As the United States has discovered in Iraq, as in Vietnam, military superiority and "hard power" do not automatically lead to satisfactory foreign-policy outcomes. Of greater importance today is "soft power,"[113] or the power of ideas and the appeal of a nation's political and social values. The ascendance of the United States to global primacy owes at least as much to its soft power than to military coercion, especially in an age of asymmetrical warfare whose weaker antagonists exploit non-military assets, including popular sympathy, to mitigate deficiencies in resources and firepower. But even in the absence of the unilateral turn in US foreign policy and widespread opposition to recent US actions, the expectation of global consensus as a result of global democratization is as misguided as the presumption of universal US moral principles and foreign-policy interests.

The United States, in short, faces both the fulfillment and contradictions of its historic mission to achieve primacy in the system of states. Reconciling those contradictions, within American society and government, will be vital if the United States is to overcome the paradox of its own world power.

Notes

1 Thomas A. Bailey, *A Diplomatic History of the American People* (New York: F.S. Crofts, 1940); William Appleman Williams, *The Tragedy of American Diplomacy* (New York: Marzani & Munsell, 1959); John Lewis Gaddis, *Strategies of Containment: a Critical Appraisal of Postwar American National Security Policy* (New York: Oxford University Press, 1982); Walter McDougall, *Promised Land, Crusader*

State: the American Encounter with the World Since 1776 (Boston: Houghton Mifflin, 1997). See also Jutta Weldes, *Constructing National Interests: the United States and the Cuban Missile Crisis* (Minneapolis: University of Minnesota Press, 1999), and David Campbell, *Writing Security: United States Foreign Policy and the Politics of Identity* (Minneapolis: University of Minnesota Press, 1992).

2 See Kenneth B. Waltz, *Theory of International Relations* (Reading, MA: Addison-Wesley, 1979); ibid., *Man, the State, and War: a Theoretical Analysis* (New York: Columbia University Press, 1959).

3 Robert Gilpin, *War and Change in World Politics* (Princeton: Princeton University Press, 1981).

4 Paul Kennedy, *The Rise and Fall of the Great Powers: Economic Change and Military Conflict from 1500 to 2000* (New York: Random House, 1987).

5 These pressures, it should be noted, do not diminish a third, *individual* level of analysis. It is obviously critical who holds the keys to such formidable world power, a point contradicted by only the most rigid structural determinists. A case can be made, however, that voters' electoral choices, themselves a subject for political psychology, are intimately linked to societal values. In this regard it is worth emphasizing that the two post-Cold War US presidents, George W. Bush and Bill Clinton, came to power with little world experience or apparent interest in foreign policy as a primary concern of their administrations. An additional question to be considered is to what extent such indifference toward world politics as expressed by US leaders, a curious phenomenon in the world's most powerful state, contributes to the paradox of American power. See Daniel Byman and Kenneth Pollack, "Let Us Now Praise Great Men: Bringing Statesmen Back In," *International Security* 24 (Spring 2001): 107–146.

6 See Steven W. Hook and John Spanier, *American Foreign Policy since World War II*, 15th edn (Washington, DC: CQ Press, 2004).

7 Fred Anderson and Andrew R.L. Cayton, *The Dominion of War: Empire and Liberty in North America, 1500–2000* (New York: Viking, 2005), 423, 424.

8 Lisa L. Martin, "An Institutionalist View: International Institutions and State Strategies," in *International Order and the Future of World Politics*, T.V. Paul and John A. Hall (eds) (New York: Cambridge University Press, 1999), 78–98; James G. March and Johan P. Olsen, *Rediscovering Institutions: the Organizational Basis of Politics* (New York: Free Press, 1989).

9 G. John Ikenberry, *After Victory: Institutions, Strategic Restraint, and the Rebuilding of Order after Major Wars* (Princeton: Princeton University Press, 2001).

10 Graham Allison and Philip Zelikow, *Essence of Decision: Explaining the Cuban Missile Crisis*, 2nd edn (New York: Longman, 1999).

11 National Commission on Terrorist Attacks Upon the United States, "The 9/11 Commission Report" (2004). Online, available at: www.911commission.gov.

12 George Kennan, *American Diplomacy, 1900–1950* (Chicago: University of Chicago Press, 1951), 59.

13 Charles Krauthammer, "The Unipolar Moment," *Foreign Affairs* 70 (Winter 1990–1991): 23–33.

14 Stephen E. Ambrose, *Rise to Globalism: American Foreign Policy Since 1938* (New York: Penguin Books, 1988).

15 Richard Grimmett, "Instances of Use of United States Armed Forces Abroad, 1798–2001," Washington, DC: Congressional Research Service, February 5, 2002.

16 These regional military commands cover North America (USNORTHCOM); South America (USSOUTHCOM); an arc connecting western Africa through Europe and across Russia (USEUCOM); the region surrounding the Persian Gulf (USCENTCOM), and southeast Asia and Australia (USPACOM).

17 US Department of Defense, *Base Structure Report: Fiscal Year 2003 Baseline* (Washington, DC: Department of Defense, 2003).

18 Steven W. Hook and David Rothstein., "The Global Arms Market after September 11th: New Rationales and Old Concerns about U.S. Export Policy," in *Guns and Butter: the Political Economy of International Security*, Peter J. Dombrowski (ed.) (Boulder: Lynne Rienner, 2005), 153–178.

19 Center for Defense Information, "Last of the Big Time Spenders: U.S. Military Budget Still the World's Largest and Growing" (2003). Online, available at: www.cdi.org/program/index/ cfm?/ProgramID=15&issueID=34.

20 Richard F. Grimmett, "Conventional Arms Transfers to Developing Nations, 1996–2003." Washington, DC: Congressional Research Service, August 29, 2005.

21 World Bank, *World Development Indicators* (New York: Oxford University Press, 2005).

22 The concept of hegemony rather than empire is used in this chapter as the former term better describes the goal of the United States to establish spheres of influence without assuming sovereign control over territories outside of the United States. The colonization of the Philippines was a stark exception to this rule.

23 Robert W. Tucker and David C. Hendrickson, *Imperial Temptations: the New World Order and America's Purpose* (New York: Council on Foreign Relations, 1992).

24 Melvyn Leffler, *A Preponderance of Power: National Security, the Truman Administration, and the Cold War* (Stanford: Stanford University Press, 1992), 19.

25 "Excerpts from Pentagon's Plan: Prevent the Re-emergence of a New Rival," *New York Times* (March 8, 1992), A14.

26 The White House, "The National Security Strategy of the United States of America" (September 2002). Online, available from: www.thewhitehouse. gov/nsc/nss.pdf.

27 Michael Hirsh, *At War With Ourselves: Why America is Squandering its Chance to Build a Better World* (New York: Oxford University Press, 2003), 27.

28 Clifford Geertz, *The Interpretation of Cultures: Selected Essays* (New York: Basic Books, 1973), 89.

29 Charles Lockhart, *The Roots of American Exceptionalism: Institutions, Culture, and Policies* (New York: Palgrave Macmillan, 2003).

30 "Culturalists" who have studied the United States have advanced diverse, but often overlapping, conceptions of the key elements of the nation's political culture. To Samuel P. Huntington, "American Ideals Versus Institutions," *Political Science Quarterly* 97 (Spring 1982): 14, the "American Creed" consists of constitutionalism, individualism, liberalism, democracy, and egalitarianism. Herbert McClosky and John Zaller, *The American Ethos: Public Attitudes Toward Capitalism and Democracy* (Cambridge: Harvard University Press, 1984), identified capitalism and democracy as two "traditions of belief" that have "dominated the life of the American nation from its inception." More recently, Seymour Martin Lipset, *American Exceptionalism: a Double-Edged Sword* (New York: W.W. Norton, 1996), based the "ideology" of the United States upon five concepts: liberty, egalitarianism, individualism, populism, and laissez-faire. This conceptual ambiguity, combined with the inherent difficulties in "measuring" political culture, is a central problem raised by critical international relations scholars.

31 For a critique, see Joseph Lepgold and Timothy McKeown, "Is American Foreign Policy Exceptional? An Empirical Analysis," *Political Science Quarterly* 110 (Fall 1995): 369–403.

32 Bernard Bailyn, *The Origins of American Politics* (New York: Vintage, 1968), 52.

33 This quote, attributed to Massachusetts Governor John Winthrop, is from Loren Baritz, *City on a Hill: a History of Ideas and Myths in America* (New York: John Wiley and Sons, 1964), 17.

34 Quoted in Robert W. Tucker and David C. Hendrickson, *Empire of Liberty: the Statecraft of Thomas Jefferson* (New York: Oxford University Press, 1990), 30.

35 McDougall, *Promised Land, Crusader State*, 112.

36 Quoted in Gideon Rose, "Democracy Promotion and American Foreign Policy," *International Security* 25 (Winter 2000–2001): 186.

37 Quoted in ibid., 187.

38 Pew Research Center for the People and the Press, "Foreign Policy Attitudes Now Driven by 9/11 and Iraq" (2004). Online, available from: people-press.org/reports/display.php3? ReportID=222, 23. This view is most strongly held (86 percent) among white evangelical Protestants, a key part of George W. Bush's electoral base in 2000 and 2004. See ibid., 25.

39 Ronald Inglehart, Miguel Basanez, and Alejandro Moreno, *Human Values and Beliefs: a Cross-Cultural Sourcebook* (Ann Arbor: University of Michigan Press, 1998).

40 Daniel Yankelovich, "Poll Positions," *Foreign Affairs* 84 (September–October 2005): 2–16. This "divine divide" closely parallels a second cleavage in public opinion – party identification – with Republicans self-identifying as more regular church goers and stronger supporters of current US foreign policies. The religious dimension has not been as strong in the past, and it reinforces a deepening polarization in public opinion in which few survey respondents take moderate or undecided positions. Thus the presumed consensus of Americans in their world views and preferences for US foreign policy, a basic presumption of the exceptionalist thesis, is lacking in current public as well as government discourse.

41 David Skidmore, "Understanding the Unilateralist Turn in U.S. Foreign Policy," *Foreign Policy Analysis* 2 (July 2005): 207–228.

42 See Gabriel Almond, *The American People and Foreign Policy* (New York: Harcourt, Brace, 1950), and Thomas A. Bailey, *The Man on the Street: the Impact of American Public Opinion on Foreign Policy* (New York: Macmillan, 1948).

43 Walter Russell Mead, *Special Providence: American Foreign Policy and How It Changed the World* (New York: Knopf, 2001), 7.

44 These survey results are drawn from Michael X. Delli Carpini and Scott Keeter, *What Americans Know About Politics and Why it Matters* (New Haven: Yale University Press, 1996).

45 US Department of Education, *The Nation's Report Card, 2001* (Washington, DC: Office of Educational Research and Improvement, US Department of Education, 2001).

46 Almond, *The American People and Foreign Policy*, 71.

47 John E. Rielly (ed.), *American Public Opinion and U.S. Foreign Policy* (Chicago: Chicago Council on Foreign Relations, 1999), 11.

48 Richard Sobel, *The Impact of Public Opinion on U.S. Foreign Policy Since Vietnam* (New York: Oxford University Press, 2001).

49 Steven Kull and I.M. Destler, *Misreading the Public: the Myth of a New Isolationism* (Washington, DC: Brookings Institution Press, 1999).

50 Pew Research Center, "Foreign Policy Attitudes," 38.

51 Chicago Council on Foreign Relations, "Global Views 2004: American Public Opinion and Foreign Policy" (2004). Online, available from: www.ccfr.org/globalviews2004, 18.

52 Kull and Destler, *Misreading the Public*.

53 Steven Kull, Clay Ramsay, and Evan Lewis, "Misperceptions, the Media, and the Iraq War," *Political Science Quarterly* 118 (Winter 2003–2004): 569–598.

54 Alexander Todorov and Anesu Mandisodza, "Public Opinion on Foreign Policy," *Public Opinion Quarterly* (Fall 2004): 343.
55 Chicago Council on Foreign Relations and the Program on International Policy Attitudes, "The Hall of Mirrors: Perception and Misperception in the Congressional Foreign Policy Process" (2004). Online, available from: www.ccfr.org/globalviews2004.
56 Pew Research Center, "Foreign Policy Attitudes."
57 James Kitfield, *War and Destiny: How the Bush Administration in Foreign and Military Affairs Redefined American Power* (Washington, DC: Potomac Books, 2005), 346.
58 Doris A. Graber, *Mass Media and American Politics*, 6th edn (Washington, DC: CQ Press, 2002).
59 Wilson Dizard, Jr., *Digital Diplomacy: U.S. Foreign Policy in the Information Age* (Westport: Praeger, 2001).
60 Magazine Publishers of America, "Fact Sheet: Average Circulation for Top 100 ABC Magazines 2001. Online, available from: www.magazine.org.
61 Edward Herman and Noam Chomsky, *Manufacturing Consent: the Political Economy of the Mass Media* (New York: Pantheon, 1988). See also Daniel C. Hallin, The *"Uncensored War": the Media and Vietnam* (New York: Oxford University Press, 1986).
62 Chris Mooney, "The Editorial Pages and the Case for War: Did Our Leading Newspapers Set Too Low a Bar for a Preemptive Attack?" *Columbia Journalism Review* 42 (March–April 2004): 29.
63 See Bill Katovsky and Timothy Carlson (eds), *Embedded: the Media at War in Iraq* (Guilford: Lyons Press, 2003). Fox News emerged from the war as the most popular cable news network – and the most supportive of the Bush administration's war effort. Among news consumers, the viewers of Fox News were most enthusiastic about Operation Iraqi Freedom, but also the most likely to exaggerate the threat posed by Saddam Hussein's regime. A prominent survey found that among Fox viewers, "greater attention to news modestly *increased* the likelihood of misperception." See Kull, Ramsay, and Lewis, "Misperceptions, the Media, and the Iraq War," 585–586.
64 See Pippa Norris, Montague Kern, and Marion Just (eds), *Framing Terrorism: the News Media, the Government, and the Public* (New York: Routledge, 2003).
65 Robert M. Entman, *Projections of Power: Framing News, Public Opinion, and U.S. Foreign Policy* (Chicago: University of Chicago Press, 2004); David A. Lewis and Roger P. Rose, "The President, the Press, and the War-Making Power: an Analysis of Media Coverage Prior to the Persian Gulf War," *Presidential Studies Quarterly* 32 (September 2002): 559–571.
66 Michael Hunt, *Ideology and U.S. Foreign Policy* (New Haven: Yale University Press, 1987).
67 John Lewis Gaddis, *Surprise, Security, and the American Experience* (Cambridge, MA: Harvard University Press, 2004), 25.
68 Ikenberry, *After Victory.*
69 Fears of abandonment were greater than domination at the time since the United States, by its democratic nature and stated intentions, would be a *benign* hegemon.
70 See Skidmore, "Understanding the Unilateralist Turn," 213.
71 Pat Buchanan, *The Great Betrayal: How American Sovereignty and Social Justice Are Being Sacrificed to the Gods of the Global Economy* (Boston: Little, Brown, 1998).
72 Domestic issues dominated the 2000 presidential race between Bush and Vice President Al Gore. In the 2004 election, even as the United States was at war in Iraq and Afghanistan, the outcome of the election was attributed to public differences over domestic social issues, including abortion and gay rights.

73 See Condoleezza Rice, "Promoting the National Interest," *Foreign Affairs* 79 (January–February 2000): 45–62.
74 Pew Research Center, "Foreign Policy Attitudes."
75 See Stephen M. Walt, *The Origins of Alliances* (Ithaca: Cornell University Press, 1987). Russo-Chinese solidarity has been institutionalized through the Shanghai Cooperation Organization, also involving several countries in Central Asia, whose ambition includes diminishing the degree of US primacy in the post-Cold War balance of power.
76 Harold K. Jacobson, *Networks of Interdependence: International Organizations and the Global Political System* (New York: Knopf, 1979).
77 See Peter Evans and Theda Scocpol (eds), *Bringing the State Back In* (New York: Cambridge University Press, 1985).
78 Stephen D. Krasner, *Defending the National Interest: Raw Materials, Investments and U.S. Foreign Policy* (Princeton: Princeton University Press, 1978).
79 Huntington, "American Ideals versus Institutions," 18. This concern dates back to Alexis de Tocqueville (1835), who found democratic governments "decidedly inferior to others." See Tocqueville, *Democracy in America*, J.P. Mayer (ed.) (New York: Perennial Library, 1988), 228.
80 For example, Sven Steinmo, "American Exceptionalism Reconsidered: Culture or Institutions?" in Lawrence C. Dodd and Calvin Jillson (eds), *The Dynamics of American Politics: Approaches and Interpretations* (Boulder: Westview Press, 1994).
81 John W. Kingdon, *America the Unusual* (New York: St. Martin's, 1999); Steven R. Smith, "The Role of Institutions and Ideas in Health Care Policy," *Journal of Health Politics, Policy and Law* 20 (1995): 385–389.
82 Kingdon, *America the Unusual*, 80.
83 Amy B. Zegart, *Flawed by Design: the Evolution of the CIA, JCS, and NSC* (Stanford: Stanford University Press, 1999), 53.
84 Edward S. Corwin, *The President: Office and Powers, 1787–1957: History and Analysis of Practice and Opinion*, 4th edn (New York: New York University Press, 1957), 171.
85 Huntington, "American Ideals versus Institutions."
86 US Commission on National Security/21st Century, "Roadmap for National Security: Imperatives for Change" (2001). Online, available from: www.nssg.gov/Reports.html. Several federal agencies issued dire warnings in the spring and summer of that year, including a President's Daily Brief entitled, "Bin Laden Determined to Strike in US." The White House, "The President's Daily Briefing," August 6, 2001 (Washington, DC: The White House, 2001).
87 Warren E. Miller and Donald E. Stokes, "Constituency Influence in Congress," *American Political Science Review* 57 (March 1963): 56.
88 Barbara Hinckley, *Less Than Meets the Eye* (Chicago: University of Chicago Press, 1994), 13.
89 Bert Rockman, "America's Departments of State: Irregular and Regular Syndromes of Policy Making," *American Political Science Review* 75 (December 1981): 911–927.
90 Ivo Daalder and I.M. Destler, *A New NSC for a New Administration, Policy Brief 68* (Washington, DC: Brookings, 2000), 7.
91 Quoted in Richard Morris, *Great Presidential Decisions* (Greenwich: Fawcett, 1966), 43–44.
92 US Department of State, *A Short History of the U.S. Department of State, 1781–1981* (Washington, DC: US Government Printing Office, 1981), 9–10.
93 See Nicholas Lemann, "The Next World Order: the Bush Administration May Have a Brand-new Doctrine of Power," *The New Yorker* (April 1, 2002): 42–48.

94 Bob Woodward, *Plan of Attack* (New York: Simon and Schuster, 2004).
95 To Zegart, *Flawed by Design*, the CIA and other post-war agencies were "flawed by design" because of the prevalence of bureaucratic self-interests, a lack of congressional oversight, and a lack of public attention during this institution-building process.
96 Condoleezza Rice, "Testimony of Condoleezza Rice Before 9/11 Commission," *New York Times* (April 8, 2004), A6.
97 Bruce B. Auster and David E. Kaplan, "What's Really Wrong with the CIA?" *US News and World Report* (June 1, 1998), 27.
98 See James Bamford, *A Pretext for War: 9/11, Iraq, and the Abuse of America's Intelligence Agencies* (New York: Doubleday, 2004).
99 Douglas T. Stuart, "Ministry for Fear: the Evolving Debate over Reform of the U.S. National Security Bureaucracy," paper presented at the annual meeting of the International Studies Association, March 24, 2002, 14.
100 See William T. Gormley and Steven J. Balla, *Bureaucracy and Democracy* (Washington, DC: CQ Press, 2004).
101 See www.publicintegrity.org.
102 Michael Crowley, "Playing Defense: Bush's Disastrous Homeland Security Department," *New Republic* (March 16, 2004): 17.
103 Markle Foundation, "National Security in the Information Age," Task Force Report (2003). Online, available from: www.markletaskforce.org.
104 Gilmore Commission, "Forging America's New Normalcy: Securing Our Homeland, Protecting Our Liberty," Task Force Report (2003). Online, available from: www.rand.org/nsrd/terrpanel.
105 Karin von Hippel, "Democracy by Force: a Renewed Commitment to Nation Building," *Washington Quarterly* 23 (Winter 2000): 95–112.
106 Francis Fukuyama, *State Building: Governance and World Order in the 21st Century* (Ithaca: Cornell University Press, 2004).
107 Tony Smith, *America's Mission: the United States and the Worldwide Struggle for Democracy in the Twentieth Century* (Princeton: Princeton University Press, 1994).
108 Steven W. Hook, "Building Democracy Through Foreign Aid: the Limitations of United States Political Conditionalities, 1992–1996," *Democratization* 5 (Autumn 1998): 156–180.
109 Fareed Zakaria, "The Rise of Illiberal Democracy," *Foreign Affairs* 76 (November–December 1997): 22–43.
110 Thomas Carothers, *Aiding Democracy Abroad: the Learning Curve* (Washington, DC: Carnegie Endowment for International Peace, 1999), 306.
111 Anderson and Cayton, *The Dominion of War*, 423.
112 See Freedom House, *Freedom in the World* (New York: Freedom House, 2004).
113 Joseph S. Nye, Jr., *Soft Power: the Means to Success in World Politics* (New York: Public Affairs, 2004).

9 Soft power, hard power, and the Pax Americana

Lawrence Sondhaus

Editor's introduction

This chapter examines the nature of US power under the post-Cold War Pax Americana, critiquing the neoliberal premise that soft power now matters more than traditional hard power. The author concludes that soft power theory has significant weaknesses, some of which may be traced to Joseph Nye's aversion to long-cycle theory, others to the general liberal preference to play down the significance of military strength in the international arena. Just as the soft power aspects of British hegemony ultimately could not save the Pax Britannica a century ago, the soft power aspects of US hegemony today are no more likely to be decisive in the long run.

The present debate over the nature of the power of the United States, and of power in the international arena in general, dates from the eve of the collapse of the Soviet Union, when Samuel P. Huntington published an article in the winter 1988–1989 issue of *Foreign Affairs* in response to Paul Kennedy, whose best-selling book, *The Rise and Fall of the Great Powers* (1987), contended that "imperial overstretch" had caused the United States to fall into "relative decline," just as similar over-commitments inevitably had brought about the decline of all other hegemons.[1] Far from being alone, Kennedy reflected the tendency of Western experts of the mid-1980s to take for granted that the US was in some sort of state of decline, locked in a permanent Cold War stalemate with the Soviet Union and certainly losing its economic competition with Japan. Huntington disagreed. While the USSR was a "one-dimensional superpower," warranting the designation only because of its military might, and Japan likewise was a superpower only in the economic sense, Huntington suggested that the sheer diversity of American power made the United States uniquely immune to decline. Foreshadowing the liberal soft power arguments of the 1990s, Huntington observed that the US "ranks extraordinarily high in almost all the major sources of national power: population size and education, natural resources, economic development, social cohesion, political stability, military strength, ideological appeal, diplomatic alliances, [and] technological achievement."[2]

Joseph Nye joined Huntington in criticizing Kennedy's work, and in doing so focused on the non-traditional aspects of power that made Huntington's list. Co-author with Robert Keohane of *Power and Interdependence* (1977), Nye already had established himself as a leading critic of realist concepts of power by the time *The Rise and Fall of the Great Powers* appeared in print. Writing during the brief period of détente, Keohane and Nye laid the foundation for subsequent neo-liberal opposition to realism by proposing a theory of "complex interdependence." They argued that military force mattered less than it had in the past and really only mattered most when there were "no constraints on [a state's] choice of instruments,"[3] in other words, only on the rare occasions when international regimes collapsed and total war broke out. Nye subsequently articulated the concept of soft power in a book and two articles published in 1990,[4] using the term to refer to all aspects of power beyond military and economic measures. Initially he labeled the concepts of hard power and soft power as "command power" and "co-optive power," defining the latter as "getting others to want what you want." In elaborating upon the concepts, however, he quickly introduced the terminology that would endure: "culture, ideology, and institutions ... can be thought of as soft power, in contrast to the hard command power usually associated with tangible resources like military and economic strength."[5] Nye's optimistic assessment of the soft power of the US and the likelihood that it would peacefully transform the world soon became the central pillar of the post-Cold War iteration of what Fred Anderson and Andrew Cayton have called "the American faith that other peoples, if offered the chance, will voluntarily adopt political systems and values consistent with those of the United States."[6]

Liberals quickly rallied behind soft power theory while realists predictably rejected it. Structural realists such as Christopher Layne characterized the standard list of examples of soft power as "second-image factors," not significant enough to be "reasons to take an optimistic view of the future," while others, most notably Aaron Friedberg, questioned the validity of the liberal faith in the inherent attractiveness of "western ideals and values," especially in the Muslim world.[7] Realist criticism aside, Nye's case suffered from significant weaknesses. Much to the detriment of his overall argument, Nye, like Kennedy, used history selectively to make his case. Indeed, his leading past examples of the diverse and changing nature of state power all proved to be problematic. Like the United States in the twentieth century, his earlier cases (Spain in the sixteenth century, the Netherlands in the seventeenth, France in the eighteenth, and Britain in the nineteenth) each exercised soft power in a cultural, ideological, and/or institutional sense, but each also had a formidable army and/or navy, at least by the standards of its century of predominance.[8] Because the most successful practitioners of soft power have also wielded hard power, as examples of the importance of soft power over hard power they are inconclusive or unconvincing. Yet the absence of a firm foundation in historical reality did not deter Nye and his followers. In just over a decade, Nye himself went from asserting that soft power was "just as important" as hard power, to arguing that it was "the means to success in world politics."[9] In contrast to Huntington's plausible observation that a state with a diverse power base (including soft power as well as hard) is more likely to rise to a position of dominance and, once there, less vulnerable to decline, they made it their cause to argue that soft power mattered more than hard power.

The notion that military power would no longer matter so much gained currency in the early post-Cold War world not only among liberal internationalist intellectuals, but also among the political leaders of the principal military allies of the United States. In the world of academia and think-tanks, the end of the Cold War freed international security studies from the bean-counting straitjacket of conceptualizing power in terms of nuclear warheads and other measures of military superiority. Meanwhile, in the real world, the demise of the Soviet Union eliminated the original and primary motive for the existence of the North Atlantic Treaty Organization (NATO), and created an opportunity for its European members – almost all of whom were members of the European Union (EU) – to chart their own course in international affairs. They were particularly well-situated to do so. Indeed, in his *Foreign Affairs* article of 1988–1989, Huntington went against the conventional wisdom of the time, which held that Japan posed the greatest threat to the dominant position of the United States, and argued instead that "if the next century is not the American century it is most likely to be the European century," because a united Europe would possess the most diverse base of power in the world other than that of the US. Indeed, "a federation of democratic, wealthy, socially diverse, mixed-economy societies would be a powerful force on the world scene."[10] But within NATO, Canada became the first individual member to publicly embrace soft power as a cornerstone of its foreign policy. During the tenure of Foreign Minister Lloyd Axworthy (1996–2000), Canadian foreign policy emphasized the use of soft power tactics not only in the service of Canada's interests but to serve the overall goal of "human security." His leading critics charged that the already underfunded Canadian Forces would soon become completely irrelevant, but Axworthy ultimately supported Canada's participation in the Kosovo campaign of 1999, condoning the use of hard power in the service of the "human security" goal of stopping Serbian atrocities against ethnic Albanians.[11] The Kosovo crisis, and the inability of the leading EU countries to resolve it without the military leadership of the United States, led to a renewed (though often grudging) appreciation of the continuing relevance of hard power in Europe as well as in Canada, an appreciation further reinforced in the wake of the terrorist attacks on the United States on September 11, 2001, and the subsequent US military campaign in Afghanistan, where European and Canadian troops fought alongside their American allies.[12]

Pax Britannica, Pax Americana

Some scholars date the Pax Americana from 1945, when the United States emerged from World War II as the only nuclear power, with an economy that produced roughly half of the world's industrial goods. Between 1944 and 1949, the US laid the foundation for the postwar capitalist economy in the Bretton Woods system, sponsoring the World Bank and International Monetary Fund; took the lead in establishing the United Nations, headquartered on its own soil; and established NATO, the prototype for other, less successful Western or pro-Western alliances. But, by the end of 1949, the Cold War had clearly begun, the Soviet Union had joined the nuclear club, and China – at the time, home to a quarter of humanity – had become communist. Some continued to use the term Pax Americana at least to describe the military and economic structures under which the Western world lived, but throughout the Cold War, the United States clearly did not enjoy the sort of global hegemony that warranted the label. To the few who still used the term, the Pax Americana ended in 1973, when the US withdrawal from Vietnam coincided with the ultimate breakdown of the gold-backed regime of fixed exchange rates under the Bretton Woods system.[13] The collapse of the Soviet Union did not bring its immediate revival; indeed, it became fashionable, especially in neo-realist circles, to predict that a multipolar system would re-emerge to replace the bipolar world of the Cold War.[14] Only slowly did the experts accept the reality that they were witnessing after the Persian Gulf War and collapse of the Soviet Union in 1991 – that the US was stronger than ever, hegemon over a unipolar world, policing the planet in a true Pax Americana that had just begun. A cursory check of the hundred or so books published as of 2006 with Pax Americana in the title bears this out. Roughly one-third appeared before 1991, one-third in the years 1991–2001, and one-third in the years 2002–2006. Reflecting the widespread interest in, and backlash against, the assertive post-9/11 behavior of the United States, the thirty-five works published in 2002–2006 include twenty in six languages other than English. As Matthew Fraser noted in 2003, "the new global reality of a Pax Americana is a fact that cannot easily be contradicted."[15]

The flaws in Nye's use of history are perhaps most glaring in his insistence that the present Pax Americana bears no resemblance to the Pax Britannica of a century or more ago. Indeed, from 1990 onward he consistently rejected what he called "inappropriate analogies between the [post-Cold War] United States and Great Britain in the late nineteenth century."[16] Nye's strong opposition to long-cycle theory, as articulated by George Modelski in *Long Cycles in World Politics* (1987), caused him to exaggerate this point, as if to admit otherwise would be to concede that the present Pax Americana would last only a few decades more, and would be succeeded by "hegemonic conflict with its attendant world wars," repeating the bloodshed of 1914–1945 that followed the breakdown of the

Pax Britannica.[17] Instead, he insisted that "there has been no global, system-wide hegemon during the past two centuries. Contrary to the myths about Pax Britannica and Pax Americana, British and American hegemonies have been regional and issue-specific rather than general."[18]

In assessing the "issue-specific" hegemony that Britain enjoyed during the Pax Britannica, Nye explained that "Britain was first in the more limited domains of manufacturing, trade, finance, and naval power," ignoring the obvious fact that these "limited domains" were the ones that mattered most.[19] In the case of naval power, Nye criticized Modelski's long-cycle theory specifically on the grounds that it overvalued the naval dimension, not just for nineteenth-century Britain but in the assessment of other hegemons over time.[20] While an extensive critique of long-cycle theory would venture far beyond the scope of this chapter, one of Modelski's strongest points clearly is his appreciation of naval power. Yet instead of recognizing the obvious importance of Britain's naval might, Nye rather simplistically equated overall military expenditure with military capability, and noted that in 1870, when Britain was "at the peak of its relative power," it trailed both Russia and France in military spending. On this basis he concluded that "nineteenth-century Britain was not militarily dominant." He also downplayed Britain's industrial might, pointing out that it trailed the US and Russia in gross national product as of 1870.[21]

But such assertions ignore the obvious: that nineteenth-century Britain, and in particular Britain circa 1870, possessed a far greater degree of usable military power than either France (which was on the verge of being humiliated on its own soil in the Franco-Prussian War) or Russia (which had already been exposed as a paper tiger in the Crimean War, likewise being humiliated on its own soil). While these two powers, according to Nye stronger militarily than Britain, were incapable of projecting power very far (if at all) beyond their own borders, Britain at the same time not only owned outright one-quarter of the world's land surface, but dominated the world's oceans without question and could impose its will anywhere within artillery range of a navigable body of water. Likewise, the agricultural factor inflates the GNP figures for the US and Russia as of 1870, obscuring the fact that Britain at that stage still held a dominant position in industry and manufacturing. Nevertheless, Nye concluded that for the post-Cold War United States, "the situation is quite different from that of Britain at the century's beginning," because while "the United States retains more traditional hard power resources than any other country, [i]t also has the soft ideological and institutional resources to preserve its lead in the new domains of transnational interdependence."[22] This statement, of course, only reflects Nye's lack of understanding of the depth and duration of Britain's domination in industrial technology; in global communication, trade, and transportation; and ironically (given his own soft power sensibilities), in the cultural realm as well.

Throughout the Pax Britannica, France pioneered the application of most new industrial technologies to sea power, but its inferiority to Britain in industrial capability doomed every challenge to failure. The French played a leading role in the introduction of the first (side-paddle) steam warships, screw-propelled battleships, armored battleships, steel cruisers, torpedo boats, and, finally, submarines, in each case pushing the British to higher levels of achievement in order to maintain their leading position. In the face of each of these challenges, Britain emerged from the competition with a quantitative and qualitative lead in the warship type in question. In some cases the French challenge even depended upon British technology. After 1815, expatriate Englishmen established so many machine shops in France that they dominated the early production of steam engines there, and the first truly successful French steam warship, the *Sphinx* (1829), was powered by an engine imported from Britain. Later, after the side-paddle gave way to the screw propeller, France benefited from further transfers of technology during its brief Crimean War alliance with Britain.[23] The nineteenth-century French fleet never commissioned a warship built in Britain, but in this regard it stood alone among the world's navies. As late as the 1890s, the fleets of Germany, Russia, Italy, Austria-Hungary, and the United States each included at least one British-built battleship or cruiser, and all of Japan's largest warships were constructed in Britain. The lesser navies of Europe and the Americas joined those of the great powers in depending heavily upon Britain for warship designs, component parts, or entire ships. Germany's Krupp became the world leader in naval ordnance as of the 1870s and armor production as of the 1890s, but the small battleship *Oldenburg* (1886) was its first built entirely from domestic resources.[24] Even after the turn of the century, when the German navy replaced the French as the most serious challenger to British supremacy, Britain maintained its lead quantitatively and qualitatively, in the latter case owing to its innovative *Dreadnought* (1906) battleship design and concurrent battle-cruiser design, as well as its superior turbine engine and gunnery range-finding technologies.[25]

As early as 1990, Nye asserted that a great deal of American soft power stemmed from the US role as the "hub of transnational communication." As his ideas continued to evolve in the age of the Internet and world wide web, he placed an even greater emphasis on the implications of the "information revolution" for American soft power.[26] But nowhere did he acknowledge that Britain in the last decades of the nineteenth century dominated global communication at least as much, by virtue of having laid most of the world's transoceanic telegraph cables. The British established the first underwater telegraph cable links to the United States and Canada, via Newfoundland, in 1866, to India via the Mediterranean and Red seas in 1870; from India to Australia via Singapore in 1871, with a branch to Hong Kong and Shanghai the same year; and from Australia to New Zealand in 1876. Britain added South Africa to the network via a branch cable down the east coast of Africa from the Red Sea in 1879, and via a second branch down the west coast of Africa from Gibraltar in 1885. By the turn of the century, British companies (subsidized by the government) owned and operated almost three-quarters of the underwater telegraph cables in the world. During the Anglo-Boer War (1899–1902), the British further enhanced their advantage by laying a new, strategically more secure cable from Britain directly to South Africa, then on to Australia via Mauritius, Ceylon and Singapore, and completed their round-the-world network by laying a Pacific Ocean cable from New Zealand to British Columbia. As Daniel Headrick has noted, "the German Reich learned in August 1914, when its cables were cut, that the world communicated on British sufferance."[27] To an increasing extent, the world also communicated in the English language, thanks to the telegraph-based information revolution. Because Britain dominated the global telegraph network, English became a standard operating language worldwide.[28]

Britain also dominated the worldwide flow of people, mail, and goods, thanks to a merchant marine which was by far the world's largest and most modern. While the primary threat to British naval predominance came from France (at least until the turn of the century), for its mercantile marine the greatest challenge came from the United States. In the quarter-century after 1815, the ready availability of inexpensive timber fueled an American boom in the construction of wooden sailing ships that Britain could not match, and by 1840 the British merchant marine accounted for barely 25 percent of the world's tonnage. But the introduction of steam propulsion combined with iron construction, then steel construction, brought a dramatic recovery in the British position, and the devastating effects of the American Civil War on the US merchant marine left it in no shape to continue the challenge. From 1850 until 1914, in any given year between 40 and 50 percent of the world's mercantile tonnage sailed under the British flag, and between 1890 and 1914, British ships carried 50 percent of global maritime trade. Even the ships that did not steam under the British flag were likely to have been built in British shipyards, which accounted for two-thirds of all new merchant vessels in the quarter-century preceding the outbreak of World War I.[29]

While Nye at least selectively looks to the past for hard power examples to compare to the present, in contrasting the United States of the late twentieth century with Britain of the late nineteenth, he underestimates not only the widespread respect and admiration for British ideals and institutions prevalent at that time, but also the "soft" cultural popularity of all things British. Aside from the much-copied British parliamentary system and concepts of individual rights, Britain asserted a tremendous influence over world culture a century before the Beatles. While Britain did not set trends in fashion, music, or art, from Germans going fox hunting to Latin Americans observing tea time, upper-class folk worldwide copied aspects of the lifestyle of the upper class in Victorian and Edwardian Britain. They also embraced British sports and games (polo, cricket, tennis, golf) along with the concept of basing these activities at the socially exclusive "club." Of course, the impact of British sports and games at the elite level paled in scope and significance to their impact at the popular level, where soccer became the world's sport and rugby or its various derivatives (American football, Canadian football, Australian football) likewise became participatory and spectator sports of widespread significance. Furthermore, in such universal pastimes as boxing, horse racing, and the collection of feats of strength that would evolve into track and field, norms and standards of competition originating in Britain became the international norms. On a more general level, the British distinction between athletic professionalism and amateurism spread to the rest of the world in the late nineteenth and early twentieth centuries, as did the general British concepts of healthy competition, fair play, and good sportsmanship.

Thus, contrary to Nye's assertions, British soft power a century ago was as extensive and as significant as American soft power today. But in the end, did it matter? In the light of 1914, all of these soft power considerations that should have worked to Britain's advantage proved to be far less important than traditional hard power considerations. It did not matter that the international networks of trade, industrial technology, and communication had centered on Britain for so long; likewise, the affinity for British elite and popular culture did not prevent Germany and its allies from declaring war on Britain. And after the peace was lost, Britain's traditional hard power advantages proved to be crucial to its success in World War I. The British navy had the resources it needed to contain the German fleet and blockade the North Sea, and the much-maligned British army proved to be resourceful enough and creative enough to take the lead in figuring out how to fight a modern ground war.[30] There certainly is reason to doubt that the present soft power advantages enjoyed by the United States will be any more relevant in preventing a future world conflict than these soft power advantages were for Britain in 1914, and reason to be confident that the hard power advantages embodied in its naval, air, and land forces will continue to be the bedrock of American hegemony in the twenty-first century. No doubt Nye's underappreciation of naval power has helped to blind him to this fact. Like Britain in the heyday of the Pax Britannica, the United States of the early twenty-first century dominates the world's oceans without question. The range of US carrier-based aircraft, ship-based cruise missiles, and ship-based expeditionary forces are factors that potential adversaries within 500 miles of the sea certainly must take into consideration.

Soft power post-9/11

Over the past two decades, academics and analysts have demonstrated a remarkable ability to cling to their favorite theoretical paradigms even when clear evidence from the real world challenges the assumptions upon which those paradigms are based. In the wake of the Cold War and the collapse of communism, proponents of realist theory predicted that Russian leaders would use Russian nationalism as the catalyst to hold together the former Soviet Union by force, and that the leaders of Japan and a reunified Germany would seek to enhance the status of their countries through military power.[31] Indeed, as late as 1993, neo-realist Christopher Layne went so far as to predict "the possibility of hegemonic war" between Japan and the United States.[32] Of course, Russia under Boris Yeltsin allowed the non-Russian republics to secede from the union, fighting (at least in the case of Chechnya) only to preserve the borders of what had been defined as "Russian" within the former USSR. Meanwhile, both Japan and Germany maintained their anti-militarist Cold War cultures, likewise confounding realist theory. Nevertheless, most realists remained faithful to their school. Indeed, in 1996 Peter Katzenstein marveled at the ease with which the realist paradigm had remained dominant, even though it had "woefully fallen short in explaining an important revolution in world politics," the dramatic changes of the years 1989–1991.[33]

Similarly, a decade later the twin shocks of the Kosovo crisis in 1999 (at least for Europe) and the terrorist attacks against the United States on September 11, 2001, cast doubt over the neo-liberal premise that soft power mattered more than hard power, and yet liberal soft power theory, like realist theory, proved to be remarkably resilient. Post 9/11, Nye's arguments remained unchanged. In his article "The Information Revolution and American Soft Power" (2002) and subsequent publications, he made a case for the central significance of soft power to both sides in the war on terror: "September 11 ... dramatized how the information revolution and technological change have ... empowered non-state actors to play a larger role in world politics." At the same time, while acknowledging the protective value of a state's hard power, he contended that "soft power will become increasingly important in preventing terrorists from recruiting supporters."[34] He elaborated upon this theme in his book *Soft Power: the Means to Success in World Politics* (2004), in which he interpreted the success of the terrorist network al Qaeda as an example of how soft power had enabled a non-state actor to become a significant player internationally; indeed, significant enough to strike a painful blow against the United States, a state possessing an unprecedented arsenal of hard power. "Terrorism depends crucially on soft power for its ultimate victory."[35]

Nye's supporters likewise remained unshaken in their convictions. In 2003, Matthew Fraser authored a classic statement of the case for soft power, grounded in the ahistorical assertion that "America's global domination has been achieved largely through non-military means." While conceding that "American hard power is necessary to maintain global stability," Fraser asserted that "American soft power – movies, pop music, television, fast food, fashions, theme parks – spreads, validates, and reinforces common norms, values, beliefs, and lifestyles. Hard power threatens; soft power seduces. Hard power dissuades; soft power persuades."[36] Fraser acknowledged the constructivist position in asserting that "the American Empire, like all empires, is essentially a cultural construction."[37] But his conclusion, that "the role of American soft power consequently has been crucial to the extension and maintenance of American imperial power,"[38] implies a compatibility between the constructivist position and soft power theory that does not necessarily exist. While both would hold that perspective and perception, past as well as present, are of central importance, soft power advocates have been slow to recognize (or have refused to recognize) that socially constructed perspectives and perceptions constitute cultural barriers that impede or prevent other aspects of soft power (e.g. the transmission of good ideas and imitation of good institutions) from working internationally in the way its advocates contend they do.

During and after the US invasion of Iraq in March 2003, soft-power advocates ranked among the most strident critics of the foreign policy of George W. Bush. In contrast to the operation undertaken by his father's administration in 1991, when the US headed a broad coalition whose actions were legitimized by the United Nations, in 2003 Bush led the US into Iraq with the help of a much smaller coalition in a campaign that lacked the support of the UN and (aside from Britain) most of the US's traditional friends in Europe. Assessing the damage after two years, Nathan Gardels argued that "soft power checkmated hard power" in that the soft power of world public opinion had rejected "the US unilateralist approach to Iraq and other issues." He concluded that "America has been demoted from a hegemon to a preponderant power by the public opinion of its own allies."[39] Gardels thus accomplished something that Nye himself had not. Their best efforts notwithstanding, heretofore proponents of soft power had found it difficult to break the perception that soft power was the mashed potatoes alongside the beef steak of hard power on the plate of international relations. Indeed, they had never succeeded in making a persuasive case for a single instance in which soft power had trumped hard power in an international conflict or crisis. By defining the collective anti-American world opinion as soft power, Gardels did just that. Amid the anti-American backlash to the invasion of Iraq, Nye acknowledged that "skeptics of soft power claim that popularity is ephemeral and should not guide foreign policy." He conceded that the image of the US had recovered from previous internationally unpopular military operations, most notably the war in Vietnam, but cautioned nevertheless that "the recent decline in US attractiveness should not be so lightly dismissed."[40] Indeed, an international opinion poll in spring 2006 revealed that in most countries surveyed – even Britain – more people considered the US presence in Iraq a danger to world peace than the nuclear ambitions of Iran.[41]

No reasonable observer, however, would argue that the soft power of public opinion, be it national or international, is as enduring a factor as hard power. A firestorm of public opinion may arise overnight but can also dissipate quickly (though usually not as quickly as it is mobilized). The history of the twentieth century is full of examples of unanticipated economic crises or military actions causing public opinion to turn 180 degrees in a matter of weeks or months, if not faster. In the opening moves of World War II, the devastation wrought by the German Blitzkrieg caused a sea change in the view that most Britons held of the once-popular appeasement policies of the 1930s, and of course the Japanese bombing of Pearl Harbor had a similar effect on the interwar isolationist views held by an overwhelming majority of Americans. More recently, we have seen that a change of leadership within one of the leading states – e.g., the election of Ronald Reagan in 1980, the rise of Mikhail Gorbachev in 1985, Gorbachev's decline and fall in 1989–1991 – likewise can bring about dramatic changes in international public opinion. Few would deny that if John Kerry had defeated George W. Bush in the US presidential election of 2004, the mere fact of the American public's rejection of Bush (even by the narrowest of margins) would have deflated much of the anti-Americanism that had grown since 2002, even before a new Kerry adminis-tration actually implemented any changes in US policy. In contrast to the ephemeral nature of public opinion – which has become more volatile, not less, because of the "information revolution" – it now takes a state a decade or more to build up an internationally significant arsenal of hard power. Once it is built, its significance is likely to endure for at least a gen-eration, even in an age of rapid advancement in military technology.

While the Kosovo crisis and, to a lesser extent, the terrorist attacks of September 11, 2001, did much to persuade the allies of the United States of the continuing relevance of hard power, the near-universal rejection of the US invasion of Iraq in European public and academic opinion reflected a renewed disdain for the use of military force. Canadian opinion was much more divided, however, as critics of the policies of the Axworthy era (1996–2000) grew even harsher in their rejection of soft power. For example, Sean Maloney praised the Martin government's pro-mulgation of a new national security policy for Canada in 2005, which acknowledged "the role of military power [as] a critical factor in the pro-jection of Canadian interests." Maloney considered the new policy "a refu-tation of soft power as championed by … Axworthy and those in the bureaucracy and academic communities who supported him." He alleged that, post-9/11, Canadian soft-power advocates had tried "to retroactively recast Axworthian foreign policy concepts to portray them as less anti-military, after the successful employment of Canadian combat forces in and over Kosovo in 1999–2000 and particularly after operations in Afghanistan."[42]

Of course, the extent to which so many of the world's Muslims identi-fied with al Qaeda's rejection of all things American posed the biggest challenge to soft-power theory post-9/11. For over a decade Nye and his followers had been arguing that the attractiveness of the culture and institutions of the United States was the key to its global power; while this may have been true within the Western world or in East Asia, clearly it was not the case in the Middle East. But Nye labeled as "hard-line skeptics" those who pointed out the obvious fact that "Osama bin Laden and his followers are repelled, not attracted, by American culture and values." In response, Nye contended that American culture and values were not the central issue at all. "The current struggle against Islamist terrorism is not a clash of civilizations," as Samuel Huntington proposed in his often-cited article (1993) and subsequent book (1996) bearing that title; rather, "it is a contest closely tied to the civil war raging within Islamic civilization between moderates and extremists." While the existence of this intra-Islamic conflict cannot be denied, Nye's solution – that the US and the West "will win" the war on terrorism "if they adopt policies that appeal to those moderates and use public diplomacy effectively to communicate that appeal" – is far less plausible.[43] Recent works on US public diplomacy in the Middle East have drawn contradictory conclusions about its effectiveness. While William A. Rugh chronicles the successes of public and cultural affairs officers of the United States Information Agency (USIA) and United States Information Service (USIS) in the Arab world since 1945, Egyptian scholar Emad El-Din Aysha discounts the effectiveness of such efforts, especially since the end of the Cold War. The governments of some Arab states actively aligned with the US during the Cold War, and even more did so after the Cold War, "bandwagoning ... in an effort to gain economic and political advantages." But throughout the Arab world "popular opinion did not bandwagon behind the US."[44]

Mark Proudman has observed that while "soft power may prove effective in intra-Western disputes, it seems less effective when the West faces conflict across what Samuel Huntington has famously identified as civilizational barriers."[45] Those placing their faith in soft power, in the universal appeal of good ideas and good institutions, assume that the goodness of these ideas and institutions can permeate culturally constructed barriers. But the "information revolution" in which Nye has placed great stock has exacerbated this problem rather than solved it. By the onset of the twenty-first century, powerful and influential news media clearly played upon and reinforced the existing prejudices of their audiences in constructing their own distinctive versions of the same reality (such as the US media, al Jazeera, and Agence France-Presse during the war in Iraq). Meanwhile, the Internet proved to be the greatest source of readily available disinformation in human history. In such an atmosphere, among populations already inclined to be anti-American, even the most educated sectors of society have shown a tendency to believe fanciful explanations for local, regional, or international events – often in the form of stories or anecdotes similar to the genre known in American popular culture as the "urban legend" – whenever such explanations cast the US in the role of villain. This tendency is especially pronounced in the Muslim world (but is not uncommon elsewhere, for example in European leftist intellectual circles). Indeed, it is not implausible to argue that the "information revolution" has left the world marketplace of ideas hopelessly polluted with widely believed distortions and disinformation. The technology that Nye and others have assumed would break down traditional culturally con-structed barriers has proven to be just as likely, if not more likely, to rein-force them. In a fair, rational world marketplace of ideas, the soft-power faith in the power of ideas would be more credible, but such a market-place simply does not exist.

"Civilizational barriers" proved not to be the only barriers insufficiently appreciated by Nye and his followers. In his initial articulation of soft-power theory in 1990, Nye concluded that such basic factors as geography and raw materials were "becoming less important" in the post-Cold War world.[46] But the operations in Kosovo in 1999 and Afghanistan in 2001 revealed the continuing importance of geography in strategy. The leading EU countries did not lack the will to intervene militarily in Kosovo but, owing to the factor of geography (even within Europe), without the help of the United States they lacked sufficient air- and sea-lift capacity to deploy significant numbers of troops to the region, and lacked the mili-tary aircraft and aerial tankers to conduct an extensive air campaign, weaknesses that accelerated efforts to form a European Rapid Reaction Force. In contrast, the first weeks and months of the campaign in Afghanistan provided an example of the unique capacities of the US in projectable power. Before alliances were forged and bases obtained in the adjacent Central Asian states of the former Soviet Union, the US effort depended largely upon sea-based air and expeditionary forces off the coast of Pakistan, in the Arabian Sea. As Rear Admiral William Gortney later remarked in reference to his service as commander of a carrier air wing in the Afghan campaign, his pilots "spent four and a half months, 24 hours a day, providing airborne artillery for the troops in Afghanistan," a landlocked country whose southern border is hundreds of miles from the sea.[47]

Meanwhile, in the area of raw materials, oil, of course, hardly declined in importance after 1990. The terrorist attacks of 9/11 and the subsequent US interventions in Afghanistan and Iraq helped to drive oil prices to unprecedented levels, and had the unintended consequence of strength-ening the hand of major oil-producing states in the international arena. Iran, already poised to become relatively more powerful in the Middle East following the elimination of Saddam Hussein's regime, benefited perhaps the most from the windfall of oil revenue, accelerating its nuclear program. Russia, in sharp decline since the collapse of communism, experienced an economic boom and began rebuilding its armed forces. In the Western hemisphere, Hugo Chavez's Venezuela became influential throughout Latin America (and the biggest regional thorn in the side of the US since Fidel Castro's Cuba during the Cold War) thanks to oil money. Oil revenue even affected the relative balance of power within Western Europe; indeed, it is difficult to imagine that Tony Blair's Britain would have been able to follow such an assertive and self-confident foreign policy if the country were not in a position to benefit from the high price of North Sea oil.

Conclusion

In 2004, Nye concluded that "America's success will depend upon our developing a deeper understanding of the role of soft power and developing a better balance of hard and soft power in our foreign policy."[48] In the same vein, early in 2006, Mitchell Smith offered perhaps the best explanation yet of the interrelated nature of the two, arguing that soft power enhanced and legitimized hard power. "The US experience in Iraq suggests that hard power, when used without a patina of soft power, can degrade if it does not swiftly produce the desired result."[49] While there is ample evidence, historical and contemporary, to support this ideal of hard power supported by soft power, there are countless examples (most recently the failed EU mediation of the crisis over Iran's nuclear program in 2005–2006) that soft power not supported by hard power is no power at all.

Mark Proudman has observed that "an emphasis on the importance of military power to international relations is thought in many circles to be unsophisticated, even simplistic," but "if counting divisions and aircraft carriers does not provide a reliable measure of state power, those qualities of culture and ideology that constitute soft power are even more difficult to measure."[50] Indeed, the nebulous nature of soft power has been at the same time its greatest asset and its greatest liability. While proponents of soft power tend to define it so broadly (including, to an increasing extent, economic factors which Nye himself initially left out of the equation) that critics have great difficulty refuting its significance, among political scientists (especially in the US) whose dominant disciplinary culture is quantitative, the "fuzzy" qualitative nature of soft power theory remains its most significant weakness.

This brief discussion of hard power and soft power in the US foreign policy of the current Pax Americana has highlighted the weaknesses of neoliberal arguments concerning the primacy or centrality of soft power, while not necessarily agreeing with the various realist critiques of the concept. It is difficult for a historian to side with either the neo-liberals or the realists, because the adherents of each perspective commonly misinterpret or misuse history (or use it very selectively) in making their case. To the extent that their ideas have shaped the debate on strategic culture, the constructivists offer the only solution fully compatible with the historical record. Perspectives and perceptions, past as well as present, are central to the factors that Nye and others have characterized as soft power. But we must recognize that perspectives are socially constructed, and perceptions are shaped by socially constructed filters or lenses. The strategic culture of the United States historically includes both hard power and soft power tendencies, present to varying degrees in each of Walter Russell Mead's four subcultures of American foreign policy (Hamiltonian, Jeffersonian, Jacksonian, and Wilsonian).[51] While it would be naive to argue that the United States today pursues substantially the same policies as Britain a century ago, the Pax Britannica and Pax Americana have more in common with one another than most international relations specialists – neoliberal or realist – are willing to admit. A historically grounded concept of strategic culture is especially important as a tool to understand the policies of a country such as the United States, which (like France and China) is culturally inclined to believe deeply in the purity or higher nature of its own motives and actions. Realist theory would explain away the evidence of such beliefs as mere rhetorical posturing, but clearly it is not. To accept them as real, rather than dismiss them as a rhetorical cover for a rational reality, helps us to better understand ourselves, our adversaries, and the world in general.

Notes

1 Paul Kennedy, *The Rise and Fall of the Great Powers: Economic Change and Military Conflict from 1500 to 2000* (New York: Random House, 1987), 515.
2 Samuel P. Huntington, "The US – Decline or Renewal?" Foreign Affairs 67, 2 (Winter 1988–1989): 90–91.
3 Robert O. Keohane and Joseph S. Nye, Jr., *Power and Interdependence: World Politics in Transition* (Boston: Little, Brown, 1977), 23, 27.
4 Joseph S. Nye, Jr., *Bound to Lead: the Changing Nature of American Power* (New York: Basic Books, 1990); ibid., "The Changing Nature of World Power," *Political Science Quarterly* 105 (1990): 177–92; ibid., "Soft Power," *Foreign Policy* 80 (1990): 153–171.
5 Nye, *Bound to Lead*, 31–32; ibid., "The Changing Nature of World Power," 181.
6 Fred Anderson and Andrew R.L. Cayton, *The Dominion of War: Empire and Liberty in North America, 1500–2000* (New York: Viking, 2005), 424.
7 Christopher Layne, "The Unipolar Illusion: Why New Great Powers Will Rise," *International Security* 17, 4 (Spring 1993), 51; Aaron L. Friedberg, "The Future of American Power," *Political Science Quarterly* 109 (1994): 17.
8 Nye, *Bound to Lead*, 33–34; ibid., "The Changing Nature of World Power," 183.
9 Nye, "Soft Power," passim; ibid., *Soft Power: the Means to Success in World Politics* (New York: Public Affairs, 2004).
10 Huntington, "Decline or Renewal," 93.
11 Joseph T. Jockel, *The Canadian Forces: Hard Choices, Soft Power* (Toronto: The Canadian Institute of Strategic Studies, 1999), 5–8, 127–128.
12 For European and Canadian perspectives on the impact of Kosovo and 9/11, see David L. Bland, "War in the Balkans: Canadian Style," *Policy Options/Options politiques* (October 1999): 18–21; Paul Cornish and Geoffrey Edwards, "Beyond the EU/NATO Dichotomy: the Beginnings of a European Strategic Culture,"

International Affairs 77 (2001): 587–603; Stine Heiselberg, *Pacifism or Activism: Towards a Common Strategic Culture Within the European Security and Defence Policy?* IIS Working Paper 2003/4 (Copenhagen: Institute for International Studies, 2003); and Florentino Portero, "The Crisis in International Relations: Some Reflections on the European Perspective," Grupo de Estudios Estratégicos, Análisis no. 53, 7 July 2003, Online, available at: www.gees.org/pdf/342/ (accessed 15 May 2005).

13 For example, C.J. Bartlett, *The Rise and Fall of the Pax Americana* (London: Elek, 1974).

14 For example, Layne, "The Unipolar Illusion," 51 and passim.

15 Matthew Fraser, *Weapons of Mass Distraction: Soft Power and American Empire* (New York: St. Martin's Press, 2003), 10.

16 Nye, "Soft Power," 153.

17 Nye, "Soft Power," 171. See George Modelski, *Long Cycles in World Politics* (Seattle: University of Washington Press, 1987).

18 Nye, "The Changing Nature of World Power," 187.

19 Ibid., 186.

20 Ibid., 191.

21 Ibid., 186, 188.

22 Nye, "Soft Power," 171.

23 Lawrence Sondhaus, *Navies in Modern World History* (London: Routledge, 2004), chapter 2.

24 Ibid., 172.

25 Lawrence Sondhaus, *Navies of Europe: 1815–2002* (London: Longman, 2002), 132–135.

26 Nye, "The Changing Nature of World Power," 183; ibid., "The Information Revolution and American Soft Power," *Asia-Pacific Review* 9 (2002): 60–76.

27 Daniel R. Headrick, *The Tools of Empire: Technology and European Imperialism in the Nineteenth Century* (Oxford: Oxford University Press, 1981), 157–164.

28 Sharon Goodman and David Graddol, *Redesigning English: New Texts, New Identities* (London: Routledge, 1996), 207.

29 Headrick, *The Tools of Empire*, 175.

30 See Timothy Travers, *How the War Was Won: Command and Technology in the British Army on the Western Front, 1917–1918* (London: Routledge, 1992).

31 For example, Zbigniew Brzezinski, "The Road to Strasbourg or to Sarajevo? Eastern Europe and the Soviet Union," *Vital Speeches of the Day* 57 (1991): 518–521; John J. Mearsheimer, "Why We Will Soon Miss the Cold War," *The Atlantic* 266, 8 (August 1990): 35–50; Jeffrey E. Garten, *A Cold Peace: America, Japan, Germany, and the Struggle for Supremacy* (New York: Times Books, 1992).

32 Layne, "The Unipolar Illusion," 51.

33 Peter J. Katzenstein (ed.), *The Culture of National Security: Norms and Identity in World Politics* (New York: Columbia University Press, 1996), xi–xii.

34 Joseph S. Nye, Jr., "Hard Power and Soft Power," in *After Terror: Promoting Dialogue among Civilizations*, Akbar Ahmed and Brian Forst (eds) (Cambridge: Polity Press, 2005), 167–168. See also ibid., "Information Revolution," 60–76.

35 Nye, *Soft Power: the Means to Success*, 22.

36 Fraser, *Weapons of Mass Distraction*, 10.

37 Ibid., 262.

38 Ibid.

39 Nathan Gardels, "The Rise and Fall of America's Soft Power," *New Perspectives Quarterly* 22, 1 (Winter 2005): 16.

40 Nye, "The Decline of America's Soft Power," *Foreign Affairs* 83, 3 (May–June 2004): 16.

41 Pew Research Center for the People and the Press, "America's Image Slips, But

Allies Share US Concerns Over Iran, Hamas" (2006). Online, available from: people-press.org/reports/display.php3?ReportID=252.

42 Sean M. Maloney, *The Roots of Soft Power: the Trudeau Government, De-NATOiza-tion, and Denuclearization, 1967–1970* (Kingston, Ontario: Centre for International Relations, Queen's University, 2005), 1.

43 Nye, "The Decline of America's Soft Power," 17. Cf. Samuel P. Huntington, "The Clash of Civilizations?" *Foreign Affairs* 72, 3 (Summer 1993): 22–49; ibid., *The Clash of Civilizations and the Remaking of World Order* (New York: Simon & Schuster, 1996).

44 Cf. William A. Rugh, *American Encounters with Arabs: the "Soft Power" of U.S. Public Diplomacy in the Middle East* (Westport: Praeger Security International, 2006); Emad El-Din Aysha, "September 11 and the Middle East Failure of US 'Soft Power': Globalisation contra Americanisation in the 'New' US Century," *International Relations* 19, 2 (2005): 195.

45 Mark F. Proudman, "Soft Power Meets Hard: the Ideological Consequences of Weakness," in *Coping with the American Colossus*, David Carment, Fen Osler Hampson, and Norman Hillmer (eds) (Oxford: Oxford University Press, 2003), 351.

46 Nye, "The Changing Nature of World Power," 179.

47 Quoted in Otto Kreisher, "Air Wings Built for Two," *Air Force Magazine* (December 2002): 73.

48 Nye, *Soft Power: the Means to Success*, 147; ibid., "Soft Power and American Foreign Policy," *Political Science Quarterly* 119 (2004): 270.

49 Mitchell Smith, "Soft Power Rising: Romantic Europe in the Service of Practical Europe," *World Literature Today* (January–February 2006): 23.

50 Proudman, "Soft Power Meets Hard," 335–336.

51 Lawrence Sondhaus, *Strategic Culture and Ways of War* (London: Routledge, 2006), 63–69; Walter Russell Mead, *Special Providence: American Foreign Policy and How It Changed the World* (New York: Alfred A. Knopf, 2002), passim.

Index

9/11 Commission 171, 185, 187, 189;
  see also World Trade Center

Abrams, Creighton, US general 134, 138
Abu Ghraib scandal (2004) 141, 192
Adae, Carl, US army officer 66
Adams, John, US president 17–18
Adams, John Quincy, US president 2, 177
Adams, Sherman, US politician 100
Afghanistan 51, 121, 173, 180, 189, 203, 211, 213
Africa 161, 206; *see also individual countries*
African-Americans 88–103
Agence France-Presse (AFP) 212
Agnew, Spiro, US politician 133, 138–9
Air Force, US 168n19, 190
Alaska 93
Albania, and Albanians 203
Alexandria, Egypt 19
Alien and Sedition Acts (1798) 17
al Jazeera 51, 212
Allin, Mort, US presidential advisor 139
al Qaeda 51, 55, 174, 179, 209, 211
Ambrose, Stephen, historian 103
American Legion 82
American Revolution (1775–83) 3, 11–12, 14–16, 21, 25–6, 73
Anderson, Fred, historian 1, 9, 37, 89, 135, 140, 169, 171, 191, 202
Anglo-Boer War (1899–1902) 207
Arabs, and Arab states 19, 212
Arabian Sea 213
Army, US 14, 19, 23, 52–3, 70, 74, 81–2, 88–97, 134–5, 168n19, 173–4, 190
Arnold, Benedict, US general 13
atomic weapons *see* nuclear weapons

Atta, Muhammad 55
Australia 33, 93, 173, 206–208
Austria-Hungary *155*, 206
automobile production *156*
Axis powers 110–11, 120, 159, *160*; *see also* Germany; Italy; Japan
Axworthy, Lloyd, Canadian statesman 203, 211
Aylett, William R., Confederate officer 64–5
Aysha, Emad El-Din, political scientist 212

Bailey, Thomas, historian 169
Bailyn, Bernard, historian 175
Baker, James, US statesman 141
bandwagoning 149, 183, 212
Barnett, Ross, US politician 100
Batavia (Djakarta) 19
Bay of Pigs invasion (1961) 117, 121, 189
Beauregard, P.G.T., Confederate general 81
Belgium 12, 77, 80
Belize 39
Bell, Steve, journalist 135–6, 139
Benchley, Peter, author 128
Benton, Reuben C., US army officer 67
Berlin Wall 118–19
Bermuda 93
bin Laden, Osama 48, 51, 174, 189, 212
Bismarck, Otto von, German chancellor 82
Black, Jeremiah S., US politician 44
Blair, Tony, British prime minister 214
Blight, David W., historian 7
Bolton, John, US diplomat 183
Bonaparte, Joseph, king of Spain 12
Bonaparte, Napoleon *see* Napoleon I

Bonin Islands 32
Boorstin, Daniel, historian 2–3, 10n6
Borland, Solon, US diplomat 29–30
Boutwell, Edward B., US naval officer 33, 37
Branch, Taylor, journalist and author 101
Brazil 50
Bretton Woods system 204
Brinkley, David, journalist 131, 144n38
Britain 13–14, 18–23, 25–7, 30, 32, 35, 37–41, 43–4, 46, 48–50, 54, 67, 72, 83, 93–4, 110, 112, 146, 149–51, 154–5, *156*, 157–8, 160–1, 175, 179, 181, 202, 204–8, 210, 214–15; *see also* Pax Britannica
British Columbia 207
Brotherhood of Sleeping Car Porters 92, 99, 101
Brown, John, abolitionist 82
Brown v. *Board of Education* (1954) 91, 98
Browne, Malcolm, journalist 129
Brownell, Herbert, US politician 99
Brownson, Orestes, journalist 39, 46
Bryan, William Jennings, US politician 76
Brzezinski, Zbigniew, US presidential advisor 187
Buchanan, Patrick J., US politician 133, 139
Buchanan, James, US president 37, 43, 45, 47
Buenos Aires 19
Bulge, Battle of the (1944) 88, 94–5, 97, 100
Burk, Robert, historian 103
Burr, Aaron, US vice president 13
Burundi 180
Bush, George, US president 140–1, 180, 182
Bush, George W., US president 4, 47–9, 125, 174–5, 179–80, 182–3, 188–90, 195n5, 198n72, 210–11
Bush Doctrine (2001) 176

Calderón de la Barca, Angel, Spanish diplomat 39, 42
Calhoun, John C., US politician 82
California Gold Rush (1849) 30, 32
Cambodia 127, 134, 139
Canada 13, 18, 20–3, 25, 173, 203, 206, 208, 211
Caribbean Sea 20, 43

Carlisle Commission (1778) 16
Carter, James "Jimmy", US president 187
Cass, Lewis, US politician 43–4
Castle, Henry, US army officer 66
Castro, Fidel, Cuban leader 214
Catherine the Great, Russian empress 12
Catholics, and Catholicism 48–9
cavalry 151–2
Cayton, Andrew, historian 1, 9, 37, 89, 135, 140, 169, 171, 191, 202
Central Intelligence Agency (CIA) 188–9
Ceylon (Sri Lanka) 19, 207
Champlain, Lake 21–2, 25
Chancellor, John, journalist 140
Chavez, Hugo, Venezuelan president 213
Chechnya 209
Cheney, Richard "Dick", US vice president 188
Cherokee 16, 19
Chesapeake Bay 19
Chile 50, 93, 192
China 5, 36, 38, 66, 110, 117, 151, 167n14, 182–3, 199n75, 204, 215
Churchill, Winston, British prime minister 122n7
Cincinnati, Society of 16
Cioffi, Lou, journalist 129
Civil War, American (1861–5) 13, 37, 82, 157, 161, 163, 207; veterans of 64–84
Clarendon, William Frederick Villiers, Earl of, British statesman 37, 40
Clausewitz, Karl von, Prussian general and strategist 140
Clay, Henry, US politician 22
Cleveland, Grover, US president 72
Clinton, Sir Henry, British general 12
Clinton, William "Bill," US president 176, 180, 182, 195n5
Coast Guard, US 188
co-evolutionary argument 148, 151–2, *153*, 161, 163–4
Cold War 97, 106–7, 109, 111–22, 162, 172–4, 176, 180, 182–4, 192, 201, 203–4, 209, 212
Colombia 24, 49
Colson, Charles, US presidential advisor 138–40
Communism, 107, 110, 112–21, 129, 153, 164, 174, 209

Comprehensive Test Ban Treaty
(CTBT) 179
Confederation, Articles of 16
Congress, Continental 14–16
Congress, US 17, 19, 21, 23, 32, 35, 38,
40–1, 95, 117, 132, 138, 162–3, 174,
176, 179, 182–7, 191
Constitution, US (1787) 16–17, 31, 46
constructivism 210, 214–15
Costa Rica 46, 48–50
Cottam, Richard, political scientist 108
Crabb, Henry, US filibuster 39–40
Creek 19
Crimean War (1853–6) 41, 205–6
Cromwell, Oliver, Lord Protector of
England 13
Cronkite, Walter, journalist 128, 131,
137, 140
Crowley, Michael, journalist 191
Cuba 32–5, 37, 39–42, 44–7, 49, 53, 54,
67–9, 71–4, 76, 192, 214
Cuban Missile Crisis (1962) 117–18
Cummins, J.A., Confederate officer 80
Custine, Adam Philippe de, French
general 12

Dallas, George Mifflin, US diplomat
50
Davis, Jefferson, Confederate president
53, 82
Dearborn, Henry, US general 22
Declaration of Independence (1776)
14, 73, 175, 192
Defense Intelligence Agency (DIA) 188
Democratic party 41, 45, 72, 83, 97,
130, 132, 185
Depression *see* Great Depression
Derna, Battle of (1805) 19
détente, US–Soviet (1970s) 202
Dewey, George, US admiral 70
Dillon, Theobald, French general 12
Dobbin, James C., US politician 30
Dole, Robert, US politician 139
Dominican Republic 42
Douglass, Frederick, African-American
leader 35
Dreadnought, British battleship 206
Dulles, John Foster, US statesman
114–16
Dunmore, John, Earl of, governor of
Virginia 20
Du Pont, Samuel Francis, US naval
officer 31
Duvall, Jed, journalist 137

East Asia 212
East India Company, British 19–20
East Indies 19
Eastern Europe 26
Eaton, William, US army officer 19
Ecuador 50, 54
Egerton, Douglas, historian 18
Egypt 19
Eisenhower, Dwight D., US general and
president 88–103, 114–16, 120, 190
El Salvador 46–7, 50
Engels, Friedrich 3
Enlightenment 120
European Rapid Reaction Force 213
European Union (EU) 183, 203,
213–14
Evans, Clement A., Confederate
general 71
exceptionalism, American 1–6, 11,
25–7, 175, 191
expansion and imperialism, American
2, 20, 25, 31, 36–7, 41, 201, 204,
209–10; *see also* Manifest Destiny

Fabens, Joseph W., US diplomat 30–1
Farmer, Don, journalist 132
Farragut Association of Naval Veterans
68
fascism 153, 164
Faubus, Orval, US politician 100, 102
Federal Bureau of Investigation (FBI)
188–9
Federal Emergency Management
Agency (FEMA) 191
Federalist party 16–23
Field, David Dudley, US politician 45
Fiji 33, 37
filibusters 20, 33–5, 37–55
Fillmore, Millard, US president 32
Fitzgerald, Frances, historian 36
Ford Motor Company, and "Fordist"
mass production *154*, 155–6, 159–60,
167n12
Formosa *see* Taiwan
France 2, 13, 17–21, 25–7, 32, 38, 40–1,
43, 47, 49–50, 72, 110, 149, *155–6*,
181, 202, 205–6, 215
Franco-Prussian War (1870–1) 205
Fraser, Matthew, political scientist 204,
209–10
French and Indian War (1754–63) 13, 36
French Revolution (1789) 12, 51
French Revolutionary and Napoleonic
Wars (1792–1815) 12, 22, 27

Friedberg, Aaron, political scientist 202
Fukuyama, Francis, political scientist 5
Fulbright, William, US politician 128

Gaddis, John Lewis, historian 169, 181
Gadsden, James, US diplomat 47, 52
Gandhi, Mohandas (Mahatma) 83, 95
Gardels, Nathan, political scientist 210
Garibaldi, Giuseppe 44
Gates, Horatio, US general 12, 16
General Dynamics corporation 190
George I, king of Great Britain 13
George II, king of Great Britain 13
George III, king of Great Britain 13
Germany 4, 72, 77–80, 82, 96, 109–10,
   113–14, 116, 118, 121, 149, 153–5,
   156, 167n10, 206–9, 211
Gettysburg, Battle of (1863) and
   reunions at 64, 68, 76, 32, 84
Gibraltar 207
Giggans, Jim, journalist 135–7, 139
Gillem, Alvan, US general 95
Gilmore Commission (2003) 191
Gilpin, Robert, political scientist 170
Goldwater–Nichols Act (1986) 190
Good Neighbor Policy 36
Gorbachev, Mikhail, Soviet leader 211
Gordon, John, Confederate general
   81
Gore, Albert, US politician 198n72
Gortney, William, US admiral 213
Gould, Eliga, historian 27
Gramsci, Antonio 3–5
Grand Army of the Republic (GAR) 65,
   67–9, 71, 78, 84
Granger, Lester, African-American
   leader 101
Grant, Ulysses S., US general and
   president 84
Great Depression (1929) 83, 162
Great Lakes 21
Greece 112–13
Greenberg, Amy S., historian 37
Greene, Nathaniel, US general 16
Gregg, David L., US diplomat 35, 46
Greytown (San Juan del Norte) 29–34,
   38, 43–4
Guatemala 46–8, 50, 121, 192

Hagel, Charles "Chuck", US politician
   186
Haiti 12–13, 25, 192
Haldeman, H.R., presidential advisor
   133–4, 138–9

Hamilton, Alexander, US general and
   politician 17, 23, 26
Hamilton, W.D., US army officer 74
Hamiltonian strategic subculture 215
Hammond, William, historian 134
Hartz, Louis, historian 2–3
Hastie, William, US civil servant 92–3
Hawaii 33, 35, 38, 46, 67, 93
Headrick, Daniel, historian 207
hegemonic stability theory 170
Heider, Fritz, psychologist 107–8
Herrmann, Richard, political scientist
   108
Hersh, Seymour M., journalist 55
Hietala, Thomas, historian 36
Hinckley, Barbara, political scientist
   186
Hirsch, Michael, political scientist 174
Hispanic immigrants to US 5
Hitler, Adolf 4, 102
Hoang Xuan Lam, South Vietnamese
   general 136
Ho Chi Minh, North Vietnamese leader
   130
Ho Chi Minh Trail 136
Hofstadter, Richard, historian 2–3
Hoganson, Kristen L., historian 68
Hollins, George N., US naval officer
   29–33, 38
Homeland Security, Department of
   190–1
Honduras 24, 38–9, 44, 46, 50
Hong Kong 38, 206
Horseshoe Bend, Battle of (1814) 19
Howard, Oliver O., US general 70
Hughes, Emmett John, journalist 102
Huntington, Samuel, political scientist
   5–6, 184, 201–3, 212
Hussein, Saddam, Iraqi leader 179–80,
   198n63, 213

Iceland 93
India 5, 177, 189, 206
Indian Ocean 19, 160
Indians *see* Native Americans
Indonesia 173, 192
Industrial revolution 154
interdependence theory 202
International Criminal Court 179, 182
International Monetary Fund (IMF)
   204
Internet, and "information revolution"
   206, 209–13
Iraq 46–7, 51, 121, 140, 176, 189

Iraq War (2003) 125–6, 141, 173, 178–80, 182, 188, 191, 193–4, 210–14
Iran 47, 117, 121, 189, 192, 214
Iran–Contra scandal 187
Ireland 12, 33, 54
isolationism, American 2, 66–7, 211
Islam, and the Muslim world 5, 48, 121, 192–3, 202, 211–13
Israel 179
Italy 44, 67, 153, *155*, 167n10, 206

Jackson, Andrew, US general and president 19
Jackson, Robert, US jurist 184
Jacksonian strategic subculture, 37, 215
Jamaica 38, 54
Japan 32, 36, 109, 153, *156*, 167n10, 173, 201, 203, 206, 209
Jay, John, US diplomat 26
Jefferson, Thomas, US president 15, 17–18, 22, 175, 187
Jeffersonian strategic subculture 215
Jews, American 48, 101
Johnson, Bradley T., Confederate general 71–2
Johnson, Lyndon, US president 117–18, 120, 126–33

Kanagawa, Treaty of (1853) 32
Katrina, hurricane (2005) 174, 191
Katzenstein, Peter, political scientist 209
Kellogg-Briand Pact (1928) 106
Kennan, George, US diplomat and historian 172
Kennedy, John F., US president 103, 117–19
Kennedy, Paul, historian 170, 201–2
Kentucky 17, 22, 34
Kentucky Military Institute 33
Keohane, Robert, political scientist 202
Kerrey, Robert "Bob", US politician 189
Kerry, John, US politician 211
King, Martin Luther, Jr., African-American leader 101–2
Kingdon, John W., political scientist 184
Kinney, Henry L., US filibuster 34, 39–40, 44, 46, 54–5
Kissinger, Henry, US statesman 120, 138, 187
Kitfield, James, political scientist 179
Knox, Henry, US general and politician 16
Korea 66; *see also* North Korea; South Korea

Korean War (1950–3) 97, 176
Kosovo 203, 209, 211, 213
Krupp, armaments manufacturer 206
Kuwait 140
Kyoto Protocol (2005) 179, 182

Laird, Melvin, US defense secretary 134
Laos 132, 134–40
Larson, Arthur, US civil servant and jurist 102
Latin America 36, 44, 46–7, 117, 161, 177, 192, 207, 214; *see also individual countries*
Laurence, John, journalist 129
Layne, Christopher, political scientist 202, 209
League of Nations 106, 176
Leavenworth, Fort, Command and General Staff school at 91
Lee, Fitzhugh, Confederate and US general 70
Lee, Henry, US general 70
Lee, J.C.H., US general 88, 93
Lee, Robert E., Confederate general 70, 81
Lee, Ulysses, historian 92
Leonard, Thomas, historian 46
Letcher, John, US politician 45
Lewis, George, journalist 135–9
liberalism, in international relations theory, 169, 202, 209
Liberia 93
Liholiho, Alexander, Hawaiian prince 35
Lincoln, Abraham, US president 175
Lincoln, Benjamin, US general 12, 15, 24
Lipset, Seymour Martin, historian 5–6
Lloyd George, David, British prime minister 83
Lockheed corporation 190
Long, David F., historian 33
Longchamps affair (1784) 16
long-cycle theory 147, 163, 204–5
Louverture, Toussaint, Haitian leader 18
Love, Eric T., historian 37

MacArthur, Douglas, US general 91
McBride, Harry Alexander, US army officer 93
McCarthy, Joseph, US politician 98
McConnell, Stuart, historian 65
McDougall, Walter, historian 6, 169

McGee, Frank, journalist 128–9
McHenry, Fort, bombardment of (1814) 25
McKinley, William, US president 69–70, 72, 175
Madison, James, US president 21–2
Magruder, Jeb Stuart, US presidential advisor 138
Maine, US battleship 68, 71–2
Maloney, Sean, historian 211
Manifest Destiny 31, 36, 40, 48; *see also* expansion
Marcy, William L., US diplomat 41, 47, 52–4
Marshall, George, US general and statesman 92–3, 95, 112
Marshall Plan (1947) 112
Martin, Paul, Canadian prime minister 211
Martinique 19
Marx, Karl, and Marxism 3, 40; *see also* neo-Marxism
Massachusetts 15, 22, 24
Mauritius 207
Mead, Walter Russell, political scientist 177, 215
Mediterranean Sea 19, 206
merchant marine, US 207
Merk, Frederick, historian 36
Mexican–American War (1846–8) 31, 33, 44, 52, 106, 176
Mexico 20, 24–6, 31, 34, 39, 41–3, 47, 53, 113, 192; Punitive Expedition against (1916) 76, 90
Middle East 49, 55, 121, 158, 179, 187, 212–13; *see also individual countries*
Military Order of the Loyal Legion of the United States (MOLLUS) 65–7
Mississippi, US naval steamer 70
Modelski, George, political scientist 204–5
Moltke, Helmuth von, German field marshal 82
Mongols 158
Monmouth Court House, battle of (1778) 12
Monroe, James, US president 19, 23
Monroe Doctrine (1823) 66, 177, 181
Moore, Michael, filmmaker 55
Morrow, E. Frederick, African-American leader 100–2
Musharraf, Pervez, Pakistani general and president 55
Muslims *see* Islam

Napoleon I, French emperor 12–13, 21
Napoleonic Wars *see* French Revolutionary and Napoleonic Wars
National Association for the Advancement of Colored People (NAACP) 92, 97, 99, 101
National Security Act (1947) 190
National Security Council (NSC) 186–7
Native Americans 15–17, 19–20, 22, 24–5, 108, 192
naval technology, evolution of 205–6, 208
Navy, US 17, 19, 23, 26, 29–33, 38, 67, 70, 168n19, 190, 206, 208
Netherlands 12, 18–19, 26, 149–51, 157–8, 160, 202
neo-liberalism, in international relations theory 202, 209, 214
neo-Marxism, in international relations theory 169
neo-realism, in international relations theory 170, 204, 209
neutrality, American 2, 33, 35, 52–4, 176
New Deal 2–3
Newell, William, US politician 45
New Left 4–5, 10n6
New Orleans, Battle of (1815) 25, 73
New Zealand 33, 206–207
Nguyen Ngoc Loan, South Vietnamese general 131
Nicaragua 29–31, 34–5, 38–9, 43–4, 46–8, 50–1, 54–5
Nixon, Richard, US president 120, 126–7, 132–4, 136, 138–9, 187
non-governmental organizations (NGOs) 171, 193–4
Nootka Sound Crisis (1790) 26
North Atlantic Treaty Organization (NATO) 97, 113, 178, 182, 203–4
North Korea 47
North Sea 214
Northwest Ordinance (1787) 17
nuclear weapons 115–16, 204, 214
Nye, Joseph, political scientist 9, 202–10, 212–15

oil, strategic importance of 154, *156*, 157–60, 163–4, 179, 213–14
Okinawa 32
Oldenburg, German battleship 206
Opium wars 38
Ostend Manifesto (1854) 32, 37

O'Sullivan, John L., US journalist and diplomat 34, 48
Ottawa Convention (1999) 179

Pach, Chester, historian 97, 103
Pacific Ocean 33, 38, 173, 192
Pakistan 55–6, 189, 192, 213
Palmerston, Henry John Temple, Viscount, British statesman 40
Panama 49–50, 91, 93, 140, 192
Patterson, Robert, US politician 95
Patton, George, US general 96
Pax Americana *154*, 204–5, 214–15
Pax Britannica 150, *154*, 155, 204–8, 215
Perry, Matthew C., US naval officer 32
Persian Gulf War (1991) 140–1, 204
Peru 24, 50
Philippines 36, 69, 71, 73, 76, 91, 175–6
Pierce, Franklin, US president 30–1, 38, 40–2, 44, 47, 52–5
Plessy v. *Ferguson* (1896) 90, 98–9
Poland 12, 84
Porter, Bruce, political scientist 153
Port Hudson, Battle of (1863) 70
Portugal 12, 34, 149, 151, 157, 160
Potsdam Conference (1945) 111
Potter, David, historian 31
Powell, Colin, US general and statesman 134–5, 140, 188
Protestants, and Protestantism 1, 48
Proudman, Mark, political scientist 212, 214
Prussia 32
public diplomacy, US 212
Puerto Rico 74
Putin, Vladimir, Russian president 193

Quasi War, US–French (1798) 17
Quebec 22
Quint, Bert, journalist 127–8, 130, 137
Quitman, John A., US general and politician 33–5, 53–4

Rabel, Ed, journalist 137
railways 26, *154*, *159*
Randolph, A. Philip, African-American leader 92, 95–6, 101
Randolph, V.M., US naval officer 47
Rather, Dan, journalist 125–6, 129, 140–1
Reagan, Ronald, US president 211
realism, in international relations

theory, 169–70, 202, 209, 214–15; *see also* neo-realism
Reasoner, Harry, journalist 136
Red Scare (1920s) 110
Red Scare (1950s) 10n6
Red Sea 206
religion, in US 175–6, 197n40; *see also* Catholics; Protestants
Republican party (Democratic-Republican) 17–18, 20–1, 23
Republican party (1854) 45, 97–9, 102–3, 133, 138–9, 182–3, 197n40
Reynolds, Frank, journalist 126
Rhode Island 16, 22–3
Rice, Condoleezza, US secretary of state, 187–8
Richardson, Elmo, historian 97, 103
Rives, William C., US diplomat 40, 47
Robinson, Jackie, professional athlete and African-American leader 102
Rogers, William, US statesman 187
Rome, and Roman Empire 152, 175
Roosevelt, Franklin D., US president 2, 36, 84, 109–10, 118, 120
Rugh, William A., political scientist 212
Rumsfeld, Donald, US secretary of defense 125–6, 141, 188, 190
Russia, and Soviet Union 12, 41, 49, 97, 107, 109–12, 114–20, 150, 153, *155*, 167n10, 178, 181, 183, 192–3, 199n75, 201, 203–5, 209, 213
Rwanda 180

Safer, Morley, journalist 128, 130
St. Lawrence River 21, 23
Sardinia-Piedmont 50
Saudi Arabia 55–6
Scali, John, journalist 132, 140
Schieffer, Bob, journalist 134
Schlesinger, Arthur M., Jr., historian 162
Schuyler, Philip, US general 12
Scott, Winfield, US general 13
Seminole War, First 19
Serbia, and Serbs 203
Shanghai 206
Shays' Rebellion (1786–7), 23–5
Shepard, Gary, journalist 135
Sheridan, Philip, US general 77, 82
Sherman, William Tecumseh, US general 77, 82
shipbuilding 207; *see also* naval techology
Singapore 206–7

slaves and slavery 20, 44, 82, 192
Slidell, John, US politician 35
Smith, Howard K., journalist 128, 130, 137, 139–40
Smith, James McCune, African-American leader 35
Smith, Mitchell, author 214
Smith, Steven R., political scientist 184
Snyder, Alvin, US civil servant 138
soft power 202–3, 206–15
Somalia 180, 182, 192
South Africa 206–7
Southern Christian Leadership Council 101
Southern Manifesto (1956) 98–9
South Korea 167n14
Soviet Union *see* Russia
Spain, and Spanish America 12–13, 18, 25–7, 32–5, 37, 39–40, 42, 45–9, 52, 67–71, 75, 108, 113, 149–50, 181, 202
Spanish–American War (1898) 36, 68–76, 90, 106, 175
Sphinx, French naval steamer 206
Stanton, Benjamin, US politician 187
Stanton, Frank, CBS president 130
Stephanson, Anders, historian 48
Stevenson, Adlai, US politician 97
Stimson, Henry, US statesman 92
Strategic arms limitations treaties (SALT) 178
strategic culture 20, 26, 214–15
Streithorst, Tom, journalist 137
Strong, George Templeton 45
Supreme Court, US 16

Tahiti 38
Taiwan 32
Tajikistan 192
Taliban 55
Tenet, George, CIA director 189
terrorism 51, 55–6, 121, 169, 173, 176, 180, 188–9, 209, 213
Tet Offensive (1968) 127, 131–2
Thayer, William Sydney, US filibuster 54
Ticonderoga, Fort 14
Tocqueville, Alexis de 1–2, 4, 168n22, 172, 199n79
Trafalgar, Battle of (1805) 21
Trinidad 93
Truman, Harry, US president 95, 102, 111–14, 116–17
Turkey 113
Twin Peaks model 147–52, 163, 165

unilateralism, in US foreign policy 181–3
United Confederate Veterans (UCV) 65, 71, 73–4, 81
United Daughters of the Confederacy (UDC) 80–1
United Nations (UN) 115, 171, 178, 181–3, 192–3, 204, 210
United States Information Agency (USIA) 212
United States Information Service (USIS) 212
Urban League 99, 101

Van Alstyne, Richard W., historian 36
Vance, Cyrus, US statesman 187
Venable, Abraham, US politician 45
Venezuela 49, 93, 213
Venice 149
Versailles, Treaty of (1919) 83, 181
Veterans of Foreign Wars (VFW) 82
Viet Cong 128–9
Vietnam, and Vietnam War 117–18, 121, 126–41, 176, 182, 193–4, 204, 210
Virginia Military Institute 34

Walker, Robert J., US politician 34
Walker, William, US filibuster 34–5, 38–55
Wallace, George, US politician 100
War for Independence, American *see* American Revolution
War of 1812 14, 18–23, 25–6, 106
War Powers Resolution (1973) 186
Warren, Earl, US politician and jurist 98
Washington, George 2, 12, 14, 17, 37, 103, 177
Wayne, Anthony, US general 16
Webster, Don, journalist 136–7
West Indies 20
Westmoreland, William, US general 129, 131
West Point (US Military Academy) 70, 89–91, 97, 137, 174
Wheeler, Joseph, Confederate and US general, 70
Whiskey Rebellion (1794) 24–5
White, Walter, African-American leader 92
"white man's burden," 176
Wilkins, Roy, African-American leader 97, 101

Wilkinson, James, US general 13, 23
Williams, John Bell, US politician 90
Williams, William Appleman, historian 169
Wilson, Woodrow, US president 81, 83, 176, 181
Wilsonian strategic subculture 215
Wolfowitz, Paul, US deputy secretary of defense 188
World Bank 204
World Trade Center 51, 55
World War I 49, 76–83, 90–2, 106, 146–7, 153, 155, 157, 159, 161–2, 167n10, 176, 181, 187, 207–8

World War II 84, 88–9, 93–6, 106, 109, 111, 114, 120, 146–7, 153, 155, 158–62, 164, 181, 204, 211

Yalta Conference (1945) 111
Yeltsin, Boris, Russian president 209
Young, Charles, US army officer 90
Yugoslavia 192

Zegart, Amy, political scientist 184
Zinn, Howard, historian 4

www.ingramcontent.com/pod-product-compliance
Ingram Content Group UK Ltd.
Pitfield, Milton Keynes, MK11 3LW, UK
UKHW020355010325
455677UK00021B/463